MUSIC BUSINESS CAREERS

T0384241

The music industry offers the opportunity to pursue a career as either a creative (artist, producer, songwriter, etc.) or as a music business "logician" (artist manager, agent, entertainment attorney, venue manager, etc.). Though both vocational paths are integral to the industry's success, the work of calling songs into existence or entertaining an audience differs from the administrative aspects of the business, such as operating an entertainment company. And while the daily activities of creatives may differ from those of the music business logician, the music industry careerist may sense a call to Career Duality, to work on both sides of the industry as a Career Dualist, a concept this book introduces, defines, and explores in the context of the music industry.

This new volume speaks to the dilemma experienced by those struggling with career decisions involving whether to work in the industry using their analytical abilities, or to work as a creative, or to do both. The potential financial challenges encountered in working in the industry as an emerging artist may necessitate maintaining a second and simultaneous occupation (possibly outside the industry) that offers economic survival. However, this is not Career Duality. Likewise, attending to the business affairs that impact all creatives is not Career Duality. Rather, Career Duality involves the deliberate pursuit of a dual career as both a music industry creative and music business logician, which is stimulated by the drive to express dual proclivities that are simultaneously artistic and analytical.

By offering a Career Duality model and other constructs, examining research on careers, calling, authenticity and related concepts, and providing profiles of music industry dualists, this book takes readers on a journey of self-exploration and offers insights and recommendations for charting an authentic career path. This is a practical examination for not only music industry professionals and the entertainment industry, but for individuals interested in expressing both the analytical and artistic self in the context of career.

Cheryl Slay Carr is Associate Dean and Associate Professor of Music Business at Belmont University, Nashville, Tennessee.

ROUTLEDGE RESEARCH IN CREATIVE AND CULTURAL INDUSTRIES MANAGEMENT

Edited by Ruth Rentschler, University of South Australia Business School, Australia

Routledge Research in Creative and Cultural Industries Management provides a forum for the publication of original research in cultural and creative industries, from a management perspective. It reflects the multiple and inter-disciplinary forms of cultural and creative industries and the expanding roles which they perform in an increasing number of countries.

As the discipline expands, there is a pressing a need to disseminate academic research, and this series provides a platform to publish this research, setting the agenda of cultural and creative industries from a managerial perspective, as an academic discipline.

The aim is to chart developments in contemporary cultural and creative industries thinking around the world, with a view to shaping future agendas reflecting the expanding significance of the cultural and creative industries in a globalized world.

Arts and Business
Building a Common Ground for Understanding Society
Edited by Elena Raviola and Peter Zackariasson

Performing Arts Center Management
Edited by Patricia Dewey Lambert and Robyn Williams

The Classical Music Industry
Edited by Christopher Dromey and Julia Haferkorn

Arts and Cultural Management
Sense and Sensibilities in the State of the Field
Edited by Constance DeVereaux

Music Business Careers
Career Duality in the Creative Industries
Cheryl Slay Carr

MUSIC BUSINESS CAREERS

Career Duality in the Creative Industries

Cheryl Slay Carr

Routledge
Taylor & Francis Group

NEW YORK AND LONDON

First published 2019
by Routledge
52 Vanderbilt Avenue, New York, NY 10017

and by Routledge
2 Park Square, Milton Park, Abingdon, Oxon OX14 4RN

Routledge is an imprint of the Taylor & Francis Group, an informa business

© 2019 Taylor & Francis

Library of Congress Cataloging-in-Publication Data
Names: Carr, Cheryl Slay, author.
Title: Music business careers : career duality in the creative industries /
Cheryl Slay Carr.
Description: New York, NY : Routledge, 2019. |
Series: Routledge research in creative and cultural industries management |
Includes bibliographical references and index.
Identifiers: LCCN 2018053164| ISBN 9781138577152 (hardback) |
ISBN 9781138482272 (pbk.) | ISBN 9781351058391 (ebook)
Subjects: LCSH: Music trade--Vocational guidance.
Classification: LCC ML3795 .C32 2019 | DDC 780.23--dc23
LC record available at https://lccn.loc.gov/2018053164

ISBN: 978-1-138-57715-2 (hbk)
ISBN: 978-1-138-48227-2 (pbk)
ISBN: 978-1-351-05839-1 (ebk)

Typeset in Bembo
by Taylor & Francis Books

This book is dedicated to: My mother, whose wisdom calls to me, The memory of my dad, who taught me authenticity, My husband, Jeff, whose love inspires me daily, And to Dualists everywhere: Find your light, then be a city on a hill.

CONTENTS

List of Illustrations   *ix*

Acknowledgments   *x*

Foreword   *xii*

Introduction   1

PART I

Understanding Career Duality   **7**

  1 The Career Duality Dilemma: An Early Tale   9

  2 Defining Career Duality   16

  3 Telling Other Tales   44

PART II

The Impetus for Career Duality   **79**

  4 Vocational Calling: The Directional Axis of Vocation   81

  5 The Case for Contextual Calling   102

  6 Call and Response   121

PART III
The Impact of Career Duality: Synthesizing Possibility   **137**

7 Authenticity   139

8 Writing Your Own Tale: Charting Your Authentic Career   156

9 A Community of Dualists   181

PART IV
Empowering Others and Living Empowered   **197**

10 Teaching and Advising for Duality   199

Epilogue: Living Empowered   211

About the Author   *213*
Index   *215*

ILLUSTRATIONS

Figures

2.1	The Career Duality Model	18
2.2	The Duality Exploration Grid	38
7.1	Authenticity map	154

Table

9.1	Entertainment industry sector comparisons	183

Boxes

Exercise Set 1:	Pivotal Moments	13
Exercise Set 2:	Exploring Duality	41
Exercise Set 3:	Telling Your Own Tale	77
Exercise Set 4:	Calling Contemplation	99
Exercise Set 5:	Customizing Context	118
Exercise Set 6:	Response to Calling	135
Exercise Set 7:	Authenticity Mapping	154
Exercise Set 8:	Career Duality Assessment	179
Exercise Set 9:	Orientation	193

ACKNOWLEDGMENTS

Many thanks to the following people who supported the writing of this book: Holly Slay Ferraro, thank you for suggesting that I pitch my proposal to David Varley. This might not have been possible without you! Thank you also for inspiring me as the true researcher you are. You have taught me much, perhaps without fully realizing it. David Varley, this book *definitely* would not have been possible without you. You believed in my concept, saw its potential, and worked with me with such understanding that I will not soon forget, and which I deeply appreciate. Jeff, thank you for taking over all housekeeping, cooking, and other domestic tasks in the final weeks of writing (can we keep that going?), for always, always, always encouraging me, and finding little and big ways to let me know you support me. You really are the wind beneath my wings. Stop blushing now. Thank you to all "my" Dualists who were interviewed for the book. You are all just stellar human beings. Really. Our interviews were an opportunity to be inspired, which is pretty much my favorite thing in the world to do and to be, and I was genuinely inspired by every one of you. I wish readers could hear every sagacious word you shared with me. I am looking forward to bringing us all together; you all *must* meet each other. Thanks to Tracy Maddux at CDBaby for introducing me to Joel Andrew. Special thanks to you Joel, for so graciously facilitating introductions to several of the profiled dualists, and for introducing me to Drew Shoals. Drew, thank you for sharing your story. Thank you to the Belmont University community: with special thanks to our music business students who served as a source of inspiration for this book, and Dean Doug Howard, Mike Curb College of Entertainment and Music Business at Belmont, for your ongoing support. Thanks to Dr. Bob Fisher, Belmont University President, Dr. Susan West, Vice President and Chief of Staff, and Dr. Thomas Burns, Provost, for your leadership. Thank you to all the students, colleagues, friends, family, and others who have expressed interest in a book like this. Now, go out and buy a copy… so I can thank you again! Thank you to the team at Routledge/Taylor Francis – Mary Del Plato, Brianna Ascher, Dawn Preston, and Miriam Armstrong for all of your support. Lastly, I live in the realm of the God who makes all things possible and am ever grateful to Him for guiding this effort, and me.

FOREWORD

My journey from musician, to lawyer, to musician began in Portland, Oregon, where I grew up. My parents placed me in drum lessons because my mom wanted someone with whom to jam. I enjoyed going to the basement to practice drums after school each day, finding out what kind of voice I wanted to create on my instrument. I learned jazz, rock, R&B, and gospel. The voice I found academically in school led me to student government, mock trials, constitutional debate team as well as school band, drama and choir. In college, I picked African American studies as a major because I enjoyed the interdisciplinary nature of studying race and class in America. This major gave me an academic language to form my own racial identity as a half black/half white kid from Oregon, while also helping me develop the critical, analytical, rhetorical, and writing skills that would ultimately lead me to law school. Furthermore, African American studies showed me the historical, social-political context for the different genres of American music I had come to love – from jazz, to rock, to hip-hop.

While attending Whitman College, I worked booking bands like *Maroon 5, Death Cab for Cutie*, Ben Folds, *OAR, Blackalicious*, and Matt Nathanson to play concerts at our school (I've since been lucky enough to become friends with several of these artists). Additionally, I played drums in the jazz band and in almost every campus band. During my junior year, I studied abroad in Botswana and toured with an afro-beat artist there. Getting the chance to tour around Botswana with musicians from all over Africa helped me discover that I wanted to be a touring musician after I graduated from college. After Whitman, I moved back to Portland and started gigging, recording, and touring with various jazz, rock, blues, and pop artists, eventually touring with Pat Monahan, the lead singer of the band *Train*, in 2007 when he led a solo-record tour. We stayed in touch when I decided to transition from music to a career in the law.

I wanted to continue developing the academic skills that I had honed in college but in a more targeted, professional setting. Law school was always something I had thought about pursuing, but after focusing on music for three or so years after college and achieving some success, it felt like a good time to switch gears and focus on law. I believed I was checking back in with my other skills and passions instead of taking a complete career detour. Seeking advice, I reached out to friends of mine who had gone to law school and to any lawyers I could meet to look for mentors and guidance for my new career path. After moving from Portland to New York City to work as a court advocate for an alternative to incarceration non-profit for a year while applying to law school, I was lucky enough to gain admission to the prestigious top-ten law school, the University of Pennsylvania Law School in Philadelphia.

Law school was challenging at first, but ultimately a very rewarding experience. Everyone at Penn Law came from impressive schools and most were used to being the sharpest students in undergrad. Some people had already achieved successful careers in finance, education, and the non-profit sector. Every student was remarkable. But law school is an equalizer, and everyone has to retrain their brains to think like lawyers. The Socratic method can be intimidating, and being graded on a curve can be either exhilarating or heartbreaking. In the end, everyone comes out on the other side with the ability to ask insightful questions, to identify potential problems in any situation and come up with proactive solutions, and to respect the rule of law. I made life-long friends who have gone on to work at top law firms, companies, and public interest organizations all over the world.

During law school, I served as the editor-in-chief of the *Penn Journal of International Law*, participated in the Frederick Douglass Moot Court competition, and held the pro bono and community service chair for the Penn Black Law Student Association. I even played a weekly jazz gig at an Ethiopian restaurant in West Philly. Most importantly, I met my now wife, Nicole. After law school, I became licensed to practice in New York State and moved to New York City where I worked at an international law firm called Shearman & Sterling in the litigation and mergers and acquisition practice groups. At Shearman, I served as co-chair of the professional affinity group for black lawyers at the firm.

Things were going well at the law firm and I had no intention of leaving at the time, but I certainly missed having more of a creative musical outlet. When I received a call from my old friend Pat Monahan to see if I was interested in leaving law to come back to music to be the drummer for *Train*, it was an exciting but intimidating decision to make. I had worked hard over several years to earn a spot working at a prestigious New York law firm and it's not a job to walk away from lightly. But I knew in my gut that it was my once-in-a-lifetime chance to tour the world playing with a Grammy Award-winning and multi-platinum band like *Train*. I was lucky that when I discussed the decision with my wife, close friends and mentors, and the partners at the firm, most people agreed that this was a rare opportunity. I had the ability to practice law down the line, but drumming for *Train* was too good to pass up.

Drumming for *Train* is an invigorating and rewarding job that gives me the space to play songs that resonate with people from all different backgrounds from all around the globe. I work with talented musicians, crew, management, and drum companies on a daily basis. I get the chance to play drums while also networking with artists and other professionals throughout all sides of the music industry. I hope to play in *Train* as long as it's creatively and professionally satisfying and I am contributing meaningfully to the band. But it's possible that further down the line, a new professional opportunity might present itself. I'm open to redefining my vocational title and professional identity as I make my career journey throughout life. It's an ongoing process.

I trust the path that led me to my forks in the road and used the decision-making process that seemed best to me at the time. Yet making career decisions can be challenging. If I could change anything about the means I used to guide my transitions, a go-to set of questions, like those offered in this book, would have been helpful to make it less overwhelming to figure out the "right" thing to do. Having more of a concrete framework for approaching these career junctures that exist between the artistic and analytical paths would have been helpful to me in the past and could be helpful to me in the future when the next major career decision arises. The intersection of scholarly research from experts and personal narratives from entertainment industry professionals working both analytically and creatively in the industry gives readers the chance to consider both theory and real-life experiences. Yet part of the book's real value is its encouragement to anyone at their own crossroads. Professor Carr has created a language for articulating the challenges of duality decisions, to give voice to that dialogue we all have within ourselves when we're trying to figure out what to do. You can sense that her goal is not only to offer practical information and strategies to consider, but to empower you to discern a path that is right for you by encouraging that inner dialogue.

As you take stock of your own journey, be open to the possibility that an exciting new opportunity might come up at a seemingly inopportune time. Sometimes you have to take a big risk to gain a big reward. I feel fortunate to be dually abled, to be able to traverse both creative and analytical career paths and to recognize that both sides express all of me, fully and authentically. Though I have chosen to focus on one path at a time, I try to keep as many of my creative and analytical skills as sharp as I can at all times, since different jobs force you to focus on the most necessary skills needed at the moment.

This is who I am, and who I want to be. But I also want to be a constantly growing person, striving to be the best version of my personal and professional self. This process will take a lifetime and I'm excited for the challenge. I'm appreciative of what I've been able to accomplish so far, and wish you the best on your career journey in the music and entertainment business.

Drew Shoals, Esq.
Former Drummer, *Train*
Entertainment Attorney
Franklin, Weinrib, Rudell & Vassallo, P.C., New York, NY

INTRODUCTION

When I became a professor teaching undergraduate law courses in a music business program I started offering students in my classes the opportunity to talk with me about careers. They took me up on it. A student responds to my classroom invitation, visits my office, and a conversation that goes something like this ensues:

> "Professor, I'm discovering that I really like studying the business and law of music, even more than I thought. Now I'm torn: should I pursue my musical career, or should I work on the business side of the industry?" I respond: "You're like me, partly analytical and part artist. You have abilities in both spheres and are drawn to both. Let's talk about what it means to live and make career decisions around this divided self."

Then I go on to tell my own tale of duality as a lawyer-singer, recalling and sharing my encounter with the all-too-familiar axiom within the legal community that has declared for centuries that "the law is a jealous mistress." It is a turn of phrase that dates back to 1829. During his address at Harvard when appointed a Dane Professor of Law, Supreme Court Justice Joseph Story told his audience that "the law is a jealous mistress and requires a long and constant courtship. It is not to be won by trifling favors, but by lavish homage."[1] The adage has become a byword for depicting the often severe, all-consuming nature of a profession in the law. The colorful mistress language serves as a kind of warning – or encouragement – that you must be totally devoted to the law. Yet for some of us the siren call of pursuits beyond our primary profession can be heard above the clamor of conventional career demands, beckoning us to an alternative path despite harsh analogies to committing career adultery. I hear that call. I am a singer-lawyer-professor-administrator. This book chronicles tales of those who, like me – and possibly like you – hear the call of the artistic/analytical divide and face the Career Duality (CD) dilemma. This preamble discusses the scope and nature of this book and offers an overview of what lies in the pages ahead.

Seeds of the Tale

This is a book about music and entertainment industry careers, but this is not a book about finding a job within that industry or describing an array of specific industry positions or how to pursue them. Before identifying or applying for jobs there is an important entity who is being readied for the workplace: you. You are the nucleus, the epicenter of your career. Who you are may determine what you will do, why, and whether it will prove satisfying or contribute to your well-being and the well-being of others. Therefore, this book examines career decision making, calling, and authenticity in the context of the entertainment industry. Its purpose is twofold: (1) to discuss the impact of CD, a concept the book originates, on individuals working in the music industry and the impact of such individuals on the entertainment industry itself, and (2) to invite readers to a personal exploration of their own duality, with a view toward managing and maximizing the duality experience.

I began contemplating the underlying idea for CD, defined and discussed in Chapter 2, as a research project called "Singing Lawyers, Professors, and Accountants: The Music Business Professional as Artist," presented as a working paper at an academic conference in 2011. Some aspects of that research are reflected here. Consequently, this book explores the music business as a context that may facilitate CD.

However, the chief inspiration for this book derives from two experiential sources: (1) creating an autoethnography, i.e., a story, of my own continuing journey of CD and what drives it, and (2) regularly encountering others who share this analytical/artistic blend of selves that creates a specific type of career challenge-opportunity, who therefore want to know how or whether to direct these two sometimes equally capable identities. A large number of these interactions stem from my role as a university professor and pre-law advisor, primarily for music business students, for over ten years. I have no official role per se as a career advisor at my university. Rather, my custom of offering students a listening ear on the subject of careers evolved naturally, owing to a steady but unplanned enchantment with the subject and with wanting to somehow speak to student consternations about a career in entertainment. Over the years I have had many meaningful discussions with students who discovered through coursework that they both excelled in and were attracted to their music business or undergraduate law coursework, but struggled with the idea of abandoning their artistic selves in pursuit of a non-artistic career in the business. They sensed the impending need to make a career choice that might alter future choices or require immediate sacrifices, for example, having to decide whether to take additional classes that nurtured a newfound awareness of analytical interests, or choosing an internship or summer job to further the exploration, taking a graduate entrance exam like the Graduate Record Exam or Law School Admission Test. For some students it meant deciding whether to continue with a college degree at all in lieu of pursuing a specific arts opportunity that had presented itself, e.g., going on tour to perform with an established celebrity. They were contemplating the predicament of CD without an awareness of it or its parameters. You may be at a similar crossroads or understand the predicament.

Like you, I live, comprehend, and identify with the perplexing yet gratifying, paradoxical nature of the CD quandary. The CD dilemma involves a keen awareness of one's artistic yet analytical proclivities, and feeling *compelled* to discern whether to vocationally pursue expression of the artistic self, versus the analytical self, or to somehow express both selves in the context of the entertainment industry. For some, the sheer practical difficulties of attempting to do both will lead to a break from one to pursue the other, or to pursue one as an avocation, and these may be good career choices. However, this text does not purport to suggest what is best for you. Rather, this book explores possibilities, chronicles the journeys of entertainment industry dualists, discusses pertinent research on careers, and offers insights for traversing your own inquiry by providing a specific framework and process for the exploration. The text also offers advisors, faculty, parents, and friends a means for assisting in that exploration.

Threshold Inquiries

The biblical scriptures described a phenomenon that is pertinent not only for spiritual inquiry, but one that also helps illustrate the CD dilemma. Jesus imparted a parable that ends with the admonition "No one can serve two masters. Either you will hate the one and love the other, or you will be devoted to the one and despise the other."[2] Following the logic of the parable one might ask, as I have certainly asked myself concerning my own career path: Why not simply undertake one thing at a time, transitioning from a career that uses my analytical abilities to one that uses my artistic ones (or vice versa), and frame both the personal exploration and the book's discussion in terms of career transitions? Wouldn't that simplify or resolve the CD dilemma? It may for some. When I first moved to Nashville and was meeting lots of new people I met J.R. (not his real name), a lawyer who was also new to the city. J.R. had retired from practicing law and moved to Nashville at age 65 to pursue his dream of being a singer-songwriter (there really are lots of singing lawyers out there), now that he had the time and financial security to do so. He chose the path of serving his analytical "master" first, then his artistic one. I admire his choice and see this kind of transition as a viable option.

But is this the path for you? If not, what are the other paths? How will you know? And how, when, or why will you start walking it? What if you prefer not to wait for retirement to express your artistic side in ways that require substantial time and effort? Or what if you currently *are* expressing your creative self but get opportunities to work on the business side of music and are drawn not just to a salary, but to the work itself? I wonder about J.R. I wonder about the songs he did not write but wanted to.[3] I wonder what he did with his artistic self all those years before retirement. I wonder how J.R. made his music industry career decisions. I wonder how you will make yours. These are all threshold inquiries that have shaped the focus of this book.

The vision of CD presented here extends beyond the idea of *doing* any two things, rather to explore *being* dually artistic and analytical, which may be inescapable regardless of what one chooses to *do*. Consequently, making career decisions is not just a matter of figuring out what to do for a living, or what class to take, or making time for an arts hobby that has personal significance, or choosing to do two things at once. If you are seeking a book about principles for balancing multiple life priorities you will find a peripheral discussion here, but the text focuses on engaging a specific process of inquiry for personal exploration with a view toward creative authenticity and calling.

A Broader Framework

Since part of the inspiration for this book is attributable to my observations about the prevalence of singer-lawyers and also comes from my work as a pre-law advisor and professor of law in a music business curriculum, music business, law, and academic contexts are all intended focal points here. It is my hope that this work will speak to music business professionals, academics, lawyers, and lawyer-aspirants who may be facing the question of what to do with the self that is artistic yet authentically analytical.

However, the question of creative career authenticity through CD is a much broader one, relevant to every career interest and inquiry. We all have career choices to make. Therefore, this text is intended for *anyone* contemplating their own duality, as well as teachers, parents, and advisors who counsel any of the foregoing. To illustrate: *singer/lawyer*[4] can (and, when applicable, should) be substituted for *musician/music business executive*, or *actor/entertainment journalist*, or other artistic/analytical combinations in the entertainment industry, and even outside entertainment. Whatever the context, the principles offered here will still apply. I encourage you to make the substitutions necessary to customize your reading and render the book's principles applicable to your individual aspirations, as it is intended to extend to this broader framework.

An Even Broader Framework

The creative industries, which include music, film, books, visual art, gaming, performing arts, and digital media, account for a large percentage of national income for many countries. One of the objectives of this book is to consider the impact of CD on the entertainment industry itself, including the global industry outside the United States. According to the 2015 creative economy report commissioned by the International Confederation of Societies of Authors and Composers in partnership with UNESCO, the creative economy accounted for 29.5 million jobs worldwide. This figure exceeds the combined number of jobs for the automotive industries of Europe, Japan, and the United States. The creative industries generated $2,250 billion in revenue – or 3 percent of the world's GDP – in 2013. This is more than the global telecommunications industry, which generated $1,570 billion.[5] Just as the creative industries expand around the globe, the concept of CD expands across creative industries, and across cultures. Correspondingly, the principles discussed here will resonate with readers from all countries and cultures who are contemplating their role in the future of those industries. Chapter 9 is specifically directed to those working within the creative industries outside the music business and globally.

Getting the Most from This Book

In addition to research on careers and the entertainment industry, this book includes the stories of dualists I interviewed to supplement my own experiences, and to provide narrative accounts that explore commonalities between dualists everywhere. They include an array of individuals whose backgrounds range from executive vice presidents and lawyers to entrepreneurs of startup companies, or music business logicians who have worked with major record labels, as well as those who gig only a few times a year. Their experiences are inspiring and compelling. Yet this book is designed to leave room for personalized, individual exploration to facilitate constructing a narrative of your own. Reflective exercises are provided at the end of each chapter for personalizing that chapter's concepts. If you are a busy, tell-me-but-cut-to-the-chase reader, then the inclination may be to fast forward to the text that provides the how-to's and bottom lines. I cannot say this strongly enough: resist that temptation. Every journey is unique. What was or is right for one person may be merely illustrative for another. In other words, the "answers" you seek are to be personally derived.

Therefore, if you believe this book applies to you, *take it all in*. Do the exercises. You will need a journal (whether electronic or paper) to complete them. Go on the journey. If you are a spiritual person (e.g., that is an important aspect of my own journey), consider making this a quasi-spiritual quest that incorporates prayer, study of scriptures, or meditation. *Commit* to a small block of time daily (say, 20–30 minutes each day) to complete the exercises, though not all require the same amount of time. Then schedule it on your calendar. The frequency is up to you depending on your availability, how long you want to take to complete the book, and how much priority you choose to accord to the exploration. Whatever the frequency, regular intervals will have the most meaningful impact.

This text is also intended for use within a university-level senior capstone or culminating experience class, as well as other entertainment industry courses.

Chapter 10 provides suggestions for teaching the material and designing the class for this kind of exploration.

Whether through a course or on your own, you may find that you genuinely enjoy setting aside some dedicated time for self-discovery. Just as importantly, you owe it to the calls within you.

Notes

1 Joseph Story, *A Discourse Pronounced upon the Inauguration of the Author as Dane Professor of Law in Harvard University* (Boston, MA: Hilliard, Gray, Little, and Wilkins, 1829), 29, https://babel.hathitrust.org/cgi/pt?id=njp.32101068036142;view=1up;seq=3, accessed September 13, 2017.
2 The Bible, Matthew 6:24, New International Version. The context of this passage is endeavoring to serve both God and money.
3 If we were still in touch I would have interviewed him for this book.
4 Or *author*/lawyer, or *actor*/lawyer; you get the idea.
5 "Cultural Times: The First Global Map of Cultural and Creative Industries," www.worldcreative.org/#overview, accessed October 15, 2018.

PART I
Understanding Career Duality

1

THE CAREER DUALITY DILEMMA

An Early Tale

I was a singer, in fact I was musical, long before I ever contemplated a career in the legal profession or academia. Every phase of my life has included producing music for as long as I can remember.

Like many, my musical experiences began during the elementary school years. My parents are of a generation and culture who believed that every home should have a piano.[1] Ours was a handsome walnut-grain spinet that resided in our living room. I was about 5 or 6 years old when they purchased it new, and have a pretty vivid recollection of the excitement associated with having one enter our home. I started lessons at around age 6 with various teachers and methods over the years. I kept up with some mix of lessons, diligence, and inconsistent practice until about junior high school. Then at that crucial juncture of adolescence, with my parents weary from paying for lessons for a student who was musically astute but lukewarm in my affection for discipline, the study gradually tapered off, though playing remained a constant.

Throughout high school and college I would sit down at the piano when visiting my folks, keeping my ability to read music alive. I later purchased my own piano so that the musical seed that was planted early on could continue to grow, albeit with pretty scant watering. However, learning to play had shaped me and still calls to me to continue to play and to maintain those early music reading skills. I learned not just musical notes but pieces of music I still remember and play, and learned composers as well – all a suitable foundation for singing. Yet the most influential foundation for the early study of singing was laid for me in glee club. Glee club seemed an odd name for a singing class, but it deeply affected me, even gleefully, though the origin of the term is broader.[2] It was part of my early call to music.

Singing at the Ford Auditorium[3] in Detroit, where I grew up, as part of a national assemblage of glee clubs from all across the country was a particularly unforgettable glee club moment. We practiced for weeks (perhaps months) learning specific music for that singular event. The descant to *America, the Beautiful* was one of the songs we learned. I still remember singing it proudly in my white blouse (a ruffly pirate design popular in the 1970s) and plain A-line black skirt, the ubiquitous uniform for glee clubs and choirs. It was a memorable experience that ignited my love of singing. I also learned other little-known descants, like the one written for *Silent Night*.[4] That glee club experience was foundational, providing the opportunity to learn many well-known and lesser-known songs I still sing today. It is an experience that taught me about arrangements and harmony, and engendered an appreciation for music as a participant, part of the tradition of making music as well as consuming it.

In junior high school I played viola for the school orchestra, having started playing viola in elementary school; I also sang in a church teen choir. In high school I auditioned for "the gospel team" (an acting and musical team of young adults) at my church. In college it never occurred to me to be a music major, perhaps because I loved literary writing too and was pretty certain I would be a journalism major. Nevertheless, I was briefly a member of a girl group practicing for a popular dorm talent show at the University of Michigan. Playing piano and viola, singing in the glee club or church and in any other context that arose were but extensions of my original call to music.

I offer this glimpse into my early experiences to suggest that for me and other artist-music business *logicians*,[5] discarding this array of musical experiences would approximate discarding a part of myself, inauthentically. Moreover, I believe that these experiences not only shaped me, but that music was beckoning me.

A Jealous Mistress, Indeed

Even so, I made choices about what music would mean and the role it would play in my life that often silenced or at least quieted music's call. We live in a world where art is still not perceived as the "safest" way to make a living, pecuniarily speaking. Not that I was thinking about that in junior high school when I elected to leave orchestra; I doubt that I was. But I shifted my attention back to my non-music studies in part because music was not easy. And by that I don't mean that the difficulty was with the academic study or mastery of music, harmonies, or notes. Rather, performing had an unpredictability that felt both personal and identity threatening. For example, talent is often judged and as actors and others in the arts know, hearing "no" is just part of the arts game, as I experienced after auditioning for the gospel team in high school when I did not make the team. It takes focused determination to persevere after hearing "no," though rejection is clearly not restricted to music. To invoke a lawyer turned author (a creative industries dualist for a time), John Grisham heard 28 no's before his first publisher agreed to print *A Time to Kill*, which sold 5,000 copies in its first print run from Wynwood Press.[6] Unlike Grisham, for a time I didn't focus on persevering to incorporate music in my life and career.

Besides, I heard other internal leanings and influences and listened to them, in part because those pursuits seemed to me more practical and more apt to serve as vocations. For example, I was drawn to writing early on, to the intricacies of using words, whether persuasively or otherwise. I was also instinctively attracted to methodical questioning and challenging of assumptions – analytical predispositions that I did not label or really recognize as such until I went to graduate school to obtain a Master of Public Administration (MPA). It was then that my analytic receptors were first turned on, with the help of attentive professors, and engaged around public policy issues that seemed a natural precursor to law school.

My vocational musings were influenced by media, fueled by 1980s movies and books about glamorous careers and by my own desire to achieve in the business, rather than arts, world. (Who knew that I would be able to partially combine both ambitions as an entertainment lawyer? But that story comes later.) Dreams of corporate ascension eclipsed the world of auditions and vocal ambition that was fed less often and therefore seemed more foreign, and more distant.

Along the way, particularly while serving as a presidential management fellow[7] for the federal government, I received feedback from colleagues and friends encouraging me to consider law school. I don't recall having thought about it much until then. But I figured they saw qualities in me that might contribute to my success as a lawyer, so I decided to investigate it.

Initially, the exploration was purely pragmatic, just to see if I could afford law school, then on to taking the Law School Admission Test (LSAT). I had considered pursuing a Master of Business Administration before getting my MPA and had therefore taken the Graduate Management Admission Test (GMAT), the entrance exam for business schools. I did not do well on the GMAT, yet when I examined some of the study materials designed to introduce the LSAT and provide practice questions, it surprisingly felt like I was "home." A test based on logic and reasoning problems resonated for me in a way the GMAT had not. I don't say this to suggest that the LSAT was easy for me; I took and needed to take a prep course, and even then my score was respectable, not stellar. Rather, there was something that felt "right" about the LSAT that seemed an intellectual fit and bolstered my confidence enough to apply to law schools located near my residence at that time.

At that point, I had made an investment of time, having not only researched law schools and taken the LSAT but also having applied for financial aid, put together an application essay that I genuinely believed, etc. (lawyers reading this have done the same, so you know the drill) and was also just plain curious as to whether I would get accepted anywhere. As I have often shared when advising pre-law students, once you make an investment the compulsion to seek the investment's return can become a corollary of necessity, along with the feeling that there is no turning back after that – a phenomenon known as "escalation of commitment."[8] Here's how this concept played out in my case: once I was admitted to law school I saw admission as an opportunity I "could not" turn down, so I "had" to go. Once I invested the time and money to attend, I felt I "had" to complete it. (Actually, I took a year off law school to contemplate a full-time singing career and considered not completing law school at all; more on that in a later chapter.) Upon graduation, I felt "compelled" to take the bar exam. Upon passage of the bar exam, I felt "compelled" to practice law, seeking the ultimate and logical return on all prior investments. You get the idea – lots of internal imperatives that spanned several years. Perhaps this is your story too, in terms of the continuing internal imperatives, whether within the context of law or outside it. You have built a case in your mind for things you believe you "must" do now that you've started down a certain path.

Once I began to practice law I felt its demands, as suggested by that adage I mentioned in the Introduction, referring to the law as a "jealous mistress."[9] Additionally, meeting its challenges can be rewarding on many levels. Public perceptions of lawyers and the legal profession are mixed; on the one hand, the profession is generally perceived as ethically challenged, accounting for a wealth of lawyer jokes and denigrations, some even derived from literary misinterpretations.[10] On the other hand, lawyers are generally seen as professionals, privileged, intellectual, integral to social justice and the rule of law. For these reasons, it is a profession that many have aspired to, and I was as drawn to that as to anything. Despite its imperfections, the legal profession has traditionally held a place of esteem and dignity in the United States, and for me it is an honor to be a part of it. When I was sworn into the Court of Appeals of Maryland (a highly meaningful ceremony to which I invited my parents, who lovingly attended) I listened carefully to the oath I was to take and took it to heart: *to uphold the law, to "demean myself fairly and honorably as an attorney and practitioner at law…"*[11]

Battle Lines: The Career Duality Dilemma

If my impassioned tribute to the legal profession seems the least bit clichéd, these perspectives were nonetheless part of an authentic call to the law for me. Yet its appeal was a double-edged sword, one that I sometimes used to battle back the call of music. The battle lines were more clearly drawn as I increasingly noticed music yielding to the priority of attending to non-music vocational pursuits, including maintaining a law practice, engendering what felt like a constant fight to keep music from disappearing from my life altogether.

This contest, perhaps an outright war, between the analytical self and the artistic self illustrates the Career Duality dilemma (CD/Di), the problem this book explores. For me, the dilemma was somewhat obscured at times since entertainment law, the primary focus for my practice, permitted me to express my analytic self within the context of the creative industries. For example, whenever attending a concert performance or music conference for my practice I felt privileged, thinking "Wow, I get to listen to music for a living!" Likewise, counseling and doing the work of entertainment industry clients offered an almost vicarious industry experience, sort of living the art through a client. But living vicariously was, at best, a temporary delight that did not facilitate use of my own creative abilities. *Listening* to music for a living, as exciting and cool as that is, was light years away from creating or performing it.

Light years! So how was it possible that I could experience this persistent, rewarding, and satisfying call to the law – and heed it – potentially diminishing my musical abilities and 20+ years of performance experience that I've described here as deeply meaningful? What to do with the enduring, original call to a correspondingly gratifying world of creativity? This is the CD/Di – the internal conflict and decisional predicament created when one perceives one's own internal duality in terms of a dual analytical and artistic self, and experiences a dual call to two different entertainment industry vocational pursuits. Theories of calling are discussed in subsequent chapters; for now, let us say that it is that internal sense of attraction I've described above as a compelling beckoning, in my case to both music and the law.

Even though CD/Di was fully at work in my vocational life, it was not until I began to persistently pose these questions to myself that an eye-opening, fierce CD/Di battle began. Valiantly performing when I could and writing music infrequently, the law was usually the victor and I began to more fully consider the importance of blending my artistic and analytical selves. Recounting my own story has an admittedly cathartic value, on a personal level, yet the purpose of sharing it and the stories of other dualists profiled in Chapter 3 and throughout the book is aimed at examining real-life illustrations of CD/Di and its impact, for the CD/Di battle is perplexing, adamant, and real.

Discussion Questions

1. What is "escalation of commitment?"
2. Define and describe CD/Di.
3. Explain the correlation between escalation of commitment and CD/Di.

EXERCISE SET 1: PIVOTAL MOMENTS

The objective of this exercise is to investigate the presence of personal CD/Di.

Perhaps you journeyed with me, recalling your own singing, or playing, or acting, or writing, or filmmaking, or (you fill in the blank) experiences. Complete the following exercise to further that exploration. Begin with identifying pivotal moments and progress to contemplating your own experience with CD/Di.

1. Starting with elementary school or earlier: What is your early big *artist* moment (e.g., my Ford Auditorium glee club experience)? What do you see? Whom do you remember? Where are you? What do you feel?
2. Perhaps your business context is artist management, or working as an agent, or in marketing, promotion, etc., either entrepreneurially or for an

---

entertainment company, in a non-artist capacity. What is your big *non-artist* moment, where you recognized and experienced the satisfaction of expressing your analytical self vocationally (e.g., my moment of being sworn in to the Court of Appeals)?

3. What is your CD/Di moment? When did you recognize the dilemma of being conflicted about whether to work as an artist versus in an analytical position (e.g., my decision to take a year off law school to explore a music career)? Identify the moment (and date/year, if possible) and the thoughts that precipitated the sense of a career dilemma.

4. If you do not sense CD/Di, have you made a career decision you are comfortable with? If you have, how did you make the decision?

Additional Journaling

1. If you identified an experience for (1) above but not (2) or vice versa, journal about why.

2. If you did not identify any experience for either (1) or (2) above, journal about why. What are your career goals? How do you envision yourself working in the entertainment industry, or another industry?

Notes

1   Mark Morris observed "not so long ago every home held a piano and everybody could play one." Mark Morris, Toni Martin, Anne Wagner, Wassily Kandinsky, Sarah Rothenberg, Erik Tarloff, Rachel Cohen, and Ethan Iverson, "A Symposium on the Piano," *Threepenny Review*, no. 119 (Fall 2009): 20, www.jstor.org.bunchproxy.idm. oclc.org/stable/25651071, accessed February 1, 2017. I believe this was particularly true for many African American homes, perhaps an underlying thought in Pulitzer prize winner August Wilson's play *The Piano Lesson* (his second Pulitzer). The play explores the life of a piano in a fictional Black home set in 1936. Harry Elam points to the piano as a central figure in the play. Harry J. Elam, "The Dialectics of August Wilson's 'The Piano Lesson,'" *Theatre Journal* 52, no. 3 (October 2000): 362, www. jstor.org.bunchproxy.idm.oclc.org/stable/25068810.

2   The origin of the word "glee" is not necessarily related to either music nor to joy, mirth. Etymology for the term glee club dates back to 1814 from the secondary sense of "musical composition for three or more solo voice." From *Online Etymology Dictionary*, www.etym online.com/word/glee#etymonline_v_6140. Gleemen were not originally just musicians. They were a variety of entertainers who combined art forms to support each other in performance. "The Material of Music. IV (Continued)," *Musical Times and Singing Class Circular* 29, no. 542 (April 1, 1888): 204, doi:10.2307/3360806.

3   Ford Auditorium now exists only in the Detroit of my memory and the memory of others. It was razed in 2011. W. Bradley McCallum, "Ford Auditorium," www.his toricdetroit.org/building/ford-auditorium/.

4   In the 40 years since I learned both descants I have not had the pleasure of meeting anyone else who seems to know or sing either of them besides my younger sister, who attended the same elementary school and later became part of its glee club. There are undoubtedly scores of other singers I have not met who know both descants, but they

appear to be unfamiliar to many, including choral directors I have known and sung with who are well-studied musicians.

5 Music business logicians are professionals whose primary vocation involves performing non-artistic work to support the operation of the music industry. This term is explored more fully in Chapter 2.

6 Oscar Collier and Frances Spatz Leighton, *How to Write and Sell Your First Novel* (Cincinnati, OH: Writer's Digest Books, 1997), 152.

7 The program was formerly known as the Presidential Management Internship Program. Instituted in 1977, the Presidential Management Fellowship Program is a leadership development initiative for advanced degree candidates. I entered the program in 1987. It was a unique and outstanding opportunity that led to a 17-year career with the federal government that included working for the Equal Employment Opportunity Commission, the National Aeronautics and Space Administration Agency, and the Centers for Medicare and Medicaid Services. See PMF.gov for additional information.

8 Barry M. Staw, "The Escalation of Commitment to a Course of Action," *Academy of Management Review* 6, no. 4 (October, 1981): 577, www.jstor.org.bunchproxy.idm.oclc.org/stable/257636.

9 Joseph Story, *A Discourse Pronounced upon the Inauguration of the Author as Dane Professor of Law in Harvard University* (Boston, MA: Hilliard, Gray, Little, and Wilkins, 1829), 29. See the Introduction to this book for the quote in its entirety.

10 For example, many have taken this line from Shakespeare's play *Henry VI* out of context: "First thing we do, let's kill all the lawyers." Henry VI, Part 2, Act IV, Scene 2, spoken by Dick the Butcher. This line has been used to generally criticize and poke fun at lawyers. However, the context in which the line is spoken recognizes that lawyers are considered keepers of the law, and would need to be disposed of or excluded from any plan to usurp or overthrow the rule of law. This interpretation flatters, rather than criticizes lawyers.

11 Josiah Henry Benton, *The Lawyer's Official Oath and Office* (Boston, MA: Boston Book Company, Rockwell and Churchill Press, 1909), 54–5, https://archive.org/stream/lawyersofficialo00bent/lawyersofficialo00bent_djvu.txt.

2

DEFINING CAREER DUALITY

Where does the Career Duality dilemma (CD/Di) come from? What exactly is CD, and how do you know if you are a dualist? These questions – examined in this chapter – are intertwined, because duality expresses someone you are, not just something you do. For example, working in two different vocational areas is an action-based way of thinking about CD, but CD begins with seeing yourself dually and recognizing the dualities within. I have introduced myself as a singer-lawyer, primarily because that is where the CD/Di is most prominent for me. But duality for me – and probably for other dualists – actually goes beyond music and law.

After graduating from the University of Michigan I moved to Atlanta at my mother's suggestion to sort through career decisions, trying to ascertain whether journalism was my vocational "calling" (I had been a communications major), or whether to apply to graduate school, or both. After a seemingly successful interview with an independent newspaper to work as a reporter, my prospects with them ended before they began when I requested a written position description, offering to draft it myself, to serve as a summary of duties and a contract of sorts. I framed my request as a tool for directing my efforts and said nothing about its contractual potential since I was really more interested in understanding my job than creating a binding document, particularly since I would be working for free, as I recall. Nevertheless, the interviewer expressed concern (that's putting it mildly) that I would need, want, or ask for a written position description. I wasn't willing to work without one, thus terminating the briefest of associations with that newspaper. Today, many employers routinely use position descriptions, but this was not the case with this particular publication, who seemed to think my request was unnecessary or unusual.

I had absolutely no thoughts of law school at the time, nor was I especially concerned about having legal recourse. In fact, the suggestion to ask for a position description was not even my own idea; it came from an older sister. But I made it my own. I readily adopted that analytical way of approaching things and it impacted the way I pursued my journalistic career interests. Interestingly, this period actually turned out to be my most prolific time for writing poetry, rather than journalistic writing. Between 1983 and 1984 I wrote 30 poems, a predisposition that would later express itself in songwriting. Both poetry and singing were expressions of artistic proclivities that coexisted with my analytical bent. The seeds of CD, or evidence of it, were being sown.

The Career Duality Model

CD has a number of elements. Chapter 1 introduced the CD/Di, a precipitating cause of CD, when I recounted a bit of my own CD story. It is my belief that my predicament is common to other dualists and therefore an important place to begin in examining CD. But what incites that dilemma? The CD model is a construct I offer to visually delineate the definition of CD, its origin, and its impact. The first four tiers describe CD and are introduced in this chapter. I developed the model and its concepts to capture and illustrate the components that are pertinent to CD. The remaining tiers describe the impetus for and impact of CD, explored in subsequent chapters. The model's first tier represents dual propensities (analytical propensity + artistic drive or A/A/D), that stimulate the CD/Di. That dilemma is the second tier of the model, and may (a possibility represented by "◊") lead to choosing CD. *CD describes the coexistence of two careers that satisfy both the analytic and artistic duality represented by A/A/D.* The CD model helps distinguish between CD as a conceptual framework versus making a CD choice. In telling my own CD tale in Chapter 1, I described the battle between my analytic and artistic selves. CD/Di is the battle, and the analytic/ artistic self is represented by A/A/D. This chapter explores the parameters of A/A/D as a precursor to taking a closer look at CD and making CD choices.

Duality Yields Duality: Analytical Propensity + Artistic Drive

The first tier of the CD model is A/A/D, which symbolizes *analytical propensity + artistic drive*. A/A/D represents an internal, personal duality of self. Specifically, it is the coexistence of dual (and sometimes dueling) propensities to work, live, behave, and perceive things both analytically and artistically, with inclinations in both realms. As Figure 2.1 suggests, having this blended, or divided, self is one of the precursors to CD. If you possess A/A/D, you are a general *dualist*, though you may not be a *Career Dualist*. A *Career Dualist* is an entertainment business logician or creative who makes a CD choice. We'll look at the distinction between the two types of dualists later in the chapter. First, let's look closely at the two components that comprise A/A/D.

Analytical Propensity + Artistic Drive = A/A/D

A/A/D → CD/Di
↓
CD/Di ◊ → CD

CD = Coexistence of 2 careers that actualize A/A/D

Calling → Desire for actualization of A/A/D (whether one responds to calling or not)
↓
Responding to calling → Authenticity

FIGURE 2.1 The Career Duality Model

Analytical propensity as defined in this book refers to a preference and inclination to engage in analysis, i.e., breaking down complex things into simpler components that are observable for resolving a problem or reaching a conclusion, particularly in thinking or reasoning. Convergent thinking is a term that researchers use to refer to this type of thought process. It involves engaging in reasoning that critiques and evaluates, even including evaluating one's own artistic work.[1] In research that examines creativity, convergent thinking has been juxtaposed against divergent thinking, which is believed to be a major source of creativity, whereas convergent thinking seeks to find an answer to a particular question through an emphasis on logic and knowledge. According to Arthur Cropley, examples of convergent thinking include:[2]

- engaging in problem solving
- being logical
- achieving accuracy and correctness
- playing it safe

Convergent thinking also involves critical processes,[3] such as synthesizing knowledge and information, akin to critical thinking. Organizations that focus on defining, teaching, and promoting critical thinking describe it in ways that are consistent with principles of convergent thinking. For example, the Foundation for Critical Thinking (criticalthinking.org) developed the International Critical Thinking Test to assess the extent to which critical thinking occurs in education contexts; the test is also intended to support faculty efforts to teach it.[4] Some of the questions included on the test are consistent with convergent and analytical thinking processes.[5] The Brookings Institution, a non–profit entity that focuses on problem solving in societal and educational contexts, suggests that critical thinking is important for independence and resisting falsehoods. The institution observes that such thinking requires inquiry or confronting the status quo and related thought processes. Music business logicians express analytical propensity by working as entrepreneurs, managing the business of their artistic pursuits, or working on behalf of entertainment companies without working as creatives for those companies.

After I began working as an attorney, colleagues or friends would often comment to me that I was approaching a particular task or situation analytically "because you're a lawyer." Having a legal education and working as a lawyer definitely sharpened my analytical propensity and penchant for evidence, logic, and looking for rule-based explanations or solutions. However, my comfort with the world of logic pre-dates law school. The newspaper job search I mentioned offers an opportunity to examine an example of my own analytical propensity. In that situation I sought clarity (problem solving) about the scope of a new job by requesting a written position description to facilitate accuracy in performing my responsibilities. I could have risked working in the position without such a document, but chose a less risky path, in that regard. On the other hand, this was a challenge to the publisher's status quo which required a different type of risk taking that typifies critical thinking.

In my current role teaching undergraduate law courses I frequently encourage students to view exam questions as logic problems that are solvable, like puzzles or math equations. This test-taking perspective existed before I took the Law School Admission Test (LSAT), which was a more comfortable exam for me than was the Graduate Management Admission Test (GMAT). When I took the GMAT in the early 1980s there was no analytical writing section on the test and the critical reasoning section was not added until the late 1980s. My performance on the LSAT was better, a reflection of my preference for logical reasoning.

These examples of convergent thinking represent an analytical propensity some individuals employ as a preferred way of approaching work as well as in academic learning. Yet these experiences only tell half the story with respect to CD. Though I have a longstanding affection and proclivity toward the world of analyses and logic, I am very much at home with the world of imagination, ideation, and creativity as a writer, poet, songwriter, and vocalist. Chapter 3, which introduces other entertainment industry dualists, explores their experiences with both components of A/A/D, and at the end of this chapter you will have the opportunity to explore your own.

Artistic drive is the second component of A/A/D. It refers in part to the artistic, creative self and the propensities associated with being artistic. However, artistic drive does not represent creativity or artistic ability alone. Rather, examining artistic propensity lays the foundation for understanding and discussing the "drive" component in artistic drive. Therefore, let's look first at the artistic component of artistic drive.

Artistic propensity is related to creativity. Just as convergent thinking is related to analytical propensity, divergent thinking is related to creativity. Divergent thinking yields new ways of looking at the familiar, or developing novel ideas and approaches. Examples of divergent thinking include:[6]

- seeing the known in a new light
- taking risks
- being unconventional
- seeing new possibilities

Using divergent thinking as a synonym for creativity is not entirely precise since they are not identical concepts, according to the research. For example, mere newness or variation from what is customary – like that generated by divergent thinking – is not necessarily or automatically creative. Cropley suggests that creativity has added components besides novelty, for example fantasy, the stuff of daydreams.[7] Although creativity can be distinguished from divergent thinking we examine them together, since divergent thinking contributes to creativity and is helpful to an understanding of artistic propensity.

In 2011, Dr. Oyvind Martinsen, a professor and creativity scholar at the Norwegian School of Management, conducted a study to develop a method of assessing and profiling qualities that identify the creative personality. The purpose of the study was to synthesize and build on prior research measures to develop a comprehensive means of measuring creative personality. Martinsen's study of 481 participants consisted of performing artists (regularly working actors and musicians) as well as managers, clerical workers, lecturers, and students from various fields. Divergent thinking tasks were among the 38 creativity constructs included in his Creative Personality Profile. Personality in relationship to A/A/D is further explored later in this chapter. Participants were also required to self-report creative achievements and activities in which they had been involved, since activity measures are considered indicators of creativity.[8] Some of the creative activities they reported on included acting, playing an instrument, writing, and visual arts activities as well as activities considered to be technical, e.g., inventing. Ultimately, the study concluded that it is possible to measure creative personality using seven factors believed to explain differences in creativity amongst different groups or personalities.[9] Five of the factors are easily understood without detailed explanation, e.g., motivation, ambition, need for originality, flexibility, and agreeableness. However, to fully appreciate the study one needs to reference Martin's explanations for all seven of the factors. One of those factors, ambition, relates not only to creativity, but to drive, which is the other aspect of artistic propensity in A/A/D.

Artistic drive as defined in this book refers to a heightened and demonstrated commitment to engage one's artistic self by *acting* on creativity or artistic propensity. This is an important distinction to make in understanding this aspect of CD. CD/ Di – the internal conflict and decisional predicament created when you perceive your own artistic/analytical duality – is triggered by expressing that duality, i.e., through action. With respect to creativity, that expression is fed by artistic drive, which can also be thought of as artistic ambition. Merriam-Webster's dictionary defines ambition as "a desire to be successful, powerful, or famous." Research by Ashley Bell Jones, Ryne Sherman, and Robert Hogan, uses the Merriam-Webster definition to suggest that ambition is an aspect of personality that predicts career success.[10] Their research also correlates ambition with grit, and "persistent striving for long term goals."[11] In the context of creativity, Martinsen's study suggests that people with high scores in ambition on his Creative Personality Profile are assertive, need recognition and attention, and want to affect others.[12]

Cropley's research observes that creativity is paradoxical in nature. One of the paradoxes of creativity is that it requires being able to accept uncertainty. Yet on the other hand, creativity emerges when closure is sought.[13] This search for creative closure is an aspect of artistic drive. Lots of people may be creative or have artistic sensibilities and interests. Yet without ambition there is no tension in career decision making, no CD/Di. To create the tension characterized by CD/Di, not only must there be ambition, it must be motivated toward the arts domain to qualify as artistic drive. Examples of artistic drive include:

- seeking to gig/work professionally as an artist on a regular or ongoing basis
- taking voice or instrument lessons to sharpen artistic acumen
- hiring a publicist, manager, or agent to maximize career options and opportunities
- creating a dedicated web presence to showcase your entertainment expertise and interest

Like the participants in Martinsen's study, you may have many artistic achievements or activities in which you actively participate. For me, CD/Di expresses itself in the areas of both writing and singing. I can comfortably posit that if I had not been a singing lawyer and had instead kept to writing as a primary career path, my A/A/D would probably still exist, regardless of the career I ultimately chose. But I experience the most CD/Di in the realm of music, where artistic drive has remained a constant over time. In other words, music is the area for me in which artistic inclination, referred to in this section as drive, becomes action-based.

Summary of Model

A/A/D, the first tier of the CD model, represents a type of personal duality. One component is analytical propensity, characterized by convergent, critical thinking that focuses on problem solving using logical reasoning. Working as an artist manager is an example of expressing analytical propensity in the music business (an artist manager solves career problems on behalf of an artist by overseeing the artist's career). Artistic drive, the second component, is characterized by creativity, divergent thinking, and artistic ambition that expresses itself through action in the arts or entertainment domain. Performing as a drummer for gigs on an ongoing basis is an example of artistic drive. Dualists possess both components of A/A/D, which can create a decisional quandary (CD/Di) about career that may ultimately be satisfied by CD. The remaining tiers of the model are explored in Part II.

Left Brain/Right Brain, Ability, and Personality

To aid in exploration of your own A/A/D, the following sections explore potential sources of analytic and artistic propensities. Where do these inclinations come from? Are they based on innate ability? Or preferences? Are your artistic and analytical proclivities an expression of your personality? Researchers Kathy J. Rysiew, Bruce M. Shore, and Rebecca T. Leeb took a comprehensive look at the research on multipotentiality and found that there was wide variation in the definition of multipotentiality amongst researchers. Nevertheless, a general definition is that it describes individuals with multiple abilities and interests, often discussed in the context of literature about people who are "gifted and talented." Rysiew, Shore, and Leeb concluded that "there is a shortage of independent empirical research in support of the concept of multipotentiality," but it is supported by anecdotal evidence.[14] A/A/D may be considered a type of multipotentiality – as this book asserts – and interviews conducted with the profiled dualists presented in Chapter 3 provide anecdotal evidence of multi-potentiality. If career decisions are based on self-knowledge, as Rysiew, Shore, and Leeb suggest, delving into these questions may assist you in reflecting on your multipotentiality, your personal dualities, i.e., your A/A/D.[15] In turn, this self-knowledge may help to sort through the CD/Di that can frustrate career decision making. The following section addresses three potential sources of A/A/D: brain dominance theory, ability, and personality. In examining these topics, the goal is to provide condensed synopses for considering their relationship to A/A/D and career choices.

Brain Dominance Theory

You ask, isn't everyone partly artistic and partly analytical anyway? Maybe. It depends on how those determinations would be made. As I was contemplating writing this book and shared with others the idea of my own experience as partly analytical and partly artistic, people often associated the idea of duality (without using that word or knowledge of this concept) with what they knew about left brain/right brain concepts. In other words, some people tend to see the idea of being analytic or artistic as an outgrowth of brain duality.

Theories suggesting that the brain has divided functionality have origins in early human history and have been studied in relationship to vocation. Gary Szirony et al. examined the relationship between brain hemisphere dominance and preferences about careers. They trace the origins of brain dominance and point out that it began with the Greek philosopher Socrates, spanning to early psychologists like Pavlov, and culminating with Roger Sperry, who won the Nobel Prize in 1981 for his discoveries concerning the functional specialization of the cerebral hemispheres.[16] The idea of left-versus right-brain dominance refers to a scientific, biologically based theory that the left or right side of an individual's brain may determine principal behavior. The theory proposes that logic and analytical behavior are determined by the left brain, while artistic, creative, or thoughtful behavior is determined by the right side of the brain.

Szirony and his colleagues' analysis of the research observes that when it comes to music, there are studies that show how highly complex the brain's operations are, suggesting that both hemispheres intertwine to process music. Therefore, contrary to popular belief, some studies assert that there may not be one dominant side of the brain that controls music processing. Questions surrounding how the brain processes music have led to further research to explore the extent to which one side of the brain controls other functions. In 2013, researchers at the University of Utah used brain-imaging technology – which sets their study apart from those that did not use this technology – to study brain functions. Their findings also challenged and questioned whether one side is more dominant than the other.[17] These amended perspectives on brain hemisphere research potentially support the idea that a dualist may have strong propensities on *both* sides of the brain, not just one dominant side. Brain science is not the province of this book or its explorations, and the concepts described here are not based on brain hemisphere theories. Nevertheless, there are some take-aways from the Szirony et al. research on brain dominance and vocation that are worth noting.

In a study with 101 graduate and undergraduate students at large universities, Szirony and fellow researchers explored self-perceptions of mathematical ability (a left-brain domain) and musical ability (a right-brain domain). The study used the Human Information Processing Survey (HIPS), which was developed to assess brain hemisphere preferences. The survey included questions about preferences for course assignments that involved left-brain functions – like logical problem solving and drawing conclusions – as well as questions about assignments involving right-brain functions, like discovery through exploration and relational thinking. The HIPS analysis showed that 44 of the participants were left-brained, 30 were integrated, and 27 were right-brained.

Since their research examined brain hemispheres in relation to vocation, the study design also incorporated a second assessment based on John Holland's career theory. John Holland is renowned for originating theories that connect personality with vocational fit and career choice. Holland identified six personality types, known as the RIASEC types, that have been a mainstay of career research for over 40 years. RIASEC stands for Realistic, Investigative, Artistic, Social, Enterprising, and Conventional. These labels represent types of personalities that engender certain vocational preferences. The RIASEC types also correspond to occupational codes. Holland's theory is discussed in the section of this chapter that explores personality as a separate factor related to A/A/D. The Szirony et al. study combined the HIPS with the Holland Self-Directed Search (SDS) form R, which assesses career interests.[18] Three brain hemisphere preferences were used – right, left, and integrated – to determine where observed correlations with ability would lie. They found a correlation between brain hemisphere and career choice in that right-brain processing related to participants who self-reported an aptitude for music. They did not find that left-brain processing related to math ability. Rather, mathematical ability related to integrated (both left and right) brain processing. Prior research had suggested that music is more of an integrated function, but that theory was not supported by this study which found that music is more right-brained.

What does all this mean in terms of A/A/D? Brain hemisphere theory could help with understanding whether you are primarily analytical or primarily artistic via an understanding of which hemisphere is dominant. And the Szirony et al. research supports prior findings that the right brain specifically correlates to music and artistic ability. However, A/A/D is not limited to focusing on whether you are primarily analytical or primarily artistic. Rather, the CD model acknowledges and explores the significance of having inclinations in *both* areas. These inclinations derive not just from a particular brain hemisphere, but from how you see yourself, according to the Szirony et al. findings. Since their research used self-reporting – the self-scoring of the Holland SDS form – to identify mathematical or musical aptitude, the study accentuates the importance of self-knowledge. In fact, the study reports that increased self-knowledge for participants was an unintended benefit of the study. Brain hemisphere dominance may be instrumental in shaping us but does not necessarily dominate when it comes to the origins of our analytic and artistic propensities.

Talent and Ability

Are the propensities represented by A/A/D innate, beyond the dictates of brain biology? The idea that we are born with certain gifts, talents, or abilities is probably familiar. How many times have family, friends, or teachers told you that you are naturally a good singer, or a natural planner? Or both? Perhaps no one needed to tell you that. Maybe you were able to play the piano at a young age without ever having received formal training. Or maybe you recognized early on that math or science classes seemed easier to you than other classes, like the participants in the Szirony et al. study.

If you believe that you are naturally talented in certain areas, or believe talent is a natural, biological ability, your view is one shared by many researchers. It is a belief that spans both artistic and analytical realms, from music and dance, to math, science, even the ability to speak foreign languages.[19] Michael Howe, Jane Davidson, and John Sloboda are researchers who refer to that belief as "the talent account." The talent account suggests not only that talent is innate, but that it explains high levels of success, i.e., the more talented you are in a given area, the more successful you will be within it. However, their research challenges that widely held belief. The talent account seems as virtuous as motherhood and apple pie, and it feels good to believe that we are naturally better at some things than other people. So why would they challenge it? The benefit of research is to dig deep, to plumb the depths of human experiences. Additionally, Howe and colleagues recognized the social implications of decisions based on talent alone. For example, what if you have a passion for math but are told by your math teacher – an expert in the field who has seen what you can do – that you have no real math aptitude? Will she support or discourage your passion? How would being told that affect your career opportunities and pursuits?

Carla Harris is a Wall Street powerhouse who is vice chairman of wealth management and senior client advisor at Morgan Stanley who appears to manifest A/A/D. Her responsibilities at Morgan Stanley require sharp analytic acumen, yet she is also an accomplished recording artist who has released three albums and performed five sold-out concerts at Carnegie Hall. A/A/D in action! When she was in high school a guidance counselor told her she should not apply to Ivy League schools. Nevertheless, she was admitted to Harvard and other Ivy League schools she applied to.[20] After entering Harvard, a professor there discouraged her from declaring economics as her major, questioning her ability to succeed in that major, telling her "she could not think."[21] Fortunately, she didn't listen. If she had listened to the voice of that professor, she might not have pursued her economics interests and Morgan Stanley (and the world) would be deprived of the expertise of a phenomenal African American woman. Her advice is to ignore what others have to say about you. Again, the importance of self-knowledge! Her autobiographical book, *Expect to Win*, is an inspiring read I highly recommend, especially for dualists. There are other stories like Harris', for example, Michael Jordan's.

Although not the focus of this book, athletic ability is another area in which talent is believed to set some sports stars apart from others. Michael Jordan, one of the greatest (perhaps the greatest) professional basketball players to ever play the game looks like the epitome of a textbook definition of talent. His accomplishments are legendary: five-time NBA Most Valuable Player, six-time NBA champion, six-time NBA Finals Most Valuable Player, and ten scoring titles, which is an NBA record. He retired with the NBA's highest scoring average of 30.1 points per game and is a Basketball Hall of Fame inductee. This is just a partial list of his achievements.[22] Commentators, and perhaps the general public, have attributed his abilities to shoot, dribble, score, and maneuver on the court to sheer talent. In fact, researchers David Feldman and Tamar Katzir point to Jordan as anecdotal evidence for natural talent, rather than practice.[23] But Jordan was initially cut from his high school team and told he would never be a very good basketball player. Determined to play the game and to play it well, his practice regimen was relentless.

The point of highlighting these examples is not to dismiss talent, but to broaden our understanding of it and of research that examines it. The negative feedback Carla Harris and Michael Jordan received are examples of why Howe, Davidson, and Sloboda were motivated to explore the influence that can come from teachers, coaches, parents, and social norms about talent. Citing the work of Jere E. Brophy and Thomas L. Good, Howe, Davidson, and Sloboda specifically point out that "children's progress can be affected negatively as well as positively by adults' expectations."[24]

In thinking about whether talent and ability are the same, the Howe, Davidson, and Sloboda investigation identifies talent through some key attributes. They characterize it as somewhat innate (i.e., genetic), a predictor of success, possessed by few, and generally limited to a specific discipline or field.[25] Merriam-Webster refers to ability as "natural aptitude or acquired proficiency." Although ability can be either natural or acquired, there is a measure of intersectionality between the Howe, Davidson, and Sloboda definition of talent and the dictionary definition of ability, since ability is the substance of talent. Additionally, the Howe, Davidson, and Sloboda definition speculates that talent – if it exists – is partly, not wholly, innate. Therefore, the terms ability and talent are used interchangeably in this book.

Howe, Davidson, and Sloboda recognized that there was no commonly accepted definition of talent within the research community and posed one to make clear just what concept they were challenging. They are not the only researchers to question the talent account. They point out that childhood experiences and sustained practice have been offered by other researchers as alternative explanations for excellence in music and other fields.[26] On the other hand, a number of researchers support the idea of talent as a natural ability that accounts for success. Given the inconsistencies in conclusions about the topic amongst researchers, Howe, Davidson, and Sloboda undertook a comprehensive review of research written about the talent account, and then penned their own findings. They analyzed each of the elements within their definition of talent and examined the beliefs associated with the talent account. They concluded that it is factors like training, effort, experience, opportunity, and practice that produce excellence, rather than natural ability alone. They also expressed concern that categorizing some individuals as talented might result in discriminatory and unfair treatment towards those considered untalented. After completing their review they invited open peer commentary from other researchers. Their invitations to provide comments offered the opportunity to consider alternative arguments in the interest of healthy scholarly debate, essentially challenging other researchers and theorists to challenge them. Thirty of some of the most well-respected researchers took up the gauntlet. For example, one of the researchers who responded to the invitation was Mihaly Csikszentmihalyi. He originated the theory of "flow," and is highly respected in the field of creativity. In his response he found no support either for or against the talent account.[27] Some of the other commenters supported the Howe, Davidson, and Sloboda conclusions, while others did not and offered theories of their own. They considered all 30 responses and published their reconsidered conclusions. The result is a detailed analysis that is briefly summarized here.

Ultimately, Howe, Davidson, and Sloboda found that the respondents to their challenge helped them think more fully about their analyses, but did not offer sufficient research evidence to alter their findings regarding the talent account. They point out that (1) the difficulty of reaching agreement on what constitutes talent points to the difficulty of measuring whether it exists; (2) they did not look at "genius" or find it necessary to examine because it is too rare to reliably measure; (3) ability can vary from person to person, and that variation can be genetically influenced, but they found no evidence that ability is not also shaped by other factors that undermine the existence of innate talent; (4) innate or hereditary influences may contribute more to persistence or determination, which may be attributable to "temperamental factors" that are akin to personality traits; (5) practice and training definitely influence ability (they cite the observation of Weisberg that even Mozart was not considered a master composer until after he had studied music for 16 years); finally, (6) they do not depart from their original concern that certain individuals who are considered talented may receive different treatment and resources than those who are not. They call attention to how inappropriate this outcome would be regarding math and science education, where equal educational opportunities for all students are valued. In the arts, however, there seems to be more willingness to focus scarce resources on only the most "gifted" or talented. They emphasize their concern that this perspective has discriminatory and divisive possibilities. This last point is particularly compelling. The United States has a history of discriminatory practices in education and other spheres. Americans have worked legislatively and socially to overcome them. Yet the kind of feedback Carla Harris and Michael Jordan received is real, particularly for persons of color. Fortunately for them, Harris and Jordan possessed determination of spirit and a sense of self-knowledge that helped them to succeed in the face of being declared "untalented."

They also possessed what is known in sports as the mindset of a champion. In her book, *Mindset: The New Psychology of Success*, celebrated professor, author, and researcher Carol Dweck develops the concept of the Growth Mindset. It refers to the determination and application of effort exemplified in the attitude of the champion and actually bolsters ability. The book details the research that undergirds her mindset theories, contrasting the stories of individuals who believed in the Fixed Mindset – believing that their abilities were fixed and that they either had a certain ability or didn't – with those who exhibited the Growth Mindset. For those with the Fixed Mindset, effort was viewed as a sign of modest or defective ability. If you possess the Growth Mindset, however, you believe that you can build on your abilities through learning and effort, seeing mistakes as opportunities for growth. For these individuals the presence or absence of talent does not impede learning. Instead, they meet new challenges with practice, or rehearsal, or whatever effort is required to improve their abilities.

How does research on whether one is naturally talented or not relate to assessing your personal A/A/D? You are free to decide! Not only are you free to interpret the significance of the research, you are free to determine your own levels of A/A/D. According to the research of Howe, Davidson, and Sloboda and others, ability is self-directed, self-assessed, and self-defined. Therefore, instead of hanging your career decisions on whether you are naturally analytical or naturally possess artistic drive, you can tune into your inclinations and preferences and can proactively choose who you are, which can influence your career choices and opens up the possibility of making a CD choice or other satisfying career decision.

The kind of self-knowledge exhibited by Harris and Jordan, by Dweck's exemplars, and by the participants in the Szirony et al. study discussed previously, is a precursor to such choice. The Szirony et al. study used self-reports of artistic and analytical ability from its participants. You must know who you are and what you are capable of achieving. When asked about their preferences and success with certain courses, the study participants had an important source of data to draw from: themselves.

I vividly recall sitting on the swings in my backyard, singing my 12-year old rendition of *We've Only Just Begun*,[28] then running off to perform it for my mother feeling I had discovered something about myself that was uniquely mine to share. I heard my own voice differently that day, something in it that seemed sonorous and somehow right. I am genuinely appreciative of those who have booked me for performances, attended my concerts, or purchased my recordings – all of which seems to indicate that others agree with my childhood assessment. But at some point, it is you who must decide not only what your abilities are, but how to use them and what they will mean for your life.

A study by Elena Gabor examined turning points in the careers of classical musicians, those pivotal moments that helped the participants decide whether they would make music a serious pursuit, either vocationally or through choosing it as a college major.[29] Gabor's qualitative study was based on interviews with 46 pairs of parent-adult child musicians reporting on the experiences that shaped their career decisions. When asked about moments in their education that marked a change they mentioned feedback from friends, parents, teachers, and audiences. But such feedback is only part of the equation as a defining moment. Ultimately, some participants transitioned from seeing themselves solely through the eyes of others or relying on parental mandates as a motivator to succeed. External input shaped self-perception, but these inputs from others served as springboards to confidence, hard work, and self-assessment of ability. How you choose to process those inputs is what determines your course of action and ultimately your success. The same can be said of ability; how analytical do *you* think you are? How much artistic drive do *you* believe you have, and are acting on?

Some artistic performers have a strong belief in natural gifts.[30] A study conducted by David Throsby and Virginia Hollister examining secondary employment amongst Australian artists found that almost one third of artists indicated that talent was "the most important factor advancing their professional development."[31] However, an issue to determine is how much weight to give to such a belief for guiding your career decisions. If you believe that you are not analytically gifted enough to achieve in law or music business, you may disadvantage yourself by not pursuing those fields. And on what are you basing that belief? Likewise, in the realm of artistic drive, telling yourself that you are not creative or capable of such ambition will affect your pursuit of career opportunities in the arts. Self-messages affect how much effort you invest, which has a proven effect on ability. It is a kind of vicious cycle: belief in your ability affects effort, and the investment of effort affects ability.

None of the research on talent discussed here suggests that everyone is equally capable of doing everything, or that there is no such thing as talent. For example, the fact that we are each born with a unique set of vocal chords – say, for use in singing – and do not determine the length of our fingers – for playing instruments – cannot be ignored. But the voice and fingers are tools. Like other tools, what they build rests in the hands of the crafter. When it comes to the idea that talent is a major determinant of success, these research findings report no uniform evidence supporting the kind of natural talent that exists apart from cultivated ability through factors like practice, training, and opportunity – even for the Mozarts and Michael Jordans of the world. Additionally, the artistic component in A/A/D refers to artistic *drive*, as previously defined. Therefore, even if you choose to believe in artistic talent, the focus of A/A/D is on how motivated you are to actually use it. Will you remain motivated to exercise your abilities when positive feedback wanes, or when feedback is negative or non-existent? How will you assess your A/A/D in order to sort through your career decisions? What we learn from the research on talent and ability is this: (1) know yourself. Self-knowledge is a persistent theme throughout the research. (2) You can discover the A/A/D that lies within you by dismissing restrictive judgments about how natural your talent or ability is. You can use that self-knowledge to direct your abilities where *you* want them to go.

Personality

We each approach things in our own way. A/A/D describes analytical and artistic propensities representing a duality of self that is common to dualists, while personality explains what shapes the self and accounts for the variation amongst individuals in how those propensities are experienced and lived.

Psychological researchers define personality through a concept known as the Big Five.[32] That labeling reminds me of reference to "the five families" in the mobster movie *The Godfather*. The term may not sound particularly research-like, yet years of research have firmly established the Big Five, also known as the Five Factor Model, as a means of understanding personality. It is a widely accepted theory that is now as influential in the research community as the heads of the five families were in *The Godfather*'s fictional America. The model builds on the work of Carl Jung, a preeminent behavioral scientist who developed his groundbreaking concepts around 1921.[33] Jung theorized that personalities can be categorized into certain types. The types are based on combinations of qualities related to introversion versus extroversion – terms he coined – and other qualities, like thinking versus feeling. He further theorized that types are expressed through certain preferences uniquely exercised by each of us. Jung's theories became the basis for the Myers-Briggs Type Indicator assessments that are popular and in widespread use today. While Jung is the father of type theory, Gordon Allport, also a leader in the field of personality, is considered one of the founders of personality trait theory.[34]

The five traits that comprise the model are openness, conscientiousness, extroversion, agreeableness, and neuroticism. They all seem fine enough when taken at face value, and we can all envision how each one might apply to us without finding any of them particularly objectionable – until we arrive at neuroticism! The image of a nervous, anxiety-ridden, pessimistic hypochondriac gives this factor little appeal, courtesy of Woody Allen-like caricatures. Such portrayals are not entirely off the mark, as anxiety and emotional instability actually are hallmarks of neuroticism. However, like weapons or power, each trait has the potential for both positive and negative expression; the variations within each of us account for how a trait actually looks on an individual level. Openness is characterized by interest in aesthetics, like art; but less openness would point to inflexibility. Examples of conscientiousness include being careful, orderly, reliable, and persevering. Confidence, ambition, and social presence are qualities that indicate extroversion, whereas introversion would be the opposite of those traits. Agreeableness is what the term implies: cooperative, easy-going, friendly. Individuals with less of this trait are said to be more argumentative, cynical, and suspicious. Last, but not least, neurotic qualities include defensiveness, insecurity, and worrying. Less of this quality indicates emotional stability and a sense of well-being.[35]

Psychologists theorize that we are all a unique mix of these qualities. That includes artistic, creative personalities. Gregory Feist comprehensively reviewed studies of personality in relation to creativity. His examination specifically looked to the Big Five and concluded that creative people are more open to experiences, introverted, more self-confident, driven, ambitious, dominant, hostile, and impulsive.[36] The spectrum of theories on creativity and personality is particularly relevant since dualists are creative personalities, at least in part. The Feist study was significant because it shined a comprehensive light on the work of other theorists studying personality and creativity, which has been ongoing for over 30 years. More recently, Martinsen's efforts to develop a creative person profile, discussed previously, incorporated the Five Factor Model in his studies. He identified 38 creativity variables and extracted seven factors to measure creative personalities: instability, ambition, motivation, need for originality, flexibility, agreeableness, and associative orientation (fantasy, playfulness). He found that these characteristics are reliable ways to think about the qualities of creative personalities. But what does it mean for us creative types?

The Predicament and Paradox of Personality

At first blush, some of the literature on creative personality seems to pit scientific or analytic personality against creative personality. Martinsen's study compares artists to marketing students, as if to imply that the qualities that differentiate such students do not exist in the same person. But what if they do, as for me and possibly for you? What if you are an artistic marketing student? John Holland, the psychological researcher known for the idea of vocational fit and personality, found that the six RIASEC types discussed earlier have a relationship to each other. Some are closer to each other; for example, the realistic type and the investigator type are closely related to each other because they resemble each other. Yet the artistic type and the conventional type are as far apart as his measures can show because they do not resemble each other. Holland's theory leaves room for combinations and recognizes that it is simplistic to say that there are only six personality types. Rather, he recognized that you may be primarily artistic, secondarily investigative, thirdly social, and so on, a mix of all six factors. Yet possessing what appear to be opposite combinations is not so obvious to everyone. Nor does it matter to everyone. But it matters to you and me. It matters so much that you and I have chosen to journey together through a book on how and whether to engage multiple selves vocationally. Personality is what makes the difference in how our brains and abilities are directed, how we each approach using or perceiving our analytical and artistic propensities, and whether these qualities meld or divide.

Though artistic drive and analytical propensity are two separate qualities, Cropley's work examined the role of convergent (analytic) thinking in creativity and found that *both* logic and knowledge are necessary for creativity. Specifically, he found that divergent thinking, the intellectual ingredient that leads to creativity, actually requires convergent thinking too. That explains some things for me, and perhaps for you. It makes so much sense that the artistically driven part of me would want to make music, write poetry, sing! Yet it also makes sense that my approach to creativity would not escape the analytical side of me. It all ties together: the creative personality actually has – and needs – its analytical side.

One of the ten most read articles of *Fast Company* magazine in 2013 was titled *10 Paradoxical Traits of Creative People* by Faisal Hoque,[37] in which Mihaly Csikszentmihalyi, professor of psychology and management mentioned previously, observes that creative people are paradoxical and complex. He observes that more and more artists are becoming entrepreneurs, and more things are converging.[38] We artistic types can run our own music companies, practice entertainment law, bring a scientific eye to the creative world. Yet we can do this innovatively because of the creative juices flowing through us. This is particularly relevant for the future of the music business and other creative industries, and is discussed in Chapter 5. Likewise, those analytical instincts impact how and who we are creatively. Possessing A/A/D can be good, a type of multipotentiality that inspires a sense of gratification and confidence in being dually abled. It can also be a source of internal conflict, one that I have experienced.

Though I started singing early, solo public performances came in my 20s and was something that began largely because of encouragement from others. During congregational singing in church someone seated near me would often comment to me about my voice, ask me why I wasn't singing solos for the church, or suggest that I should. Eventually, I volunteered to do just that, which led to more

and different opportunities. The more I performed, the more I began to contemplate how to improve my singing skills, to combine knowledge with artistry.
I started studying with voice teachers, attending classes, practicing drills, and
learning techniques. Somewhere in my quest for knowledge the analytical side of
me seemed to take over my focus, to edge out creativity. In those early days of
performing, my technical perspective diminished my joy for singing for many
years. Appreciation from audiences was a motivating factor that urged me on, but
I performed primarily because I believed it was something I was supposed to do
since I had the ability to do so, and the analytical side of me was determined to
do it "right." But it was work, mostly the work of convergent thinking.

When I initially started working on an album in the 1990s my producer, Ron
Smith, suggested that I consider writing some of the music for it. I had never written
any songs and initially resisted the idea of writing music, believing that was something only people with that gift could do; I believed in the talent account. As it turns
out, songwriting is something you can teach and learn. It is possible to train yourself
to channel your own creativity. My university has an excellent songwriting major
that produces successful writers every year. The discipline of training and coursework
requires convergent thinking that is channeled into divergent thinking to produce
creative songs. I am grateful to Ron for helping me see that the creative inclination I
had for writing poetry could be directed toward learning to write a song.

You can study scat (an improv style of singing jazz), breath control, phrasing,
and other vocal techniques. Vincent Van Gogh studied painting. Mozart studied
music. The question of paradox in a creative personality is whether a technical
approach impedes creativity or stimulates it. In the case of Van Gogh and Mozart
study was complimentary, rather than obstructive. Mozart composed over 600
works, including masses, operas, symphonies, and concertos. Van Gogh produced
over 900 paintings. I do not compare myself to either of these masters, but like them
have a creative personality that is paradoxically prone to study. Being logical helps
me tackle performing a song that initially seems difficult. Figuring out how to
approach it requires some analysis; I systematically break the song down into smaller
parts to find ways to modify it to fit my style and ability. Both study and artistry are
involved. Will the result be a technical-sounding performance? Or will it yield a
sense of mastery? Cropley's research suggests that creativity "requires goal-directed,
logical (convergent) thinking, but must simultaneously go beyond it."[39]

I am happy to have entered a phase of life as a performer where I am exploring
what it means to go beyond the technical, to reclaim both my joy of singing and
a measure of creativity that balances with the analytical side of my personality.
Cropley's work and the work of other researchers helps us to better understand the
dilemma dualists experience as a result of the paradox of the creative personality.
How you experience and manage the dilemma of duality is a matter of who you
are, and how those paradoxes operate within your personality. Discovering the
research behind my experience was a Eureka moment for me. I hope this understanding of creative personality is the beginning of a Eureka moment for you too.

The Power to Choose

How do the concepts of A/A/D, brain dominance, ability, and personality connect to CD? CD corresponds to an array of opportunities for addressing your CD/Di. It involves a choice that begins with first recognizing and understanding your A/A/D, an inner duality. A/A/D may not feel like a choice. We may believe we are born with analytical propensity and artistic drive. We may believe that brain dominance defines us. We may believe in the talent account, and what we perceive to be our natural abilities. We may believe our abilities oppose, rather than complement each other. However, personality – how one uniquely approaches inclinations, interests, and abilities – is where our preferences are exercised and where we can express our choices. We can choose to acknowledge the duality that lives within and seek an awareness of how to express that duality vocationally. That is why this book was written. The CD choice represents an option to exert influence over your career destiny by opting to maintain two concurrent careers that satisfy A/A/D, as the CD model suggests. But what does CD look like? And why does it involve two careers?

If A/A/D is a type of duality, maintaining two careers is a corresponding duality to fulfill it. Nevertheless, grounding CD in the idea of maintaining dual careers may appear to doom dualists to an existence of way too much hard work! Or may look like a "requirement" perpetuating the type of busyness that has become a watchword for social significance. My intent and the concept of CD could not be more different. CD is about finding satisfaction, authenticity, even a sense of purpose. It is also about keeping your options open. It involves being more intentional about some choices dualists are already making but may not be choosing from conviction or self-knowledge. The reality for some dualists is that they will either seek to express their A/A/D or spend a lifetime wishing they had, imagining an unlived past. However, you have the power to choose, to consider what you believe is best for you today and for your future. While opting for two careers is not the only path open to dualists (as explored in Chapter 8), the following research on avocation and related concepts provides some helpful insights on why a CD choice is worth considering. Yet this is not a choice to be dictated by scientists or other experts. CD is a choice that involves maintaining two careers in a way that is custom made, personally tailored, to seek a balance that resonates with your own A/A/D and how you wish to express it.

Avocation, Semi-Professionalism, and Professionalism

I really thought, though I am not sure I fully believed, that being an entertainment lawyer would scratch my A/A/D itch. I have previously described the excitement and sense of privilege I felt when attending a concert or other performances for work, and realized how blessed I was to be able to blend my love for the art world with my job. I still feel that way when I reflect on my current work in an entertainment and music business curriculum, the other artists I engage with, the impact I hope I am having on the industry by training future entertainment business professionals – all very rewarding. My analytical propensity is satisfied, in spades. But my artistic drive cannot be sated by these activities, nor was it satisfied when I worked as a practicing lawyer. There is no stage for musical performance, no audience to connect with as an artist when one works on the business side of the industry. If you work for a music publishing company as a copyright administrator, you are being paid to obtain licenses and manage royalty computations and payments, not sing or play. If you work in A&R, your job is to look for and promote someone else's talent, not your own. If you work as an artist manager, the energy you expend on directing a career in the entertainment industry will benefit your client, rather than your own artistic ambition. And this will be reflected in your day-to-day responsibilities. Consequently, the sense that something is missing – attention to your own artistic drive – will be real unless you find a way to fulfill it.

This imbalance is normal for those with multiple abilities, like dualists, and is experienced outside the arts as well, as the research on multipotentiality suggests. Researchers have found that those with multiple abilities should think more broadly than expecting a single, life-long occupation to fully meet all their needs.[40] Yet those with a wide array of abilities are the very types of people who want to express themselves fully in utilizing as many of their abilities as possible. As a subset of the multipotentialed, dualists experience the same kind of dilemma when it comes to making vocational choices. Even though the business side of the music and entertainment industries provides opportunities for creativity, the type of creativity required for the administrative aspects of such positions leaves a gap when it comes to artistic drive. Likewise, the satisfaction one receives working as a vocalist, producer, or songwriter is different from the fulfillment derived from running an entertainment company, strategizing for litigation, trying and winning a case, or managing an artist. How, then, does one satisfy both sides of A/A/D?

Two recommendations from the research on multipotentiality support the CD model and have been found to contribute to career satisfaction: 1) keep your career options open; and 2) consider consecutive or concurrent career paths.[41] A consecutive, or serial, career path is one in which you move from one job to another to gratify your many interests. In contrast, a concurrent path involves holding more than one position at a time. The concurrent path is a CD choice. The research of Justin M. Berg, Adam M. Grant, and Victoria Johnson suggests that engaging in leisure and job-crafting activities is a specific way to implement the concurrent approach, to help fill the gaps left missing by a job that does not allow for maximum self-expression.[42] CD is an example of the concurrent approach that can incorporate avocation as a type of "leisure" activity that helps quench the compelling thirst of A/A/D.

Avocation is defined by Merriam-Webster's dictionary as "a subordinate occupation pursued in addition to one's vocation, especially for enjoyment."[43] This is the primary definition to bear in mind whenever the term is used throughout the book.

Avocation is also defined as "customary employment" or vocation. This second aspect of the definition is reflected in a study conducted by Neil Alper and Gregory Wassall for the National Endowment for the Arts. They examined the practice of moonlighting, defined by Merriam-Webster's *New World Dictionary* as "the practice of holding a second regular job in addition to one's main job."[44] Alper and Wassall expanded this secondary meaning to align with the definition of avocation by delineating the relationship between primary and subordinate employment. Specifically, they incorporate an element of time, thus clarifying that "a moonlighting worker's main, or primary, job is defined as the one in which he or she works (or usually works) the most hours."[45] Using this definition, they found that artists routinely hold more than one position. Their study was based on data from the United States Current Population Survey for the years 1970 to 1997 and grouped artists into four categories: 1) architects and designers; 2) performing artists; 3) visual artists (painters, sculptors, photographers, and the like); and 4) other artists (authors, college and university teachers of art, drama, and music, and artists not classified elsewhere). These categories were derived from aggregating 11 artist occupations reported through the census.[46] During the years covering the study period, 7 to 14 percent of artists engaged in moonlighting. When comparing artists to non-artist occupations they found that artists moonlight about 40 percent more frequently than all other workers.[47] Other findings that are interesting in relation to CD:

- Artists averaged spending 12 hours per week on their second job.
- The stereotype of artists working primarily in service occupations (e.g., waiting tables) as a second job was not supported. Rather, just under 20 percent of artists' moonlighting jobs were in sales, clerical, or service occupations, while 55 to 75 percent of artists held second jobs in a professional or technical field; this includes holding a second job as an artist.
- In fact, the second job held is often as an artist. Performing artist was the most common choice for a second job from amongst the four artist-occupation categories.
- However, since 1985 the number of artists moonlighting as artists fell from three in five to one in three, while the number of artists holding second jobs other than as artists rose from one in ten to one in three.
- The most frequently cited reason for working a second job was to supplement income. The second most common reason for a second job was enjoyment of the work, particularly for non-artists working as an artist in a second job. In fact, for non-artists working a second job as an artist, the need to supplement income was cited less often as a reason for moonlighting.

Financial need as a motivation for moonlighting amongst artists is not so unexpected. The starving artist archetype is, unfortunately, all too familiar and the need to support oneself is a practical reality. In their study of secondary employment amongst artists, Throsby and Hollister found evidence that when artists in

Australia and other countries were asked what factors impeded their advancement as professional artists, they indicated "financial problems and time constraints."[48] The Alper and Wassall moonlighting study and Throsby and Hollister data provide helpful information about how artistic drive looks, particularly in conjunction with other employment. It also allows us to acknowledge the role of compensation and earning potential in a dialogue about making career choices in the entertainment industry.

However, moonlighting departs from a CD-inspired definition of concurrent employment, in that moonlighting is characterized as simply holding two jobs at once. A goal of CD is not merely to engage in moonlighting, but to explore avocation, which involves pursuits that extend beyond financial need and even beyond enjoyment. Additionally, as the CD model suggests, calling is an impetus for CD that is examined in Part II of this book and authenticity is the goal of CD, not mere concurrent engagement.

If enjoyment is an element of an avocational pursuit and if avocation is secondary to primary employment, how is it different from a hobby? The dictionary defines avocation and hobby similarly, wherein hobby is defined as "a pursuit outside one's regular occupation engaged in especially for relaxation."[49] The Throsby and Hollister study separated "amateurs from hobbyists" by distinguishing *professional* artists as "serious practitioners operating at a level and standard of work and with a degree of commitment appropriate to the norms of professional practice within their artform."[50] Though the dictionary definition of "professional" includes being paid for your work, the Throsby and Hollister definition does not include pay at all; in fact, they expressly reject it as a necessary criterion for defining professional behavior. Nevertheless, it is the perception of the dualist that matters most. This chapter has previously mentioned the importance of self-knowledge in career decision making, from identifying your abilities, to choosing a major in college, or in interpreting feedback from others. Therefore, if you see your concurrent employment as a hobby, then so it is. Conversely, if you bring to it the level of commitment and "norms of professional practice" implicit in the definition of professionalism – such as time spent regularly working in your craft and maintaining your skills and abilities in a manner that renders them with excellence, a sense of self-respect, and diligence – then you are a professional, even if your pursuit is part time.

Over the years when I have been asked if I am a professional vocalist, I have opted for the term "semi-professional," since performing as a singer has always been a secondary pursuit for me. I am often paid but have never been signed to a record label, or worked at it full time, nor worked with celebrities as a singer. Yet I adopted that label because of how I construe it. The "semi" prefix acknowledges the secondary component of concurrent employment and is combined with the term "professional" to indicate the standard I endeavor to apply to my pursuit. If conventional notions of semi-professionalism have historically implied a lower standard of professionalism, I chose to repurpose that term to fit my own journey. Dropping the "semi" altogether could apply to my work as a vocalist as well.

Chapter 3 profiles other dualists, including Career Dualists, who have made choices about avocation. Kevin Bruener, vice president of marketing for CDBaby, is one of the Career Dualists profiled in that chapter. He discussed his level of professionalism for music and distinguished between avocation and hobby very clearly in terms that speak to a commitment that transcends money and time.

> *Everything I do with music I pursue at a professional level. So I may not be getting paid full time, but the quality of the product, the people we employ to engineer and record, the way we go about presenting ourselves is always at a professional level. Even when I've just been in local bands here in the Portland scene, same thing. It's not just guys going around because we want to get together and play music; we're very serious about writing songs, recording them in a way that we think represents the sound we're going for, doing our best to promote and market to our ability with whatever means we have that we can afford to put into it. When I think about a hobby I think of something more to just pass the time or to find a little bit of personal enjoyment. But to me, the way I pursue it, the level I'd say of Smalltown Poets – that's the band that was signed to an EMI label – especially the way we do it, even though our time together is far more limited than when we were basically living together on the road, we still take it very seriously and are still, we think, making great music with the amount of time and effort that we can.*

Bruener and I, and the other dualists you will read about in Chapter 3, have established our own definitions of avocation and professionalism. Therefore, here is where I repeat my mantra about CD choices, a message that I hope resonates throughout this book: you, too, are empowered to choose how you approach and perceive your vocational pursuits. You have a whole range of career options that stretch before you, waiting to be explored. This extended discussion distinguishing moonlighting, avocation, and semi-professionalism has been presented because CD is an avocational approach (where avocation is uniquely self-defined) to concurrent employment that facilitates fulfillment of A/A/D through career exploration. That exploration is just around the corner.

What Color Is Your Duality?

Creative personalities have some traits in common, but how they are expressed in each of us is different. Variation is the heart and soul of personality. Likewise, your experience and expression of A/A/D will differ from mine and so will your CD or duality experience. Having described A/A/D and the source of its variation, this section examines how CD can look and proposes a method for assessing your own Duality.

The Duality Exploration Grid

If you possess A/A/D, you are a dualist. But are you a Career Dualist? I have created the Duality Exploration Grid (Figure 2.2) to serve as a tool designed to

	Low analytical propensity (low amount of time spent in analytical career activities)	High analytical propensity (high amount of time spent in analytical career activities)
High artistic drive (high amount of time spent in artistic career activities)	Artistic Explorer (Music business creative)	Career Dualist
Low artistic drive (low amount of time spent in artistic career activities)	Career Explorer	Dualist Explorer (Music business logician)

FIGURE 2.2 The Duality Exploration Grid

assist you in efficiently making that determination. The grid helps illustrate the interplay of artistic drive and analytical propensity as they relate to actualizing A/A/D to facilitate CD. As you examine the different grid identities remember that the terms "drive" and "propensity" as used in this book relate to choice and inclination, not ability.

The grid uses time as a measure of commitment to career pursuits. Time reflects how you are choosing to express your A/A/D; this is supported by the moonlighting research discussed earlier. Every quadrant within the grid represents a duality of time. Accordingly, the amount of time you spend on artistic activities versus the amount of time you spend on analytical career activities determines into which quadrant you fit. A numerical representation of how much time separates you from fitting in one quadrant versus another is 51 percent. In other words, if you spend a minimum of 51 percent of your time on artistic career activities that constitutes high artistic drive.[51] Likewise, if you spend a minimum of 51 percent of your time on analytical career activities, that constitutes high analytical propensity. How is the time allocated? This varies by individual, as do the actual percentages, which can be much higher. In a study by David Throsby and Anita Zednik examining how Australian artists spend their time on non-arts activities, they found a three-way split in time allocation, noting that artists in the study spent 53 percent of their working time on creative work (preparation, practice, rehearsal, research related to their creative work), 27 percent on arts-related work (not related to their core creative work but using artistic skills in areas like teaching their art), and 20 percent on non-arts work (waiting tables in a restaurant, driving a taxi, etc.). "In terms of hours per week, the time devoted to work outside the arts amounted to about 8 hours in an average working week of about 41 hours."[52] The three-way split they found may be true for some but not for others, or will vary in percentages or types of non-arts activities.

For the High/High or Low/Low quadrant combinations, there is an even split in the allocation of time; this is discussed below in the quadrant descriptions. The grid labels identify each quadrant and offer insight into the range of possible duality choices. The label Explorer is used in three of the quadrants and connects to aspiring to resolve CD/Di. Since CD/Di compels dualists to satisfy their A/A/D, referring to that search as an exploratory one makes sense. Therefore, the term *Explorer* is not used to label the CD quadrant, since CD represents balanced career satisfaction and thereby can resolve CD/Di. The overall context for the grid is working within the music business. Chapter 9 examines duality within the broader entertainment industry.

The *Artistic Explorer* represents the individual who is low in analytical propensity and high in artistic drive. The Artistic Explorer is primarily a *music business creative.*[53] He is the most likely of all dualists to have a career as a full-time, professional artist. He chooses to spend little time on analytical career activities despite having that propensity. Traits: he spends at least 51 percent of his work week on artistic career activity, i.e., working as an artist, whether performing, auditioning, recording, producing, creating, rehearsing, or other artistic activity. The 51 percent figure is the minimum amount of time spent on artistic activities. In other words, the Artistic Explorer spends more of his time expressing artistic drive than analytical propensity. The actual amount of time spent in artistic activities could be 90 percent. The rest of his work week is spent in analytical activities, e.g., marketing and promoting his art (probably not someone else's), analyzing his fan base/audience, or booking his own gigs. The Artistic Explorer may not engage in all of these activities since he chooses to spend more time on his art. For example, he may use a booking agent, or may hire someone else to assist him with marketing and promoting his art. However, his analytical propensity permits him to perform analytical tasks with proficiency and enjoyment, as an avocational interest or by necessity as an entrepreneur.

The *Dualist Explorer*, the opposite of the Artistic Explorer, represents the individual who has high analytical propensity and spends more time (at least 51 percent) on analytical career activities. For example, she works professionally as an artist manager, music publisher, entertainment company administrator, or entertainment lawyer, probably five days a week. Utilizing her analytical propensity through budgeting and accounting, starting and managing a new arts venture, analyzing industry trends, or similar work is her primary work focus. Less than 50 percent of her work week is spent working as an artist, and she may view artistic work as an avocational, semi-professional pursuit. She may engage in artistic work periodically, e.g., only on the weekends or seasonally. Her avocational artistic activity is likely to be regular, engaged in at a professional level, and with a commitment to maintaining art as an integral part of her work and life. This approach fulfills the enjoyment aspect of the definition of avocation. It may also serve as a means of experimenting with her art on a part-time basis to determine whether she wishes to transition to it as her full-time work.

The *Career Explorer* represents an individual who has both low artistic drive and low analytical propensity, as determined by the amount of time spent on each. He spends less than 50 percent of his time on artistic activities and less than 50 percent of time performing analytical work. He may be working as a waitress, writing and performing music, and starting a new entertainment venture all at the same time. However, less than 50 percent of his time is spent on any one of those activities. The term *Career Explorer* fits because he may be experiencing ambivalence about career identity and is likely in the midst of career decision making, exploring, and trying on different career options to figure it all out. On the one hand, he may recognize his creative personality and bent but is not driven to commit much time to artistic pursuits, possibly because he is not sure he wants them to serve as a career. On the other hand, he recognizes his analytical propensity and may find a measure of satisfaction in exercising these skills. This quadrant represents a time of transition and less focus or sense of direction for career identity.

The *Career Dualist* represents the individual whose analytical propensity and artistic drive are expressed evenly, simultaneously, and entirely in the context of the music or entertainment industry. Therefore, she spends 50 percent of her time devoted to the expression of artistic drive and 50 percent of her time expressing analytical propensity, and has this time allocation as a deliberate goal, as the Career Dualist works toward this allocation from a place of internal purpose. Impossible to have a 50/50 split, you say? You will meet Career Dualists in Chapter 3 who characterize their work in the industry in precisely that way. The 50/50 time allocation represents the cleanest way of determining placement in this quadrant. However, there is another factor that helps to determine placement in the quadrant. There is the immeasurable element of passion toward a particular domain. This passion element is described in the vocational sense in this book as a *calling* that heightens your artistic drive or analytical propensity. For example, I have categorized some of the dualists profiled in Chapter 3 as Career Dualists because I discern this heightened passion and calling, despite the absence of a precise 50/50 split. However, a word of caution is in order here. Time spent on activities is the first and primary determinant of which quadrant best characterizes your A/A/D identity. Do not be quick to identify with this (or any other) quadrant because of passion that you construe as a calling. Discerning your calling requires self-knowledge, honesty with self, time, and an understanding of the concept. Therefore, three chapters in Part II of this book are devoted to the subject of calling. As a practical matter, the individuals categorized as Career Dualists in Chapter 3 who do not have a 50/50 split have a split that is close to 50/50 or spend on average about 20 hours per week on artistic activities if working in a full-time job on the business side of the music industry. They demonstrate that the true test of passion is time commitment, so that time spent on activities is still a crucial element in determining whether you are a Career Dualist.

The Soul of Duality

CD is an ideal, and an achievable one, as this book suggests. Yet every quadrant is a good place to be if it is the right place for you, and it is the right quadrant for you if it is an authentic fit. The goal of career decision making is to strive for authenticity in our work. Therefore, there is more to determining our duality identities than characterization on the Duality Exploration Grid, particularly since there may be movement for you amongst the quadrants, depending on what's happening in your life at a given time. However, the Duality Exploration Grid is a helpful tool for surveying the spectrum of duality, providing you with a snapshot of where you lie along the spectrum. You can choose which quadrant you occupy and move from one quadrant to another, depending on the opportunities you have or are seeking. In Chapter 3 we meet some dualists to learn how they have lived out their own duality. But first, complete the exercises below to begin taking a look at your own.

Discussion Questions

1. What does the CD Model describe? Define each of its components.
2. What does the Duality Exploration Grid describe? Summarize each quadrant without using the name of the quadrant.
3. What do left/right brain, personality, and talent/ability represent? How do these concepts relate to the CD Model?

EXERCISE SET 2: EXPLORING DUALITY

The objective of this exercise is to explore the colors and contours of your duality.

1. How much time per week do you devote to analytical activities in the music industry? Outside it?

    a   What kind of analytical activities do you enjoy?
    b   List as many of them as you can.

2. How much time per week do you devote to artistic or creative activities in the music industry? Outside it?

    a   Do you daydream?
    b   What are your daydreams about?

3. Using the Duality Exploration Grid, identify the quadrant into which you believe you fit best.

    a   Now that you have identified it, how do you feel about it?
    b   As you were contemplating your quadrant fit, was there a particular quadrant that you were hoping you would land in?

4. In addition to determining your quadrant fit, it is important to ascertain if you are there by coincidence or by choice.

    a   Which is it, coincidence, or choice?
    b   Is it where you want to be?
    c   If not, begin to daydream – on paper, in your journal – about how you will determine where you want to be. Do not make a plan for getting there just yet. Figuring out *how you will decide* where you want to be comes before determining how to get there.

Notes

1   Arthur Cropley, "In Praise of Convergent Thinking," *Creativity Research Journal* 18, no. 3 (2006): 398.
2   Cropley, "In Praise of Convergent Thinking," 392. There are additional examples provided in the article.
3   Cropley, "In Praise of Convergent Thinking," 398.
4   Excerpted from a description of the purpose of the test: "The first goal is to provide a reasonable way to pre- and post-test students to determine the extent to which they have learned to think critically. The second goal is to provide a test instrument that stimulates the faculty to teach their discipline so as to foster critical thinking in the students." www.criticalthinking.org/pages/international-center-for-the-assessment-of-higher-order-thinking/589, accessed January 2, 2018.
5   Based on a review of sample questions available at www.criticalthinking.org/pages/international-center-for-the-assessment-of-higher-order-thinking/589.
6   Cropley, "In Praise of Convergent Thinking," 392. There are additional examples provided in the article.
7   Cropley, "In Praise of Convergent Thinking," 392.
8   Oyvind L. Martinsen, "The Creative Personality: A Synthesis and Development of the Creative Person Profile," *Creativity Research Journal* 23, no. 3 (2011): 198.
9   Martinsen, "The Creative Personality," 191.
10   Ashley Bell Jones, Ryne A. Sherman, and Robert T. Hogan, "Where Is Ambition in Factor Models of Personality?" *Personality and Individual Differences* 106 (2017): 26.
11   Jones, Sherman and Hogan, "Where Is Ambition," 27.
12   Martinsen, "The Creative Personality," 197.
13   Arthur Cropley and David Cropley, "Resolving the Paradoxes of Creativity: An Extended Phase Model," *Cambridge Journal of Education* 38, no. 3 (September 2008): 357.
14   Kathy J. Rysiew, Bruce M. Shore, and Rebecca T. Leeb, "Mutipotentiality, Giftedness, and Career Choice: A Review," *Journal of Counseling and Development* 77 (Fall 1999): 428.
15   Rysiew et al., "Mutipotentiality, Giftedness, and Career Choice," 427.
16   Szirony, Gary Michael, L. Carolyn Pearson, John S. Burgin, Gerald C. Murray, and Lisa Marie Elrod, "Brain Hemisphere Dominance and Vocational Preference: A Preliminary Analysis," *Work* 29 (2007): 323.
17   Researchers at the University of Utah reexamined how this theory may work and agreed with prior research about what functions are on the left side and which are on the right. However, they proposed that one side is not necessarily stronger than the other. Jared A. Nielsen et al., "An Evaluation of the Left-Brain vs. Right-Brain Hypothesis with Resting State Functional Connectivity Magnetic Resonance Imaging," *PLoS ONE* 8, no. 8 (August 2013): e71275, https://doi.org/10.1371/journal.pone.0071275.
18   You may be able to take this assessment, if interested. If you are a college student, your school's career development office may already have a university account, so you may wish to check with them for assistance.
19   Michael J.A. Howe, Jane W. Davidson, and John A. Sloboda, "Innate Talents: Reality or Myth?" *Behavioral and Brain Sciences* 21 (1998): 399.
20   Marguerite Ward, "Morgan Stanley Exec: The Career Advice I Would Give My 20-Year Old Self," The Definitive Guide to Business, CNBC, September 27, 2016, www.cnbc.com/2016/09/27/morgan-stanley-exec-the-career-advice-i-would-give-my-20-year-old-self.html.
21   Andrea J. Will, "Carla Harris, Vice Chairman and Managing Director of Morgan Stanley," LifeChats Series in Finance and Accounting, Fuqua School of Business, Duke University, June 3, 2014, www.colelifechatscollection.com/portfolio/carla-harris-vice-chairman-and-managing-director-of-morgan-stanley/.

22 Legends profile: Michael Jordan, NBA History, www.nba.com/history/legends/profi les/michael-jordan#.
23 Howe et al., "Innate Talents," 414.
24 Jere Brophy and Thomas Good, *Individual Differences: Toward an Understanding of Classroom Life* (New York: Holt, Rinehart, and Winston, 1973), quoted in Howe et al., "Innate Talents," 399.
25 Howe et al., "Innate Talents," 399–400. This is a partial definition.
26 Howe et al., "Innate Talents," 400–1.
27 Howe et al., "Innate Talents," 411.
28 A song written by Burt Bacharach and very popular at the time.
29 Elena Gabor, "Turning Points in the Development of Classical Musicians," *Journal of Ethnographic and Qualitative Research* 5 (2011): 140.
30 Howe et al., "Innate Talents," 433.
31 David Throsby and Virginia Hollister, *Don't Give Up Your Day Job: An Economic Study of Professional Artists in Australia* (Sydney: Australia Council, 2003): 35, www.australiacoun cil.gov.au/workspace/uploads/files/research/entire_document-54325d2a023c8.pdf.
32 Robert R. McCrae and Oliver P. John. "An Introduction to the Five-Factor Model and Its Applications," *Journal of Personality* 60, no. 2 (1992): 175–215.
33 "Psychological Types," Wikipedia, https://en.wikipedia.org/wiki/Psychological_Types
34 Ian Weinstein, "Learning and Lawyering across Personality Types," *Clinical Law Review* 21 (Spring 2015): 429.
35 These summaries of each trait are highly abbreviated.
36 Gregory J. Feist, "A Meta-Analysis of Personality in Scientific and Artistic Creativity," *Personality and Social Psychology Review* 2, no. 4 (1998): 299.
37 Faisal Hoque, "10 Paradoxical Traits of Creative People," *Fast Company*, September 4, 2013. www.fastcompany.com/3016689/10-paradoxical-traits-of-creative-people.
38 Hoque, "10 Paradoxical Traits."
39 Cropley and Cropley, "Resolving Paradoxes of Creativity," 358.
40 Rysiew et al., "Mutipotentiality, Giftedness, and Career Choice," 427.
41 Rysiew et al., "Mutipotentiality, Giftedness, and Career Choice," 427.
42 Justin M. Berg, Adam M. Grant, and Victoria Johnson, "When Callings Are Calling: Crafting Work and Leisure in Pursuit of Unanswered Occupational Callings," *Organization Science* 21, no. 5 (September–October 2010): 984.
43 zMerriam-Webster's Collegiate Dictionary, 10th edition (Springfield, MA: Merriam-Webster, 1993).
44 Neil O. Alper and Gregory H. Wassall, *More Than Once in a Blue Moon: Multiple Job-holdings by American Artists*, Research Division Report #40 (Santa Ana, CA: Seven Locks Press, National Endowment for the Arts, 2000).
45 Alper and Wassall, "Executive Summary," *More Than Once in a Blue Moon*, 1.
46 Alper and Wassall, "Executive Summary," *More Than Once in a Blue Moon*, 32.
47 Alper and Wassall, "Executive Summary," *More Than Once in a Blue Moon*, 33.
48 Throsby and Hollister, *Don't Give Up Your Day Job*, 36.
49 *Merriam-Webster's Collegiate Dictionary*, 1993.
50 Throsby and Hollister, *Don't Give Up Your Day Job*, 13.
51 The Throsby data, pertaining to Australian artists, suggest that "on average artists spend only about half their time on creative work in their own or another artform." Throsby and Hollister, *Don't Give Up Your Day Job*, 39.
52 David Throsby and Anita Zednik, "Multiple Job-Holding and Artistic Careers: Some Empirical Evidence," *Cultural Trends* 20, no. 1 (March 2011): 11.
53 Music business creatives are professionals whose primary vocation involves performing artistic work to support the operation of the music industry.

3

TELLING OTHER TALES

Some 30 plus years after receiving encouragement to do so from fans and supporters I released *Invocation*, an album that embodies its own brand of duality as jazz-themed music blended with secular and sacred inspiration.[1] Though I had been performing publicly for pay since my mid-20s, working with voice teachers and coaches, and otherwise supporting my vocal ambitions, my attention to the law meant that creating a recording took a long time. Years.

I heard a dual call to music as well as law and felt the compulsion to heed both, in my own way. Every dualist or Career Dualist has their own story. We are all so uniquely driven. This chapter is about the stories of other dualists and their career choices. Understanding Career Duality (CD) is best realized through seeing it lived out. If a picture is worth a thousand words, the following profiles help paint the Career Duality dilemma (CD/Di) battle and the spectrum of dualist life more vividly.

Process and Protocol

I have chronicled the stories of 13 dualists (subsequently referred to as "profiled dualists") through personal interviews with each individual. A selection of 13 participants, as opposed to a higher or lower number, results from an objective of this book to explore a range of dualist experiences, providing profiles of each individual while keeping the number of participants manageable enough to present their profiles primarily within one chapter. While the data compiled from the interviews constitute a type of qualitative research, the goal of this chapter is to offer actual narratives of individuals who have lived a life of duality and to understand their career decisions and paths, rather than to present a strictly scientific data analysis.[2] A key requirement for inclusion in the sample was that participants work or have worked simultaneously on both sides of the music or entertainment industry as both music industry logicians and creatives. As a result, professors or teachers were not included unless they worked on both sides of the entertainment industry concurrently with teaching. Individuals who possessed analytical propensity + artistic drive (A/A/D) but who work outside the entertainment industry were likewise excluded from participation.[3]

Each interviewee was asked a series of 35 questions. That's a lot of questions! Therefore, each profile contained in this chapter is an abbreviated snapshot of the dualist and our interview, rather than a question-by-question replication of all of a participant's responses, which would be prohibitively lengthy to include. The duration of the interviews varied, depending on how each person chose to answer the questions. Some chose lengthy responses, others chose to be more succinct. All interviews lasted at least one hour, while some lasted well over two hours. The participant pool includes a mix of young and seasoned professionals, as well as demographic diversity in gender, age, and race.[4] Participants were given the option to remain anonymous or to reveal their identities. All interviewees chose to disclose their identities except one, whose name and identifying facts have been changed to grant anonymity.

Meet the Dualists

As Chapter 2 explains, a dualist is distinguished from a Career Dualist in that a dualist is the generic term created to identify those who possess A/A/D. Whereas, a Career Dualist is an individual who has made a CD choice to use their A/A/D in the music and entertainment industry to express both sides of A/A/D through dual careers, as described at length in Chapter 2. The stories of the dualists interviewed are told in this chapter to illustrate not only how A/A/D and CD can look and feel, but to also communicate the many colors of duality. That spectrum is introduced in Chapter 2 as the Duality Exploration Grid. Accordingly, each profiled dualist is categorized in accordance with the quadrant that person occupies on the grid. The grid categories reflected for each dualist are based on my assessments, not the interviewee's.

Conducting interviews with each of the individuals you will meet in this chapter was an emotional journey for them and for me, in a good way. When people have an opportunity to reflect on their careers, contemplate their decisions, and recreate their own journeys it is like dipping into deep reservoirs of poignant personal histories. Consequently, the overflow was moving. Sometimes I felt I was observing someone in the midst of thinking about an experience for the first time and in a new way. Sometimes I saw passion for duality. And at all times I heard from individuals who are engaged in their careers in deliberate (though not necessarily calculated) ways. Since it was not feasible to include every word of these one- to three-hour interviews for this number of individuals, I have focused their stories on questions that address (1) the path to their current position; (2) why they currently are not full-time music industry creatives; and (3) whether they would change their journey, particularly to one that is a more full-time artistic vocation. Question prompts or introductions to their responses are shown here in italics. Depending on how extensively the questions relating to these topics were answered, I have also included responses to additional topics, or not included all three of the topics listed above. I have also included their responses to questions I asked about awards, honors, and recognitions, either for their work on the business side or on the creative side of the industry. Each participant shared themselves in authentic transparency. I count myself blessed to have had them share not only their time with me, but their lives as well. You will hear from them again in some of the other chapters. Additionally, two of the 13 interviewees are profiled in other chapters. Meredith Collins' profile appears in Chapter 8, where she tells the story of an individual who transitioned out of the music and entertainment industry altogether. Lana Detland is profiled in Chapter 9, providing a picture of an entertainment industry professional working in the broader entertainment industry.

Artistic Explorers

Recall that all dualists have both A/A/D propensities. Therefore, no one I interviewed (nor any dualist) could be categorized as 100 percent music industry creative. Rather, the categorization leads to classifying the individual as fitting into one category more than another, as having a *primary* occupation and therefore a primary categorization on the Duality Exploration Grid. An Artistic Explorer works primarily as a music industry creative. Since I was seeking dualists to interview – to investigate their duality – it may have been inevitable that no Artistic Explorers would wind up as part of my participant pool. However, many (perhaps all) of the Career Dualists profiled have the calling and soul of Artistic Explorers. Some have had significant careers as creatives and still derive substantial income from that source. Had I interviewed them earlier in their careers some would have fit within this category. As you read the profiles of most of the dualists categorized in the other (non-Career Dualist) quadrants you will also hear their creative spirits loudly and clearly, which are alive and well within their current careers. In fact, you will discern the call of creativity in every dualist, no matter what their current primary occupation.

Career Explorers

Kimberly Lannear (Nashville, TN), Technology Startup Entrepreneur

I have often felt that I know too few music industry professionals who are involved in creating technology for the entertainment industry. That is, until I met Kimberly Lannear. That is what she does. Yet her self-expression extends beyond her tech self.

I have a startup called Scripturally Sound and it came about through my experience as a person of faith who believes in Christ and also drawing from my experience as a worship leader, as someone who's been in the choir. I wanted to merge my interests with music, Christianity, and technology because I know that the world is becoming more tech dependent. And so I chose this profession because I just wanted to make sure that Christ's message was continuing as people became more tech dependent and I knew that music is universal. Technology has a universal appeal and the message of love in the Christian bible is very universal as well. So I wanted to make sure that I can use the talents that I have to reach the 2.2 billion Christians in the world. I know not all of them will have an app. I thought it had the potential to reach people who were not familiar with Christianity but they may be drawn to music. So I just thought there was a lot of far-reaching appeal.

I got someone else to do [the programming] and I'm currently seeking another developer… a lot of them… may not have had the passion for the vision… I don't want to possibly give up equity in the company unless the person shares that vision. So I've hired outside contractors to help.

Why did you decide not to become a full-time musician?

I really wish that musicians made a lot more money. Honestly, I think we're using antiquated law, as you probably know as a lawyer, with songwriting and royalty, I mean like the splits for how we deal with publishing and songwriting and things like that. So, I went to school for journalism and I actually would've loved to go to a school like Belmont but I thought I was just trying to be practical and you're always told to fall back on something. I just felt as though there are so many people vying for fame and doing music for things other than the music, the passion for music itself, although some people do. But I just felt like it's such a, it's like you have to have a strike of luck to do this full time. And it doesn't necessarily have to be even on the Billboard charts. Even people who are working as a full-time musician, unknown, are not signed artists or independent artists, that too can be a difficult task. So, I saw that it would've been a difficult career choice. But that doesn't mean that I still can't do it full time. I'm still looking for opportunities to collaborate and network and I don't want to speak out things as though they are, in the negative way of thinking. So, I am working with some people that are collaborating with songwriting so I think that option is still there. I am in a moment of making decisions about my career. I know that I have to be intentional with my planning and goal setting. A thing that I'm doing this year is practicing piano a lot more, 'cause I think if you're good in instrumentation you become a better vocalist.

Would you ever switch careers entirely to music/entertainment?

For music I would love to allow it to be a career. I think where I am now with music, I just want to do it for the love of it and if I find opportunities to go full time and not just make money for small-time gigs, that would be great.

Yeah. I totally would. That's really what I want to do. If I had the time to do it and not have to worry about money and if there were more viable ways to make money in music then I would do it. And I don't even necessarily have to be like making more than six figures or whatever it is, just something to sustain me and be relatively comfortable, I would do it. Honestly, another reason why I'm doing Scripturally Sound was so that I can have income to just feed my passion in music. That was definitely another reason why I went into it. Because I was thinking about how can I make money, not thinking it would be an entirely other like challenge, uphill battle, to some degree… I don't know why I thought that Scripturally Sound initially would allow me to have this income that would feed my… I mean eventually it very well can be but in the early stage it's very hard to have two kinds of like startup entities. Being a freelance musician is a startup and then having this tech startup so when you're in that early stage, even though I have been singing all my life, I mean if I want to do it full time since I don't have a huge following – until that time happens I'm going to be in the very nascent stages of both careers.

If you had it to do all over again, which pursuit would be primary, and why?

I would say music because it's the easiest for me and it's, I just think it's the most authentic. I think the best art is authentic. And I want to project my voice in a unique way. I want to tell my story of how I see the world and I just think art is about the imitation of life and what better way to share your life experiences through what I think is like the first art form which I think is music.

Awards and honors: Kimberly was nominated by the Nashville Technology Council for the Diversity Game Changer of the Year for 2017. On the creative side, she received call backs from American Idol.

Dualist Explorers

Justin Longerbeam (Portland, OR), Album Production and Audio Engineering

We meet at a restaurant/bar in a very cool Portland neighborhood. This spot is Justin's pick. He is the only one of my interviewees with whom I met outside of an office. And as soon as I meet him I sense his individuality and see him as this kind of music industry maverick who is passionate about how he engages in the business of music.

I was doing a lot of freelance work… I was doing things for free because I was interested in it. I built a studio in my basement so that I could record my own music and my friends and I could make music. It was just about chasing a passion, it wasn't about a business endeavor. And word started to sort of get out that I was doing that and more people started asking me to come over and it wasn't about money; I had a job. And it just got to a point that I was overwhelmed by how many people wanted me to do it that I had to start letting people know that "I just don't have time for this right now." And they'd say, "Well, what if I gave you $500?" And I was like, "Well I can't say no to that, and so yeah, of course I'll make you a priority." And then people just wanted me to make them a priority and so that's how money came. That's the advice I give a lot of people actually. When people are trying to pursue freelance within the creative world, just do as much as you can for free until you don't have that option any more. Just meet as many people as you can, own your own craft through experience. Eventually, if you're doing it right and you're doing it enough, someone is going to tell you that they want to give you money. And that's what happened to me. Ten years ago I was a gigging musician in Portland and that was it. And then I would say probably seven years ago is when I started getting money for freelance engineering. Five years ago I was working at the music distribution company, and also freelance engineering, and DJing. I had to sort of spread myself as thin as possible. DJ gigs paid a lot of money, so I started throwing events that also paid money. Engineering in my basement for friends' demos started bringing in money. I started getting to work at this music company so then friends wanted me to help them put out their records. All of those things, spreading myself as thin as possible, while also performing and playing in bands sort of led me through to a path where a career started to take shape.

For the last three years I have been the founder of a record label and recording studio which are joined in a certain way but they are also separate entities at the same time. They sort of like share resources. As the founding member of that label I, sort of on the business side, have had varying degrees of responsibilities from having input on how money is moved around, partitions between artists and those sorts of things. I have input on anything from the type of licensing companies that we work with to artists that we sign. And then seeking out clientele, working to maintain the schedules of the studio, versus label artists versus clientele that's paying for their time in the studio and those sorts of things. And then as an artist I've just been a musician for the bulk of my life. I play a large swath of instruments, none of them as well as someone who's stuck to just one. I started out playing trombone. My love for the trombone will never fade. And I've played in orchestra, and in jazz ensembles, even here in Portland I've played with jazz ensembles here and been hired to write brass arrangements for people's work and performing trombone from time to time. Brass is a little bit scarce around here, people just seek it out. And I've been hired to put brass ensembles together for people's projects or one-off shows.

Then also I'm an engineer and producer for other artists and a session musician. I've sort of worked my way to be able to proficiently perform most instruments that an artist may require in the studio.

Why did you decide not to become a full-time musician?

I think the realities of that require a particular lifestyle that requires... I think you have to sort of concede certain lifestyles by being a professional musician for a long time. Specifically... money isn't consistent. Not to say that I don't think that it can be, but...

Would you ever switch careers entirely to music/entertainment?

I think if I did it would be specifically for a temporary opportunity. If somebody had asked me to go on a global tour with them, some kind of opportunity that had the potential to be life changing in some way or very valuable above currency, I would certainly take that. But I think they would be more temporary in nature. *[I probe with why]* I think that I'm aware of my personal limitations as a performer. And... I don't feel a personal need to inject my personal narrative into a larger conversation right now, at this point in my life. I'm more interested in working with performers who have a message that I can get behind and support in some way. I have no interest in being in the spotlight, though at one point I did.

The absence of his need for the spotlight translates to giving the spotlight to others, to support other artists in telling their own stories. For example, when I ask him about PR for his own endeavors I learn more about his commitment to the artist community. He does press for other artists.

I've spent enough time in the back end of the industry to know what a press release needs to look like. So when my friend is confronted with a $3,000 price tag for a publicist for an album I might tell them to put that money to better use and give them my entire spreadsheet of all the media contacts that I have, and sort of sharing that information with the community without them investing massive amounts of money... I think it's very hard to talk about your own work in a way that is translatable and I think there's been this interesting movement here where we're helping each other talk, we're being one another's champions and sharing resources so that the limited amount of funds that artists do have can go to things that create tangible product or put them on the road.

He does not charge artists any fees for his PR services. Rather, this is an outgrowth of an ambition that goes beyond providing specific services for artists and extends to his broader goals as a businessperson. It's where his inner maverick lies.

You're actually talking to me at a very interesting time. I have been more interested in shifting to the non-profit sector recently. I think that personally the model of owning someone's art and profiting off of it is becoming less relevant in a world where an artist has the ability to put an album on Spotify from their home and reach a global audience immediately.

Awards or honors: one of the records that the label put out last year that I engineered and did the sound design for was just named Best Hip Hop record in Portland of 2017… And then another record that I worked on last year was third on that list.

Jesse Bobick (Nashville, TN), E-Commerce Sales Coordinator/Social Media and Marketing Coordinator, Naxos Records

Jesse is a recent graduate from Belmont University who majored in music business and minored in music (piano). If you are thinking that he was a dualist as a student, you are correct, and that means you are beginning to understand how duality works and often looks. Jesse was a student in my music industry contract law class and one of the brightest, most highly motivated students I have had the privilege to teach. He also may have been one of the first students I spoke with who was a clear dualist who realized that he had the analytical/ artistic split (A/A/D), and that was a point of commonality I could share with him and with other students who readily recognized their split and saw themselves at a career crossroads.

My title is E-Commerce Sales Coordinator, and my new title sometime in January will be a Social Media and Marketing Coordinator for Naxos. Mostly it was an opportunity that I was able to get in the music industry. After graduation I had taken some time off, which I felt was very much needed. And then after that was kind of doing the job hunt pretty seriously. And kind of wanted to apply for pretty much everything that I could probably be qualified for that was in the music industry. I was interested primarily more on the marketing side. But I also just wanted to make sure that whatever I was doing was going to have something to do with music. And I know that it's really difficult to find like the exact perfect job the first thing after you're out of college. And I knew that if I was able to get any sort of experience in the music industry like immediately after college I'd be extremely grateful for that. So I had a few interviews, and I had felt like they had gone well but I hadn't gotten those first few. But when I had the interview with Naxos it just, it really fit, and I could tell I really meshed with the culture. I knew about Naxos through my education here at Belmont. It was a resource that I had used during my music classes. I knew generally what the company was about and had some of its core competencies and I thought it'd be a really good opportunity and a really good organization to be part of.

Upon graduation he chose to go the music business route, rather than to become a full-time musician. As with other interviewees, I asked him why.

It's something that I do think about from time to time. A lot of my education here at Belmont I was more drawn to the business side of music and I really enjoyed thinking about it. I felt like I had a lot of analytical strengths on the business side of music and felt I could bring a lot of creativity to that. I loved the research part of it. I really liked looking at the legal issues and entertainment issues in entertainment law and I guess part of me also was kind of looking ahead and I wasn't sure if I wanted either the financial or life instability associated with becoming a full-time musician where your schedule and your finances are always governed by the gig. What's the next gig, and the next gig? If you're a touring musician you could be with the most successful artist but then when that gig is over, it's like you don't have a gig, and the band breaks up or something. So I was more on the side of not wanting that instability, but whatever I did I wanted to make sure that I was able to keep music a part of my life. So, actually the conversation that I had with you was extremely influential in that because I was really interested in the law side, and I was studying for the LSAT [Law School Admission Test] and [law] was something I was kind of heading towards. But putting it all in perspective that you're so much of a lawyer before you get to interact with the music side of business and how it's certainly a demanding path, whether it's always being on call or working the 70+ hour weeks, and what else do you feel like doing after that? Certainly not creative music endeavors. So I appreciate that my current role gives me enough flexibility that I can do music things on the side. We still play at Ellendale's[5] every Sunday night… I'm a staff pianist at a church in Smyrna… I have been teaching piano lessons from time to time. This year in particular, the musical director at my church is also a theatre director at a high school in Wilson county and I have done a couple of musicals with them, played piano for them. And I have also gotten one other opportunity through that connection, them knowing that I play piano… It's very demanding and time intensive at the time, but I definitely value the experience to work with these young, talented kids that are so excited and so driven and being able to support them alongside usually a larger band to make a musical happen. We have another one coming up in February… It's been fun. So I am definitely more heavy on the business side, but I appreciate that my work week is 40 hours and not 80. And I'm also forcing myself to do these music things. A lot of these musical obligations are not just when I feel like it. No, I'm committed every Sunday for Ellendale's and the church. I'm committed on a weekly basis for the piano lessons. So I'm forcing myself to do something that I want to do. That's the only reason that I got a piano minor here at Belmont as well. So I'm happy with that for now. But I also know that if I do get an opportunity at any point that's crazy good on the music side, it's probably something that I won't not consider.

Would you ever switch careers entirely to music/entertainment?

I think that if the right opportunity came up, I definitely would. I feel really good about where I am right now and what I've learned even so far and how much I've grown. In some ways I am kind of putting it in God's hands just like "lead me." I think that this next transition in January is a really good one, and I can see staying with it for a while. And even if it is an opportunity that leads me to another company within the music industry I see being in this career path for a while. I definitely see it as more of a long-term thing.

Awards and honors: won an Anderson University Orangehaus Music Business camp award for songwriting. He was also chosen to participate in the Pipeline Project, an entertainment industry research opportunity granted to select students at Belmont University.

Gina Miller (Nashville, TN), Vice President and General Manager, Entertainment One-Nashville

When Gina Miller took the podium at a music industry event I attended and told the story of her entrée into the music industry, I decided then and there that I wanted to talk with her about her career journey and interview her for this book. Our paths would not cross that evening, but I knew that eventually they would – it was a feeling that our meeting was sort of predestined, and indeed it was. Not long after the event I met Gina through a mutual friend and colleague, Ileia Hook – Belmont University alumna, staffer, and background vocalist for Christian music industry artists like Nicole C. Mullen, Todd Dulaney, and others. But nothing else about my interactions with Gina has been predictable, as she and her story embody the antithesis of the word.

I don't want to sound cliché that it [my career] chose me, but to some degree I will say that to understand how I got here I have to start at my beginnings, how I got to this place, in this seat, with this company. This is going on somewhere between my 14th, 15th year here, and I started out as a very non-traditional intern, meaning that I was already grown with children and a husband at the time. I had already been teaching some; I also have a license to teach music K-12 in the state of Tennessee. Although my teaching wasn't in music, I've been around music teachers. I have a family of music teachers. I have a family of teachers in all disciplines – principals, etc. I thought at one point that was where I was going and I embraced that. I'm a 5th-generation teacher and it was kind of the normal path, I thought. And the music part is also a part of my family history. We all played some type of instrument, as well as all of us play the piano; to some degree it was required of us to do so. So, the music part, the education part, the natural parts that were pretty much part of my DNA, if you will. And it seemed like there was no option about the route that those things were going to afford me, what kind of opportunities. So getting to Nashville I thought that perhaps there was something else that I could do. So I've played for churches, I did a lot of different things and I landed upon this one little story; I met someone that knew someone and they introduced me to someone that said that they were talking about a record label and it was a gospel music record label. I thought "even better" because this company represented songs that were not just familiar but very personal to me. And much of the music that I grew up not just enjoying personally but music that I had been teaching in choir were all birthed from this place. So I thought, "wow, here's an opportunity to work closely with people that I already admire what they do. I already know who they are and what they do, I'm gonna go for it." So I ended up having an appointment with the then president and general manager. And he said "I like you a lot, but we don't have any jobs here." And so I said, "Okay, can I still come and hang out anyway?" And he said "Sure." So it took us a while to get our schedules lined up and to figure out what that would mean and how often I would come. It started out that I was coming just a few hours a week, turned into me working every day full time without pay for almost a year.

So after that first year, I can remember vividly, he called me into his office and I was very much present, I was very much active, I was very much a participant in our day-to-day business at that point, without any regard really to the fact that I wasn't getting paid for it. But he called me into his office one day, he said "Okay, why are you still here, you're embarrassing me." And I said I figured I would keep coming until something opened up. And he said "Well, there's a lot that I can tell you about what your time here with us has done, even for me as a leader." And it caused him to take a look at some things that he probably should have addressed sooner than he had. And he said, "Okay, here's the deal, we had already done our budget for that fiscal year and still don't have any room for you." And it was a very interesting conversation. Long story short, he said "I'm gonna create a job for you. It won't be much, it'll be part time, and I'll start you at some coordinator's position that sounds good. We'll just come up with something and let me assess what we need and what you've been doing, and we'll create something." And he said, "How do you feel about that?" And I said, "I feel great about it, let's do it." So he offered me a coordinator's position, and the formal title was Radio and Retail Coordinator. And that really was the beginning of my commitment to being here. So how I got from there to here involved time spent at that position and really understanding what all of that could mean and all that we defined as we created it, to moving from a coordinator to a manager.

I moved from there to marketing manager and worked very closely with the marketing team and marketing VP [vice president] at the time and moved from marketing manager to director of sales, working with the VP of sales at the time and some other coordinators. And from there we added some things to my title: Label Relations; that seemed to be a great niche. I felt that I had gotten to a really sweet spot between sales and label relations. It allowed me to go out and really sell the product to national companies (Walmart, Kmart, record stores), and really tell them about our artists and our products. And I would assist our vice president with certain things, keeping him updated on what was going on within the gospel music industry as well as our artists, and so this whole path just ended up full circle. I left there and moved to radio promotions. It was about that time that I had a title of Vice President of Promotions and Marketing. I was Vice

President of Promotions and Label Relations. And then just a Vice President of Promotions because we then expanded our label and we added a lot of different departments as we've grown over the last 14 years. And now moving out of Promotions to General Manager has been the last addition, and I would expect for my time here this to be the last stop. There's nowhere else to go besides where I am! I'm excited and proud of that. That's probably the best way to explain how I got here.

Why did you decide not to become a full-time musician/artist?

Here's what I know at this point: the life that I'm living now and the age that I am now, my journey with God and what my own growth and wisdom has shown me: God put this music in me to do exactly what I'm doing with it. This music that I have inside of me is to absolutely worship Him. I worship God still every single day. I don't need an audience to do that. I think there was probably some point in my life when I thought "Oh, I'm gonna make it to the stage, and I'm going to have this career perhaps singing opera or singing the classical spirituals at the Metropolitan Opera House like Leontyne Price or Marian Anderson" or something like that. But along the way I never was discouraged because that wasn't the path that I could see. It wasn't the foreseeable path. But what happened, interestingly enough, I saw how the dots were actually connecting to make a different picture. Remember dot-to-dot books? The thing about a dot-to-dot book, you don't have to connect all the dots to see what's coming. And so there was a point – I can tell you very clearly in my journey – that I could see the dots forming and I understood that there was a different picture being created, one that may have been different from what I initially thought. But what I know now, I'm so glad that I didn't get locked down and disappointed in my own thoughts and my own ideas, because I don't even know that it was a dream. I really have been taught to live my life with being open and flexible and where I am is where God intends me to be... doing the jobs that I've been doing now, to the level I've been able to do them, with the artists that I'm able to connect with and work with. I understand now that all of that was put into me to be able to undergird and assist and to push them forward and to have enough understanding about the discipline required, the knowledge required, the sacrifice required... all the things that are required for them to hit the stage. I understand it more personally, I believe, because I'm a performance person but not necessarily needing the stage for my gifts to manifest and to really shine through them [artists] is the gift in it all... I would have a different view and they would probably have a different relationship with me as well if I didn't have the experience that I have. It's almost like when you go to a restaurant and you want to try the special of the day and you ask the waiter, "Have you tried it?" But the waiter has not tried it. They want to sell you the special of the day but they have not tried it. I know that there are restaurants that have their staff try the specials before they open for dinner, they have a sample, just enough… I believe that my enough is just enough to give them enough support in their day-to-day duties in the spotlight and I'm really grateful that I have those experiences to bring to the table.

Awards and honors: received the Power Moves Award for Arts and Entertainment in 2017, and received the Stellar Women of Gospel Award in 2018.

Loren Mulraine, Esq. (Nashville, TN), Professor, Belmont University; Entertainment Attorney; Vocalist/Songwriter/Producer

Loren Mulraine is a friend and colleague. When I decided to write this book, he was probably the first person I thought of interviewing. After you read his profile, I believe you will understand why.

So I never had any thoughts of being a lawyer growing up. That was the furthest thing from my mind. When I was in high school I went to a math and science high school and just figured like everybody else I'd go into engineering. I took constitutional law as an elective senior year. I wasn't particularly engaged; senioritis had already set in but it was interesting and planted a seed in the back of my mind. So I went on to college as an engineering major and – this is my story I tell everybody – went to my first day meeting with my advisor and went through the list of all the courses I would take for the next four years and I walked out of the advisor's meeting and thought to myself: "Who are you kidding? This is not really who you are," and I decided to change my major that day. So I ended up changing my major to journalism with a minor in music. Actually, a minor in music and African American studies, double minor. And went on through school and got really involved in the radio TV film piece and got a really good internship at the NBC affiliate when I was a junior in DC. Doors opened for me so that when I graduated from college I immediately got an on-air position at a local radio station. So I started off as a DJ at a local gospel station in Washington, WYCB, and absolutely loved the job. I started off working midnight to 6, then got moved up to 6 to midnight and did some afternoon stuff. And absolutely loved the job. But started looking around after about a year or so and I was looking at how the business side of it was more relevant with regard to power in the industry as opposed to the talent side of it, as a broadcaster, the talent side of it. And at that point I said, "You know what, I really want to get into the radio station owner-ship." And this is back in the 1980s when that was a feasible dream. So I said, ok, how do you do this? I probably should further my education and get some kind of graduate degree. I decided I was going to do an MBA initially, and one thing led to another. I eventually decided I would do a law degree instead of an MBA. When I went to law school, from the very moment I started law school I knew it was to go into entertainment and media law. I never wanted to be a lawyer, but once I decided to be a lawyer I knew that's what I wanted to do. So I focused on that all the way through in terms of the courses I wanted to take and that sort of thing. And then after law school I started off in contract work, working for the Federal Aviation Administration. And here and there I'd have a client on the side, but there wasn't really enough of it to build real skills as an entertainment lawyer. So after working for about three years or so in DC I decided to move here to Nashville, to get into one of the music centers to try to build my skill set and my contacts set. It was New York, LA, and Nashville. And I chose Nashville for two reasons: one is because as a musician I've always been a gospel musician, and so Nashville was the scene for that. And the other reason was a more pragmatic reason was that I didn't have a job. And so I grew up in New York and knew what it was like to live in New York and what it cost to live in New York. I knew what it cost to live in LA. And Nashville is a little more feasible for somebody who was gonna come here to try to make it on his own. So I came to Nashville, came to visit and looked around. I went to an apartment complex and said "Hey, I don't have a job, but I can give you a check for six months' rent, can we move in?" And they said "sure," so we came here and the rest is history.

Why did you decide not to become a full-time musician / artist?

I've always been involved in music in some form or other. I started performing... publicly when I was about 14. Initially I played horns all through elementary school and I played this trumpet solo in church. And halfway through the solo – it was an Andrae Crouch song – and halfway through, like on the second chorus, I put down the trumpet and sang the second chorus, and everybody in the audience was like, I didn't know he sang! They knew I played. And shortly after that – maybe a year after that – I joined a group. There was a pretty active gospel music scene in New York when I was growing up, and one of the popular groups was a group that was kind of born out of my church, called the Aestatistics, but they were a really popular group in the local scene. And one of the members of the group was my older sister's boyfriend. And he was over at the house one day and he heard me just singing around the house, you know, singing some Spinners or O'Jays song or something. And he said "Hey man, we're looking for a new member of the group; would you be interested in joining?" And at that time that was like being asked to join the Beatles! So I went on and joined the group, and that was when I was 14 when I started singing with this group, and it was really a great sort of building block for learning how to sing and how to perform. Because I think one of the things that's missing a lot with today's – I don't want to be like the get-off-my-lawn-old-man-guy – but a lot of today's artists don't spend enough time in the woodshed just working on the craft. And that group sang every weekend, usually two or three times, like three different churches: New York, New Jersey, Connecticut, and all around the tri-state area. So you really learned how to sing, how to perform. And I did that through high school. When I went into college I started my own group and started writing songs for my own group, and kind of arranging how I wanted my sound to be. And did that all the way through college. Late, I think it might've been my senior year, we started doing these various contests. They'd have the Kentucky Fried Chicken gospel music competition and stuff like that. And one year we got all the way to the finals of the contest and lost to a group from Baltimore. But we were the second runner up so we got a nice little trophy, or whatever. And one of my friends who had played piano for my band for a little while said to me, "You know, the group is good but I really think you ultimately are a solo artist." And I thought about that and decided to give it a shot. And the next year I came back to the same contest as a solo artist and won. Oh, and check this out, the guest that year that I won was Andrae Crouch, who had been one of my childhood idols. And I got to meet him and take pictures with him and the finale that evening, when they brought everyone back onto the stage; this was at the Kennedy Center in Washington. The finale – that was right around the time of *The Color Purple*, I think that was the movie that this song was from – was "Maybe God is trying to tell you something." So I knew, man, this music thing, it's always been a part of me since I was a kid, I've always loved it, it's never seemed like work. Maybe I should give this a shot. But to be honest with you I never really made it the only thing. I was always doing something else.

That continued all the way through, even in law school I kind of stepped back a little bit in law school, but I still kept performing and kind of became like the law school go-to singer-musician-guy whenever we had programs. And just kept it going, it was always kind of bubbling under but I never really gave it a shot of going full force until I decided to leave DC after those three years of working in the federal government, and I then came to Nashville. I said you know, I'm going to see if I can do something, maybe I can do some session work. And that was back in the day when session players and singers could actually make a living. So I came down and I knew a few people. I knew the guys in Take 6. Got to know their manager who introduced me to the president at Warner Bros. Records, at that time it was Jim Ed Norman, really good guy. And he believed in me without having heard anything that I did. He literally hired me to be an arranger and background vocal contractor for a couple of projects without me really showing him anything that I did, just based on the fact that this manager told him, "This guy is good." So I did a couple things with him. I did a B.J. Thomas album. I did a – it was a Black cowboy – I think he was the first Black singing cowboy like in the 1930s or 1940s called Herb Jeffries and Herb Jeffries was coming back because Jim Ed used to do some really creative stuff. It wasn't just commercial, which he was very successful at. But he would do off the beaten path stuff, which was how Take 6 made it. Nobody really thought an capella group could be that successful. He thought, "These guys are great." So he brought Herb Jeffries in to do this cowboy album, basically. He asked me to arrange the background vocals. I did most of the songs on that record, and then I did a couple of other things with Warner Bros. and that branched out into some things for some Christian labels: Star Song, and Sparrow, and Integrity, and stuff like that. It was great, but the challenge was that it was sporadic. So you and I, we enjoy both the right-side and left-side brain and the spreadsheet part of me was like "Wait a minute, I can't budget now, because I don't know when the next check is coming in!" That year was just up and down, lots of really high highs and low lows, and some of the low lows were really low. So at the end of that year I decided… I can't do this. And actually, was thinking about moving back to DC. But things happened that kept me here. I ended up staying here but making music just a part of what I did, as opposed to the only thing to pay the bills.

Would you ever switch careers entirely to music/entertainment?

I don't envision that happening. However, I'm equally at home in either world. And if there was an opportunity – 'cause as a musician and as an artist I started several years ago on this path of owning something. So I own my own production company and recording company and all of that. And if there was a legitimate opportunity to build that on a full-time basis where I become the writer, producer for other people and that sort of thing, I wouldn't rule it out that I'd do that. What I would not be interested in doing is being a full-time artist who just makes his income running around the country singing. I don't want to do that. But I would be happy to be the guy running the company, and writing songs and producing for people, and then doing a concert here and there, which is basically what I'm doing now. The thing that I haven't done at the level that I would like to do is work with other artists. That's like the "what's the thing you haven't done yet?" That's what I haven't done yet. I've done some production with some other indie people, but nobody that anybody would know… I think all of these pieces come together to create the puzzle. And once you put all those pieces together and you see my face. Because I've taken this piece here, this piece there, and I enjoy it. I love it. Yeah.

Awards: received a Grammy certificate for his performance on a Grammy-winning record.[6] "It was an Andrae Crouch album. God puts you where He wants you to be, where you need to be. And I wasn't seeking it out. Sometimes we think we have to line everything up." *Honors on the business side: Leadership Music alumnus.*

Ben Hubbird (Portland, OR), Senior Label Manager, Infinite Companion

The office space for Infinite Companion is absolutely beautiful. Modern. Spacious. Funky and hip and sleek at the same time. I meet Ben Hubbird here, and he makes me a cup of decaf coffee using a pour-over process, also pretty cool. Ben seems at home in this office. It seems to match his avant-garde ways of thinking about music and the music business. I start with my usual opening question: why this job, why now?

I had been at CDBaby[7] for ten years. About a year ago there was a job opening at another record label in town and the owner of that label had asked me to
apply for that position. I told him that I was really flattered but... told him I was
happy where I was... Thinking back on it, I felt a lot of responsibility towards
the clients that I worked with, the musicians that I worked with and didn't
necessarily feel like I could step away and leave them well taken care of. Over the
year between then we built a team that was a little better equipped to do that
stuff. Ryan, the CEO here, approached me about this position about five months
ago. We had an initial conversation and I realized that it was something that I
really wanted to do. I have a record label that I started with a friend in spare time,
sort of a postman's holiday. And I realized that I had been doing one thing for a
long time and that the opportunity to build something new was really exciting to
me. On a less inspiring note, there wasn't a lot of potential for advancement
where I was. And unless I wanted to leave Portland there weren't a lot of other
options, in a way. This was the thing that was going to allow me to make a move
that was not lateral but somewhat of an advancement for my career, and it was
here in town, and it was with a company that has really awesome space, and I get
to build something new. It was a combination of factors. I never really set out in
my mind that this is the thing that I want to do. I think I built skills that made
me a good fit for the position. And then when the position came into existence it
seemed like a logical move.

I fell into it, honestly. I had (I think it's a bit of a cliché that I use) sort of a past
life as a political and community organizer. I spent about five years doing non-
profit and candidate campaigns for environmental and progressive causes. Some of
that time was spent running an office; I'd hire staff and train them and go do
some door-to-door fundraising for environmental groups and some voter
registration work and also did community organizing work, which is more going
into a neighborhood and recruiting volunteers, and then building a team of those
volunteers and coming up with an agenda that we want to push, either legislative
or at an organizational level. And I burned out on that pretty hard. After a
while I realized that because I was motivated to do that work primarily by a love
of the work and a love of doing it, I wasn't able to shut it off and was working
80-hour weeks and got really exhausted and started to hate the work and started
to hate the cause. After about six months of just doing temp work – I didn't
know what I was gonna do, this is all I had ever done – my girlfriend at the time
worked at CDBaby and was in the customer service team and said "I can get you
a job answering emails." I said "sure." I was in a band and we had our CD on
CDBaby. But I had never thought of the music business as a possible career. It
had never occurred to me. I volunteered at a local really incredible non-profit
performing arts center in Eugene called the W.O.W. Hall that's one of the best
venues in Eugene. It has a floating dance floor, and miniature crystal ballroom,
really great sound. Really great indie acts when they tour through they play
there. So I grew up from [ages] 13 to 23 volunteering there, seeing so many great

bands and learning about how to run a small venue, and worked in college radio and did radio shows and all that kind of stuff. Through all of that time I never thought of that as a potential career. It never seemed attainable. It seemed a little bit silly to want to do that. So I got this job at CDBaby answering phone calls and emails. And I kind of realized – I think it might be putting a little too much narrative into it to say that I realized that it was possible 'cause I more realized that I liked it. I really enjoyed talking to artists and helping them make a career out of what they were doing. And I really liked the weird people that I worked with. It was a very wild operation, CDBaby was, back then. It was pumped to the extreme [chuckles]. I think that some of the same instincts or tendencies that got me to the point of burning out in politics kind of took over in this new role and pretty quickly I was just really loving it and really digging in. And I think the main difference and the reason that I haven't burned out is that rather than being discouraged and sometimes disgusted by the people around me (that's not fair), I really enjoyed the people that I was working with. I think the feeling that I got from bolstering the artistic work that really incredible artists were doing, I realized that I value that just as much as like fighting the good fight and that being part of an effort to like enable artists to make more art was inherently a societal good. And then I was pretty good at it. I love music, I've always listened to music, I have always been pretty passionate about music. I think I have an ear, I have developed an ability to communicate effectively with people. It was kind of an accident. As soon as I realized that it was possible it became pretty obvious that that's what I wanted to do.

Why did you decide not to become a full-time musician/artist?

That was very clearly, well, maybe in the same way didn't seem realistic. I had been in a couple of bands and joined another band right when I started at CDBaby and had toured and made records and put out the records and had varying degrees of success. And even at its most successful, the last band I was in we went on tour and played like a three-week tour and had just finished recording a record. And even the most successful we ever were it was laughable the idea that we would ever be able to pay bills based on being in the band. And backing up, partly, I grew up in the punk rock ethos where expecting to make a living from your art was almost frowned upon or at least the commercialization of art was very suspect. And I still think that the most interesting art isn't made for those reasons. The premise that artists have to starve to make good work is obviously flawed, but I think there is a lot to be said for art that isn't made with the intention of financial gain. There's a tendency towards predictability I guess when you have a built-in financial incentive to make art that will sell. Part of the value of that ethos is that it removes that incentive: just make art, we're not trying to make money. So I came up with that growing up. I also was never particularly talented as a musician. [*I ask if he plays or sings; he plays guitar and sings.*]

I like to think I'm good enough to know that I'm not very good. I don't have beginner's naiveté about my own skills, but I do really enjoy it. I've come to realize that it's one of the only things that I feel like really nurtures my soul. I get like a little bit of a tingly religious feeling sometimes.

What do you consider to be your primary vocational pursuit at this time?

I would really like to build structures that can more powerfully enable artists to create their best and most dangerous work, most exciting work. Anything I can do to insulate an artist from the worry about how they're gonna pay rent and let them take risks artistically I feel like is a small success. I'm not a very ambitious person personally, but if I can broaden that work or further that work in organizations and institutions that do support artists, I consider that success.

Awards and honors: none. Stated without explanations or defenses. I dig that.

Joel Andrew, Esq. (Portland, OR), General Counsel, CDBaby

I was introduced to Joel by Tracy Maddux, CEO of CDBaby, in August 2017 while attending and speaking for the CDBaby DIY conference in Nashville. I usually feel a sense of kinship with other lawyer-musicians, so I was excited to meet Joel. I have Joel to thank for facilitating introductions for me to the other interviewees who are or have been affiliated with CDBaby.

I would describe myself as an entertainment lawyer. That's the industry that I work in. Probably as a non-traditional entertainment lawyer but that's still what I am or see myself as. Working at CDBaby for the last 14 years I saw an opportunity to continue down the business path. The debate was to get an MBA or law degree just because I knew what the company was and what we needed and I saw where money was going for expenses. And so I thought that there was a lot of money here that I could help us save… This would've been 2008 or 2007 or so when the recession was really hitting. Attorneys were working very hard to get whatever work they could get. So, family law attorneys were presenting themselves as entertainment attorneys, tax law attorneys as entertainment attorneys, so I saw a lot of bad work come at CDBaby or be around CDBaby. It was there that I found myself explaining basic music law, based on entertainment law… to people that had great degrees, great careers, really sharp, but they just didn't understand this field. And because I knew it and I enjoyed it, it was a fascinating thing to understand how law works as a musician. I saw that there was more opportunity in that field in the industry than traditional business people. Where the need was for CDBaby musicians, that was really what I thought that I was going to do when I went to school was that I was going to be an entertainment attorney focusing individually on the long tail, that I was going to work with all of these hundreds of thousands of artists individually. And then while in law school – I got into a school that's here in Portland – so I was doing night school there while working here at CDBaby. And there was no promise of a position while I was in school and then as we just got closer and closer to graduation it just made itself more and more reasonable that I would stay at CDBaby at least part time, or some amount of work or have a flagship client like CDBaby or something. And then when I finally was studying for the bar [exam], this was like the easiest decision to make on both sides. Not just for me wanting work but for CDBaby as well: we've got this guy who knows our industry, he knows what our clients need, is one of our clients, all that kind of stuff. And that was kind of all the giant answer I would give to what made me want to start doing this.

Why did you decide not to become a full-time musician/artist?

I still haven't decided to not become a full-time musician. A friend of mine (I don't know, this is an anecdote) but a friend of mine that was one of the first of my friends to go to law school – he's the greatest drummer I know. His name is Drew Shoals and he went to law school, so smart, great example for me to look at how to go through law school, get a good job. He graduated and was practicing [law] and doing his thing, and I think living in New York at the time and the band Train reached out to him (again, this is totally anecdote, I don't know if you can put it in), but Train, a Grammy award-winning band reached out to him and said, "Hey we'd love it if you came and did some gigs with us, fill in work or whatever," and now he's their full-time drummer. He doesn't practice [law] anymore. He's way smarter than me, way smarter than me, way gifted as an attorney and he's doing what he does best which is being a drummer.[8] So that's in my mind. I don't know what industry he was working in but that's my world. I'm gonna continue to work around musicians with kind of this like ridiculous notion, to me, individually it makes sense. I don't know how much it would compute to somebody else but I'm around these musicians all the time and somebody always says "you know we need a bass player" and I get to do that. I just went to the East Coast for four days, I just did three days this weekend. That was all because I still keep my chops up as a musician and work around musicians. I think it would be more difficult if I went into, say, property law or something outside of music. It's just so much easier that my bass is packed up and ready to go at any time. So yeah, ultimately, I haven't made a decision that that's out of my realm. But when I did start stepping back from what is my main pursuit – because I was pursuing being a touring musician – our goal was always six months a year of touring – I just got poor and just really poor, and more poor. And we were all very young and I was the only one in the band with a credit card. And I didn't understand what a credit card… I understood what a credit card was but I didn't understand how finance like that works. I didn't realize how much damage I was really causing myself in the long run. And CDBaby was my job on the weekends when I was touring, so they just supported me. And then I said, "I need more money" and they said "You have all these skills, you know all this stuff in this industry that we work in. How about you trade some of that for a little bit more financially successful future"... It was a financial decision that made the most sense because I was just so poor, to just stop touring, stop pursuing that.

Would you ever switch careers entirely to music/entertainment?

In that way, "would I ever" I absolutely would... and I would if I could kind of, I guess it would still be a financial thing. If I could afford to do it and not really mess up. School bills. Everything was loans. That's a real thing for me. That's a real weight that I have to make decisions around. I recognize that I am super lucky to get a job right out of school, in an industry that I love, that appreciates me and values me in a place that I could see long-term career... As well as I really love working at CDBaby and what I do and I do feel very much like an entertainment lawyer for 500,000 artists, even though I'm not their lawyer and I would never want them to think that I'm they're lawyer... I did a wedding band for a while and I hated it. And if I did a wedding band and it could somehow financially pay for me to sing music and play an instrument for the rest of my career, I wouldn't do it. 'Cause there was very little personal expression in it, versus if it was one of my bands that I play in and we could somehow rock into our 80s, I would love to do that... I don't know if I would be ready to fully step away from independent musicians and law. And I feel like I provide a lot of resource and advocacy for artists that – even through volunteer lawyers of the arts associations – will not get legal representation, ever. That would be another caveat is if I did become a full-time musician I would feel really bummed that I don't get to work in that area that I feel really passionate about, which is helping independent musicians just understand basics of music industry copyright law, business law... I would feel bummed out. That stuff's very personal to me now... We had this program... the academic enhancement program at the Lewis and Clark Law School and it was designed for non-traditional students because I was starting law school in my early 30s. It was designed for first-generation law students, which I am as well... one of the things was to go back and read your personal statement [periodically] so that way you'd remind yourself... this is why you're not giving up is because of this personal statement... and I remember that the first sentence of my personal statement said "I want to be an advocate for artists for the rest of my life." So in thinking about whether I would ever quit this job to go be a full-time musician, I would absolutely do that so long as I could be an advocate for artists for the rest of my life.

Awards and honors: he asks me to mention that a local weekly newspaper gave their band an award for worst band name: "Brother Joseph or as I call him Broseph." There you go, Joel, I've mentioned it.

Career Dualists

Kevin Bruener (Portland, OR), Vice President of Marketing, CDBaby; Guitarist and Songwriter, Small Town Poets

"These questions were designed with someone like you in mind," I say to Kevin Bruener at the beginning of our interview. I mean it, though I didn't know him when I designed the questions. When I think about a prototypical (if there is such a thing) Career Dualist, Bruener fits the bill. His career passions and callings clearly lie in both places, where there is an expressed split between being analytical and being artistic.

I was an active artist, I was releasing music independently and just happened to be living in the same area as CDBaby, and I got a job here and my passion was helping artists. And I had been signed to a major label and had been releasing music independently thinking there's gotta be a better way for artists to get their music out there and that's when I came across CDBaby. So I just had a passion for helping artists understand their options and how to build fans and how to retain ownership of their music and their rights. So my first job here at CDBaby was just helping artists. I'd take calls from artists all day who were trying to release their music and understand how to navigate the changing music business. Because of that I started a podcast, the DIY musician podcast, where it's more long form where we can have those conversations.

I've always been the person in the band or the artist who's the marketer in the band or the person who is always trying to promote and has an eye for marketing and messaging and the way things look and are packaged, so it just became a natural fit when CDBaby started growing and they added a marketing department. We were originally purchased by Discmakers and so they brought somebody in to establish the marketing department but they were from the East Coast and decided they didn't want to live in Portland. So they left and they promoted me into that position and just kept working my way up.

Why did you decide not to become a full-time musician/artist?

Well I was for a while! [He laughs.] It's one of those things where I was doing it full time and then, you know, life just can get in the way. There's so many different paths in being a full-time musician with that umbrella. And I would say talent plays into that. I would say that what you're passionate about plays into that and whether or not something under that umbrella's gonna work for you, especially long term. So, for me, I'm very much a collaborator, band guy. The band I'm in we're still signed to a label, we're still making records, in fact we released a single today and it's being featured on a Spotify playlist. But I'm really a band guy, a collaborator. I'm not a solo artist, songwriter. If I could sing I probably would've still been doing it full time. But I'm not a singer, I'm someone who collaborates really well. I can write a million guitar-driven song ideas but not finish songs, so it's like collaborating with other people to create a final product. So to me it was kind of after many years, kind of doing some soul searching and realizing that's where my talents are. And I think I'm very talented in that area but that kind of limits some of the options that you have. I'm not gonna go play for the symphony, or go play being a session musician. That's just not my gifting of being able to just walk into a studio and play something. That's why I keep plugging along, if something happened where I could be full time again, you know the reality is also that touring is extremely tough. When I was at Belmont[9] I was always surprised how many people would be like "I don't want to tour" and I was like "That's all I want to do! I want to travel, I want to get out on the road, I want to play shows!" And it is a really tough lifestyle that really starts to have implications and ramifications in the rest of your life. You start to feel like you don't have any friends anymore because you're off typically on a Monday and you're working on Friday, Saturday, and Sunday, and it's just this weird thing, you're always gone and it can be tough. Our band handled it really well. But it's one of those things; when you start having kids I can't imagine having kids and being gone as often as some of my friends are, I just couldn't do it. When that transition was happening, that's around the time I found CDBaby and started playing more locally and getting in projects that were based more in a local scene; that's where I spent a lot of my time for a while. But I've never stopped playing or stopped pursuing the dream. Can't let it die.

Would you ever switch careers entirely to music/entertainment?

Absolutely. If the circumstance was the right circumstance. Like I said, the dream's not dead. I'm always curious to see what might happen in the future. You never know what each day will hold, especially with music. Actually, in all seriousness, that's one of the things I love about music is that you never know when success can strike. Sometimes it comes from very interesting and unexpected places in unexpected times. I mentioned that Rock and Roll Hall of Fame placement. That band had kind of disbanded years ago, but our music is still finding success. And then another interesting thing we had recently is two years ago on an NBC prime time TV show there was this 90-second scene with two characters, and it kept going back and forth and one of them was wearing a Small Town Poets t-shirt that hadn't been available for 15 years! And it was just like a giant ad on NBC for like 90 seconds and you're like, "Wow, I never in a million years would've thought that would happen today." So it's those kind of things where you're like there's fans out there and you never know where they work, what they might be thinking, and where opportunity can come from. So with music… it's not just that I can't give up the dream it's like you never know, and enough things happen and if I'd given up those things might not have happened.

Bruener's full-time days were filled with touring, playing with multiple bands that no longer exist but left a musical legacy. For example, one of the bands still gets song placements in film and television. In fact, he shared with me that the Rock and Roll Hall of Fame just licensed some tracks from that other band called "Hello Morning" to use in a new installation. And Bruener is, appropriately, proud of that. "I don't care if it's for a new bathroom that they're installing, our music's in the Rock and Roll Hall of Fame!"

Do you consider music an avocation?

Everything that I do with music I pursue it at a professional level. So I may not be getting paid full time, but the quality of the product, the people that we employ to engineer and record, the way we go about presenting ourselves is always at a professional level. Even when I've just been in local bands here in the Portland scene, same thing. It's not just guys going around because we just want to get together with the guys and play music. It's we're very serious about writing songs, recording them in a way we think represents the sound that we're going for. And do our best to promote and market to our ability with whatever means we have and can afford to put into it. When I think about a hobby it's something I think it's something more to just pass the time or to find a little bit of personal enjoyment. But this is to me the way I pursue it, the level that we, as Small Town Poets especially, that's the band that we were on an EMI label, especially the way we do it, even though our time together is far more limited than when we were basically living together on the road, we still take it very serious and are still, we think, making great music with the amount of time and effort we can.

Awards and honors: Small Town Poets has been nominated for two Grammys, nominated for three or four Dove awards, and nominated for a Billboard Music Video award. One of the songs he co-wrote for the band was included on a compilation album that went platinum. His band has also had three or four number one songs in his genre (Christian alternative rock).

David Smith (Nashville, TN), Vice President of Music Entertainment, Pinnacle Bank; Singer/Songwriter

David Smith understands and lives his duality very consciously. I am always on the lookout for dualists and was delighted when I discovered he would be speaking to our seminar students about working a full-time job while continuing to work as an active musician.

My mom was a singer back in the day. She came down to Nashville, made a record and back then they were called the Smith Family Singers Southern Gospel Group. So, my grandpa put instruments in everybody's hands right away, as a kid. My uncle had a stutter, so he found out if he sang it helped with his stuttering.

So that's kind of where music got started in the family. So, by the time I came around I just grew up around music. I personally didn't want to pursue that or have an idea I was gonna pursue that. But it was just always around so I learned how to sing. My mom was putting us in nursing homes and we would sing Christmas carols and stuff like that. Later I started singing and kind of rapping with acoustic guitar and stuff, and from there is when I expressed writing. And even younger, like in junior high when I listened to raps I wanted to write rhymes and I'd be in school, in English class, and I would just be writing rhymes and rhymes. So writing was very, very important to me, I would say that even started it all. So by the time the voice developed, then it just was natural, singer/ songwriter. But I would definitely say the singing helps me deliver the writing. So, singer/songwriter for sure.

Why did you decide to become Vice President of Music Entertainment?

So, the idea for that was never in my plan. I wasn't smart enough to think of something like that at the time or aware that that was even out there. I just knew that I had to pay the bills, and music wasn't doing it at the time. There was a friend who would come to my shows and she was very supportive of my music and she knew I was struggling financially, 'cause I went to her as a banker and asked, "I gotta get a plan together here, I'm struggling paying my bills." So she was kind of helping me manage money but my money was so sporadic: show here, show there. I mean I was dependent on booking a gig to pay for rent. There were times in the winter – summer was great, and winter was slow – and I didn't prepare for that. I was just a free-flowing kind of artist guy. And she was like, "Well they're hiring at the bank, you could be a part-time teller, have a little bit of a consistent income while you pursue your music." I thought well, I guess that's interesting. Maybe I could explore that. When I started thinking about it I just really dove in and thought, what could a banker be for me? And that came down to even just a guy who has a little pocket watch and a little eyeglass thing [monocle], just think of the old-time banker. I thought yeah, I could be this character. That's how I thought of it. That's how I had to think of it to get excited. I thought yeah then I could help other artists who are like me and really prepare them and say "I know what you're thinking, times are great right now. But come December they might not be. How can we prepare for that?" And I felt that since I was aware of the situations they're going through and could think the way they think, I would be able to help them better. And I didn't know music banking existed, but that was the perspective I was gonna carry with me. So when I kind of got into it, at training, at Wells Fargo down in Birmingham, one of the bankers who had had a long career in banking asked me, "What do you want to do in banking?" I told him "I want to be a banker for musicians." And he said, "There's actually a real market for that. Not in many places, but in Nashville definitely there's a market for that." He goes, "If you're fortunate enough you could probably break into that." I was like "Oh cool." So he made me aware that there was actually an industry that existed doing that. And I heard about Avenue, and so a bunch of my friends were already banking at Avenue. They had a marketed music and entertainment division. So I was like man that would be really cool, and they actually reached out to me on LinkedIn about a year into my banking career because of my picture on LinkedIn. It was a little more artistic; I was in a car, looking back. I just wanted to portray banking differently, something more approachable, and that was their vision as well. So they saw it and were like, "Hey we really think your picture is interesting, would you come in and meet with us?" And I was right there in the music and entertainment office. And I was like, wow, this would be so cool to work here. So I did get the job over in that office and I didn't know a lot about using royalties for collateral or anything like that at this time. For me, it was more to help the artist understand money better. But throughout that I was taken under the wing, basically, and I had these weekly meetings with our director of music and entertainment over at Pinnacle, and he started just teaching me about lending and the commercial world and how that applies to music and thinking instead of a big building downtown and how those guarantors relate to that lending; how music – the royalties – can be the collateral. Started opening my mind to all that stuff and it fascinated me 'cause this world was so foreign to me. I was a performer, I didn't think anything about the business; I didn't even know music business existed. So really diving in and learning this stuff, to me was absolutely fascinating. So I kept reading, kept learning, and with my connections already in the music world as a songwriter and performer it was a huge asset to the bank and they saw that, and this guy in particular. Without him, another banker could've just overlooked me and thought, inexperienced, just some singer/songwriter trying to pursue a dream. But Andy's vision really connected with mine. And after I told him my story as well he said, "Man you were born for the music business." And from there I felt more confident. 'Cause I was like this guy sees me, he knows what I'm doing, he knows my vision, and he's going to help me get there. So he was a huge contribution to my success in the banking world. Just after experience and having some success bringing people to the bank and helping songwriters, it kind of led me to that vice president office later of music and entertainment.

Why did you decide not to become a full-time musician?

Walk through the door that opens for you, or I always used to tell myself, do what pursues you. So I'm pursuing music. It's just like a girl. If I'm pursuing a girl and she's not pursuing me back, I'm a creep. It's like she's gonna be running away. And life's that way. Things in life work that way. Music pursued me back, at times, and then it didn't. It's like tug of war. And when I was doing it full time, like at Belmont things were great, it felt like music was pursuing me back. But after Belmont I wanted to be a songwriter full time because that's what I came to Nashville for – pursue the dream, be an artist. I had great success at Belmont so I thought that would just carry into the Nashville world, and it wasn't. And so after I wasn't getting paid and I was falling short on rent and I was pursuing music and these doors weren't opening, I didn't know what to do. So I had to do something that was able to pay the bills and this banking job kind of opened a door for me. So at Wells Fargo I was quickly promoted to a personal banker position from what they call a CSSR, a person who does teller work and banker work, but I was strong on the banking side of things so I got quickly promoted and I'm like "that's cool, I got promoted – hey, never had that happen before." So that was nice. And same thing started happening at Avenue. I really quickly took this leadership role and those doors kept opening for me. And Andy and I met and we talked and he offered an opportunity and I actually got put on the merger committee for Pinnacle and Avenue Bank. So once Pinnacle bought Avenue, Andy recommended me to be on this merger committee which I was scared to death of. I had three years of banking experience and I'm supposed to say how this merger goes and how that works? And I'm here with people who are executives at Pinnacle and I'm just this young guy. But it was a really great experience. Just doors like that kept opening for me. They were investing in me. And so I kept wanting to pursue that back. And I just feel it really just comes back down to my first sentence of do what pursues you, even though music is always a creative outlet for me so I wasn't ever gonna let it go. I was always gonna do music, I love it. I told myself when I got into it that I'll be a guy who just goes and plays these little random bar gigs, don't care, I love to do music. So I could work anywhere I want to and I'll still do music. If one day it chooses to pursue me back, then I can cross that road. But for now, you have to take care of your responsibilities, I gotta pay the bills. The banking job is really opening a lot of doors for me and music's not. So that's where that came about.

Would you ever switch careers entirely to music/entertainment?

I will always leave the door open for conversation for future opportunities. As I start to dive into how money flows in the music business and how we're using it as collateral, I think that gives a very unique perspective to the music business as a whole. So if there was a company that was interested in taking the things I've learned in the banking world, I'd be open to that conversation for sure, if that platform still allows me to – and we're talking music business right now as an opportunity – to reach as many people as I am at the bank. If you're talking about the artist side of things – the dream when I moved to Nashville was to be an artist. Period. Point blank. I left my family for it, I left my nephews growing up for it, you sacrifice a lot to pursue that dream because at the time I was able to; I didn't have a ton of responsibilities. If I want to pursue an artist career that decision is on me and kind of about me and my dreams, which is fine and dandy.

But the route I want to go, and I don't want to sound all high and mighty here either but I am justifying that decision on I think I have an opportunity to do more for other people in this position of being a banker and still doing music and maybe getting songs recorded by artists, I mean that opportunity is really big here in Nashville. To say hey I think this is possible for me because David did it. And I want to be that example for other people, over just pursuing the artist career.

Awards and honors: received a golden ticket (invitation to Hollywood) for American Idol. *Had a top 40 on National Songwriters. Lots of artists have cut his songs, e.g., Rayvon Owens (an* American Idol *finalist in season 14 and Belmont alumnus). Business honors:* "I was a top 50 banker in the southeast (Wells Fargo). Fun win: lip-syncing contest winner for Pinnacle. And it was competitive!" *In David's words, you have to celebrate every moment as a success.*

Chuck Harmony (Nashville, TN), Music Producer/Songwriter/CEO of Weirdo Workshop

Chuck Harmony, along with Claude Kelly, is CEO of Weirdo Workshop. He and Claude are veterans and household names in the music business as songwriters and producers. And they are dualists. Chuck's answers to my questions are precise, pointed, poignant, compelling. He packs meaning into every word.

I started Weirdo Workshop out of frustration. I never, ever wanted to... I'm not a person that always had the intention of being CEO of some record label. That was not in my realm of thinking. It was not until I saw that the music business wasn't going to service me totally the way that I felt I should be serviced as a producer and as a creative mind that I felt that I needed to house my own creativity. Just looking at the difficulties in business for a lot of people that's like me. I would consider myself one of the creatives that's so gung ho about creativity that the business can kind of fall to the back burner of your life. And for most of my career that's what it was. It was just like creativity first. In the business where commerce is the main thing those people get underserviced as it relates to business, as it relates to signing good deals, as it relates to people taking your creativity as seriously as you take it. So Weirdo Workshop was not only just to house my creativity it was also to house like-minded creatives like myself, just to give them a safe haven. If you want to be just a creative then you can come to Weirdo Workshop and be just creative and you don't have to worry about the pitfalls of bad business or people taking advantage of you or not caring about your opinions. All of the things that I felt like I experienced in the music business I was trying to remedy for people like me, piano players and songwriters and producers and singers as well.

Why did you decide not to become a full-time musician/artist?

The reason I chose not to be a full-time musician [anymore] was because I wanted to challenge myself outside my comfort zone. Since 3 years old I've been doing music and I've been kind of exploring creativity, just non-stop, through junior high, through high school, through college, and as a grown person. So when I got in the business in 2007 I saw a need to explore other sides of myself, because I really wasn't being challenged, especially creativity as is. It's kind of like a microwave society, you just turn out product after product after product. So for people that want to be intellectual and actually want to think and actually want to strategize about anything, not just music but about anything, creativity can become redundant and you can fall into a laziness about life. So part of my reasoning for wanting to split up my duties and venture off and start a company and start intellectual projects was I wanted to challenge myself. I wanted my life to be more than one dimensional.

If you had it to do all over again, which pursuit would be primary?

I would have been an artist all along. For creative freedom. But more importantly, as a music producer and trying to get into the music business I spent so much time putting artists on a pedestal, and it really stunted my growth a lot. I guess you have this ideal of what an artist is, and so how dare you even consider yourself that kind of person, especially if you have insecurities, if you're coming from a point where you didn't get the encouragement so you're kind of just feeling your way through, trying to figure stuff out. I knew at an early age that I could've definitely been an artist and I prevented myself from that because I didn't want the heartache of it and I didn't want the rejection of it. And I never say this but it's so true, like in all honesty my music-producing career was me taking the safe route. I knew I could put music together so it's a no-brainer that I could make money from that. But the artist route would've charged me to be bolder sooner. It would've demanded that I revealed a lot more about the wholeness of my creativity earlier. So I really regret that, knocking on 40 now. Now I understand who I am totally as a creator. But I wish I had done that from the beginning. Really do.

Do you have any joys/rewards that you attribute to being blended (i.e., a dualist)?

The reward is that I have the final say over the product. And it's not that I feel like I know it all, but I do feel like I will fight for what's best for my creative and for my product. So the joy is in knowing that I will have the final say so there's at least gonna be the best of me in everything that Weirdo Workshop does, because I'm not gonna allow any less. It's also a joy to watch things that you create come into fruition. Tiny Book Club, for example, when we got that Billboard article about Tiny Book Club I found so much pleasure in knowing that not only was that a brand that we created, but it was powered by our business mind. And I feel like one of my secret initiatives in life is to remind people that musicians are intellectual people. Like we are smart and sharp people. I think this culture actually diminishes that side of a musician. As long as you're good at social media or however people are getting discovered musically, you're safe… that was always a little thorn in my side in terms of music production. I could never be satisfied because I was always like, nobody ever sees the intellectual side of a musician any more. The joy for me… is that people get to see how we think and how we consider things as it relates to business, that power these beautiful things we are able to accomplish. So that's my biggest joy. I definitely think at the end of the day, at the end of my career I would definitely want to be known as the CEO of Weirdo Workshop more than a music producer, more than a songwriter, more than it all. I think everybody should… own the rights to their work, however they do it. We all, at a certain point, have to work for somebody else as it relates to getting income. But I think in the totality of your life I think people should own the rights to their work. They should build a thing, a service, build something that helps them make it through life financially.

Would you ever switch careers entirely to music/entertainment?

Never again. Because at this point I feel like I have to take care of the business aspect of my career for the rest of my career. And I have artists signed to me that I have to take care of their careers for the rest of their careers. I'm super dedicated to those missions.

Awards and honors: Dove award for best contemporary gospel song; NAACP award for best song. "I've been Grammy nominated for Mary J. Blige, Growing Pains, Neo-O, Ledice, Fantasia, Leandria twice – six Grammy nominations." *Honors on business side – Leadership Music alumnus.*[10]

Claude Kelly (Nashville, TN), CEO, Weirdo Workshop; Musician; Emerging Inspirational Figure

Claude Kelly is a visionary. And a weirdo. A visionary weirdo. I already knew the story behind the Weirdo Workshop name, having interviewed him for a seminar at Belmont. So it is not a question I ask during the interview. Suffice it to say the "weirdo" moniker has to do with bringing your authentic self to the music industry, boldly and unapologetically. I ask how he became CEO of Weirdo Workshop.

I had a lot of issues with the music business. I definitely had a chip on my shoulder around the time I was thinking about quitting. I was successful, but I was very much perturbed by some of the nonsensical ways in which the music business still operates. So when we started talking about creating a company to support the music that Louis York[11] was doing, we [he and Chuck Harmony] had equally as many conversations about how we were going to do things busi-nesswise differently. And not just "Oh, we're gonna be an independent company and we'll take care of it ourselves and we won't go to the majors." That's still like the low hanging fruit. It was more about how people are viewing entertainment.

There is more to this response. Much, much more. The rest of Claude's perspectives, captured in Chapter 5, speak not only to his and Chuck's perception of how the music business operates, but to how a dualist can challenge the music industry through their duality.

How do you describe yourself to others when asked "what do you do?"

I describe myself as a CEO of a company and I describe myself as a musician, not a singer, 'cause I think that's too limiting. But ideally, I'm trying to graduate from musician to I guess the best word would be teacher or inspirational figure, not looking for the praise or pastoral sense of it. But I understand that the songs are really just the outer crust of a message. So I'm so much more concerned with people hearing what I'm trying to tell them, as opposed to "oh that was pretty, the way that you did that." And "singer" implies that I just want you to love my trills. And "musician" implies that you have a deeper understanding of the whole track, the whole study. But there's still a deeper layer than that. There are musicians who understand that the title "musician" is just the vocation and that really your calling is delivering a message and teaching, a philosopher at best. It might be too big shoes to fill, but definitely there's something in that. I'm always trying to bottom line to the little nugget of truth that I think will get people through the day. And the music just gets you focused on that… In fact, I used to call myself a songwriter and I know that's the right term. But now when I listen to what I do, even compared to people I don't respect as much, I try to value myself as a poet more than as a songwriter. Because I value so much every single word, every single comma, every single inflection and emphasis of the word 'cause it changes the meaning. And I don't think most people take that into consideration. It's just words to rhyme or a prettiness thing. And we spend way too much time, surgically like, are they getting what we're saying? Is that the right word? Is it gonna turn some people off? And sometimes you just have to trust yourself. But it's so much more about them getting the message, than them loving the beat, or them loving the fact that I have a pretty voice. So whatever the title that I get from that is where I want to be in the end, hopefully.

Why did you decide not to become a full-time artist?

I would say that I was a full-time musician until about five years ago. My business world or the way I viewed being a musician drastically changed. My reason for even being in Nashville now is obviously Weirdo Workshop and Louis York. But before that I was getting ready to quit the business. And to even pre-cede that, the way it was set up before was that on the pop side, especially in

New York and LA, it's broken down into departments very, very specifically. So I was a songwriter, of course, and I had a manager, and my manager kind of did all the business talking for me. I was more astute than I would give a lot of musicians credit for. I was naturally more inquisitive and did my homework and knew stuff. But for the most part, the everyday business stuff that happens I didn't have to worry about. For example, when interns or employees were clocking in and clocking out, or payroll, really managing the calendar – I was allowed to be as creative as possible. And when I decided to "quit" my manager was still there, but that's when I started to realize that I was overlooking some of the fine print. I certainly wasn't one of those cautionary tales of being cheated in the business. I just recognized that the business was changing. Things as they were weren't gonna work anymore, so I'd better start paying attention to what's happening so I can find my legacy in this changing business, which led to Louis York and Weirdo Workshop. It would start with creative control first, start taking more creative control. And then after we started doing great songs I was so proud of them in a way that I hadn't been proud of them before because it was all my money, also my idea – with Chuck (Harmony) of course, and my time. When you're writing for someone else you're on their time, so you're kind of just a work for hire. But once this music was done, I felt that I owed it to the music to be as responsible as possible with how I handled the business of that art. And that's what forced me to stop being 100 percent just a musician, and more of a 50/50, which I definitely consider myself now. I used to write all day every day, seven days a week. And now I hardly write like I used to. I think it's more meaningful, but I spend a lot more time strategizing and organizing and outreach. And it may sound kind of childish, but we spend a lot of time dreaming, which you don't get to do when you're on other people's time because it's about ful-filling their dream, or what makes the other artist the best. But for us we spend a lot of time with vision boards, and chalk boards, and erasing things and coming up with ideas and potential equations. And it's a part of my brand I never got to use before, and I love it. So for me, I decided five years ago to do that but I'm grateful that my decision to do that wasn't because the music side wasn't working out. It was actually because I was adamant about protecting the music side that I was so proud of. So now I feel like I have a balance. I understand that in order for the great music I'm working on to not be in vain, I have to divide my time so that after it comes out of me I'm thinking about the care for it, the parenting of it, which in itself is a business. And sometimes I'm dying to be in the studio and be singing and just being free, but I don't feel so bad because I know that I'm doing the right things to make sure that what I'm working on will get a fighting chance, which is already hard in this business. But I say this all the time: even if you're the very, very best it's still very hard to cut through all the noise here. So you'd better make sure that you at least do your best to be as aware and prepared and as business savvy as you can, to give yourself a fighting chance. Or it becomes such a one in gazillion chance that you're almost wasting your time. I love being 50/50.

Would you ever switch careers entirely to music/entertainment?

If there's one I had to choose it would be entirely music, I would definitely not go entirely to business. I'm absolutely a creative brain. I can't turn that off even if I wanted to. I also think I'm unique because I'm good at both. I've seen a lot of people in record labels kind of lose their musical edge when they get behind a desk all the time. And I think it skews how they handle their business in the music business, because you have to have the heart for it to take the right kinds of risks. 'Cause sometimes, like in every business, you have to do things that don't make sense. You're betting on someone who doesn't really have the numbers, or the fans yet and instinct has to take it and say this person could be Prince, this person could be Paul McCartney or this person could be Beyoncé, or whoever it is that you're discovering and that doesn't always make sense. If there is a death to the music industry, which I don't believe, but if there is a killer, a cancer to the music business the cancer is a lack of creative professionals who are sitting behind desks, or creative professionals who haven't decided to split their time healthily between still being creative and doing their business. They were musicians before, they don't sing anymore. Or they don't play. Even if it's gigging on the weekends. I go to record labels sometimes and I hear no music playing. None. I mean, dentist offices have music playing. And you're like, is this Wall Street? Or is it the music business? And it requires you loving music all day to think about business correctly for music that you love all day. So I could not be a full business person. I reign in the side of me that's 100 percent music because that means I think it translates some odd times to irresponsibility. But if I had to choose I would give up all the wealth trappings, but I know I would be 100 percent happy if I was in a third-world country island or somewhere, if I could sing in a choir or teach music or sing in a small club. I love music that much that I would do that. I think I have messages that need to be heard, so if business is included because, like I said at the beginning, I feel like what we're doing is so potent that you ought to think businesswise about it. But [if forced]… I think I would choose music 100 percent.

Awards and honors: "I've been nominated for Grammys several times. Everyone says being nominated is the win. I haven't won a Grammy but I was nominated for five or six of them, I believe. I've won plenty of BMI awards. I was songwriter of the year in 2014, I believe. I have an NAACP award and a Dove award." *Honors on the business side: Leadership Music Alumnus.*

Everyone is unique. I was inspired by every story, and every twist and turn in each person's journey. These profiles do not purport to tell an individual's entire story, but together paint a portrait of duality.

Amplifying the Grid

Why is Justin a Dualist Explorer, rather than a Career Dualist? Why is David categorized as a Career Dualist rather than a Dualist Explorer? Categorizing human beings, with all their complexities and uniqueness, in one of four quadrants is not one dimensional. For example, because I am aware of the level of seriousness, professionalism, and experience Loren takes to his artistic pursuits, I originally placed him in the Career Dualist quadrant. Kevin seemed right on the cusp between Dualist Explorer and Career Dualist. And David also seemed borderline Dualist Explorer. In the end, I based my placements on the quadrant descriptions in Chapter 2. To belong in the Career Dualist quadrant a dualist must have a 50/50 A/A/D allocation of time. Alternatively, the Career Dualist is very close to that 50/50 allocation + passion + approximately 20 hours per week of time spent expressing artistic drive if working in a full-time position as a music business logician. Review Chapter 2 for a complete description of the Career Dualist quadrant.

Calling is that passion element that amplifies the Duality Exploration Grid. What role does passion play in your story? Let the journeys of each of the dualists inspire you to complete the exercises in this chapter. Dip into the reservoirs of your own experience. Explore and expand your own self-knowledge. This helps to lay the foundation for the exploration of calling in Part II of this book.

Discussion Questions

1. What do the Career Dualists have in common?
2. What do the Dualist Explorers have in common?
3. What strikes you about the Career Explorer's profile?
4. Review the Duality Exploration Grid found in Chapter 2. Distinguish the definitions. Would you categorize any of the profiled dualists in different quadrants than where the author has placed them? Why or why not?

EXERCISE SET 3: TELLING YOUR OWN TALE

The objective of this exercise is to begin constructing your own narrative concerning duality.

1. Whose story or stories do you most identify with? Why? Identify the elements in each story that sound like the story you are beginning, have begun, or want to begin.
2. Listen. Listen for calling. Listen to you. Whose story do you hear?
3. Think about the terminology *Music Business Logician* versus *Music Business Creative*. How do you feel about choosing to be primarily one versus the other?

Notes

1 Liner notes and album available at musicarr.com. Individual downloads available on iTunes, Amazon. Streams available on YouTube and Apple Music.
2 The data collection was submitted to and approved by the Internal Review Board of Belmont University.
3 For example, there are many medical doctor-singers, scientist-musicians, and engineer-actors who may possess similar experiences as those profiled here, and may also experience CD/Di. A few who knew of my study offered to be interviewed, but because they fall outside the target sample have not been interviewed for this book.
4 Participants included four women, nine men, seven white dualists, one Latino dualist, and five Black dualists. The age range for profiled dualists spanned from 20s to 50s.
5 A Nashville restaurant that closed its doors shortly after this interview.
6 He pointed out that a Grammy certificate is granted in lieu of a Grammy award when the artist is not considered a featured artist on a record, e.g., a background vocalist.
7 CDBaby is a resource for independent artists, headquartered in Portland, OR. See www.cdbaby.com/ for more information about the company and services offered. I have been a CDBaby artist since approximately 2015.
8 Drew has been written about by "Above the Law." His biography appears at drew shoals.com.
9 Bruener studied music business at Belmont University, Nashville, TN.
10 Leadership Music: https://leadershipmusic.org/about/overview/.
11 Name of his music group with Chuck Harmony. The name comes from a combination of both musicians' hometowns. Harmony is from St. Louis, Kelly is from New York, hence Louis York.

PART II

The Impetus for Career Duality

4

VOCATIONAL CALLING

The Directional Axis of Vocation

There are musicians who understand that the title "musician" is just the vocation and that really your calling is delivering a message and teaching, a philosopher at best.

(Claude Kelly)

Moving from an academic understanding of analytical propensity + artistic drive (A/A/D) to a career decision that actualizes it involves establishing clarity, the kind of clarity that is personal, that speaks to your individuality. Where will that clarity come from? How will you know whether to focus on expressing your analytical propensity or your artistic drive, or both? What voices do *you* hear? An objective of this book is to explore potential solutions to the Career Duality dilemma presented by possessing A/A/D. What if the solution is to simply go with what you want to do most? Or choosing what gives you the greatest sense of purpose and meaning? Or to use the strongest abilities you have? All those possibilities invoke the concept of calling, which is the fifth tier of the Career Duality model. Calling is a means of understanding the directional axis of vocation. Therefore, this chapter and the next two chapters explore calling as a lens through which to consider career direction.

Career theorists and researchers have defined calling in a variety of ways. Shoshana Dobrow Riza and Jennifer Tosti-Kharas define calling as "a consuming, meaningful passion people experience toward a domain."[1] Amy Wrzesniewski et al. described calling as "a focus on the enjoyment of fulfilling and socially useful work."[2] Bryan J. Dik and Ryan D. Duffy concluded that calling is "a transcendent summons, experienced as originating beyond the self, to approach a particular life role in a manner oriented toward demonstrating or deriving a sense of purpose or meaningfulness and that holds other-oriented values and goals as primary sources of motivation."[3] Hagmaier and Abele's calling construct says that calling is "the realization of one's full potential in the world of employment that is guided by a transcendent force and goes along with the experience of sense and meaning."[4] Taken together, characteristics of calling include: an emotional (passion-centered) connection to career, a less rational component, orientation to purpose, and a spectrum of calling experiences ranging from partial calling to no calling at all. The existence of multiple definitions suggests not only that the concept has many components, but that as a practical matter, calling may be individually discerned and lived out, referred to herein as "living called."

For example, Gina Miller is a music industry logician and singer who performs publicly about eight to ten times a year. I didn't ask her about calling during our interview. I asked her what she considers to be her primary vocational pursuit. She didn't say "the music industry" or anything remotely close to that. It was much broader. And bigger.

> *Purpose. [Long pause] That's it!*

She laughs. But I just smile, because I need to understand it. I know there is more to be said, and ask what she means.

> *For the most part, when it comes to the things I'm spending my time doing, [it means] that they are absolutely in line with what God has for me to do with the gifts He has given to me. And that's really what I believe. I also believe that it could mean, even with my artists, I say to them all the time there are so many people who could sit in this seat that I get to sit in. There are so many people with qualifications to do music maybe better and maybe better musicians and even maybe have more business knowledge. And I say this quite often: I'm so glad that that's not the requirement that's needed for me. That's not why I'm here. I really absolutely believe with everything in me that I'm here to help make sure that everyone understands their purpose more and reaches their more effective purpose in life. If we can get to purpose we can get everything we're supposed to get, and that includes our business.*

Somehow, this does not sound like what you are likely to hear in your music business classes. And perhaps it does not sound like either the analytical or artistic side of her A/A/D is even engaged. Or does it? Can we quarrel with her ascendency to the position of vice president and general manager of Entertainment One? Not if we understand that her job extends far beyond her title, which reframes yet utilizes her A/A/D.

> *So I can embrace that that's my job. I'm a manager of purpose and expectation. That should be my title! Because if I keep everybody focused on purpose and real expecta-tions, everything else that this company needs, everything that I need, everything that the artist needs will absolutely follow. I think it's when we go outside of purpose and try to force ourselves down paths that God never intended for us to have and work he*

never designed us to do, creating something that's not for us to be, all those things are contrary and create more work than is necessary to do. If we just follow the will He has for us we would absolutely get what we're supposed to get… God used music so I could connect with these great people so I could help them in the way that He really designed me to do. We call it music but music's really just a vehicle to get us in the car together to give me an opportunity to help them see that they're here for something perhaps bigger and bolder and different than they had even considered. That's my primary vocation right now.

At first blush, Gina's perspective makes the business of finding a calling-like purpose sound easy, so straightforward. Just find your purpose and live it, she seems to say. But if we listen more closely to her words, her mission to help others find their purpose suggests that people need help with the whole purpose journey, so it may not be so straightforward after all. This chapter introduces the concept of calling, explores its origins, and describes some of the benefits and potential challenges associated with searching for and finding a calling, as well as considerations for *not* doing so.

Called to What?

The terms vocation and career are used interchangeably throughout this book to refer to the work we do. At one time in history, work was mostly about work. Not passion. You were pretty much a cog in a wheel that existed to churn out products for your employer or provide services to customers who were "always right." You were paid for that. That was the exchange – work for pay – and employers were expected to provide little more than that. Then an industrialized society created organizational hierarchies that led to seeking promotions and increased pay. Career is a modern notion that builds on the idea of working for financial sustenance and expands it to include identifying with our work to derive meaning and purpose from it. That's where calling comes in. If we are called, we are called to our work, and calling offers a perspective that makes the work meaningful beyond economic survival.

So we search for calling to find the meaning a satisfied calling can provide. Not everyone conducts a search. But some do. Justin Longerbeam, a profiled dualist, did. I asked why he decided to work on the business side of the music industry.

That sort of came from I think struggling through freelance work. I wanted to not have to work a day job that wasn't relevant to this passion that I seek and that led me to a job at the music distribution company CDBaby, with an entry level position there. And I spent a few years there and learned a ton about the back end of the industry and that sort of sparked a desire to further that. And that knowledge and interest of all that stuff led me to future endeavors.

Justin gives us the words: "seeking a passion." That is what is meant here by searching for calling. Not knowing what your calling is, whether there is a specific calling for you, or knowing how to discover it, if it exists at all, can render the whole concept meaningless or simply be frustrating. Yet we are often left to ourselves to figure it out.

We typically do not collect data on ourselves, but we could. Parker Palmer did. His well-known and much beloved book that I highly recommend, called *Let Your Life Speak*, chronicles the journey of his own calling. His was an arduous, sometimes beleaguered and vexing search. He traversed a path from aspirations to work in advertising, to full-time ministry, to aviation, to community organizer and activist, to teaching as a university professor, and ultimately to activist and teacher for those in the teaching profession. He recounts his story of a gradually unfolding discovery through a journey that includes seeking self-knowledge – a consistent theme in this book and in the idea of calling. We might imagine that to finally discover one's calling is the supreme, shining end of such a journey. Yet what makes his story so compelling and inspirational is the transparency with which he reveals discoveries of the soul and spirit along the way. He shares his depressions, missteps, the fog of bewilderment he encountered. It is not a fairy tale. It is a volume of truth and reality. Of life. Ultimately, he reached what he believes to be his unique career destiny, but there was nothing simple about it.

It may be that in the pursuit of calling the best discovery and real destiny is learning who you are, because that person may actually *do* anything anywhere and everywhere, so long as when she does it she knows who she is, for she can draw upon that personal power to be, not merely to do. And being is the essence of living called. In Palmer's words, "Teaching, I was coming to understand, is my native way of being in the world. Make me a cleric or a CEO, a poet or a politico, and teaching is what I will do. Teaching is the heart of my vocation and will manifest itself in anything I do."[5]

Embarking on a search for calling sounds like something big and monumental. In some respects, it is. And perhaps it should be. A sincere look at one's life to fathom its meaning cannot be like making instant oatmeal; plopping a mixture into a bowl, stirring it, and using the fastest means to boil, microwave, or otherwise get it cooked so that it can be eaten. It took Parker Palmer many years and a great deal of soul searching. His investment of time involved the proverbial trial-and-error methodology scientists value and expect before making a big discovery. But it's not the process we non-scientists choose if we want a quick answer. Searching also requires vulnerability and risk, one potentially fraught with questions: Is searching worth the trouble? Is calling worth the trouble? What if you seek but do not find a calling? What if you find the wrong one? How can you know whether what you find is really authentic and best for you? How long will it take? What do you do while figuring out the answer? Where does one begin? Some might argue that a calling is really not something you have to look for, that the whole point of being called is that there is something already speaking to you, a summons that may be internal or external.

Sources of Calling

The Divine and Transcendent

Calling was originally associated with hearing a call from God, and the call involved doing work for God. Gina's references to "what God intended" and working "in line with what God has for me to do" are examples of the "transcendent force" that is part of Hagmaier and Abele's calling construct. Biblical examples of calling include: God's call to Moses to lead the Israelites out of Egyptian bondage;[6] a call to Noah to build an ark;[7] a call to Jonah (the prophet who wound up in the belly of the whale) to preach to the Ninevites;[8] and the call to Samuel to be a prophet.[9] Calling has spiritual roots, yet in the last decade or so, the literature and research on calling have increased, expanding the number of theories about the nature of calling and its sources. This includes research about the transcendent origins of calling. The literature has used the transcendent/divine approach to refer to an external source like God as a springboard to more broadly examine external sources beyond God, as pertinent to calling. Calling theory anticipates that a belief in God is not part of everyone's ideological framework. Therefore, external sources have been generalized to include any variable that might impact career decision making, leading to research that examines additional external influences and motivations for work, e.g., poverty. Some research has focused on defining calling without focusing on the source of calling, e.g., Wrzesniewski et al., who defined a calling as the desire to serve a greater good.[10] Even without focusing on a divine source, calling is associated with the intangible, more perpetual potential for work.

On the other hand, some early calling research suggested that calling emanates only from an external source, theorizing that you cannot call yourself, and suggested that to have a call there must be a caller. This is the perspective of Robert McKenna et al., theorists who maintain that implicit in the definition of calling is the requirement for there to be a caller, and that you cannot therefore call yourself. However, other researchers allow for a different conceptualization of calling as internally motivated. Though McKenna et al. disagree with the idea of internal calling, they acknowledge the theories that suggest that you can be called by your own sense of your abilities and interests.[11]

Ability

Chapter 2 examined ability as a component of A/A/D and described the talent account – the idea that abilities are innate – and explored research that shows that even inborn talent can be enhanced when cultivated. Cultivating ability requires a belief that it can be enhanced, and that belief begins a cycle: the more you work at your talent, the more you believe in it. Likewise, the more you believe in your ability, the more you work at it. There is a similar connection between ability and calling. On the one hand, calling is not dependent on ability and can exist apart from it. Your passion to pursue a particular field may be triggered by an experience, or heightened interest, or inspiration from witnessing a role model's success in a given discipline without respect to whether you possessed any ability in the discipline at the time of the calling. This makes particular sense with respect to fields like medicine and law wherein one is not born with the ability to wield a scalpel to heal or to know how to develop a legal argument that accords with legal frameworks.

Conversely, early ability can lead to development of a calling.[12] Researchers Shoshana Dobrow Riza and Daniel Heller conducted a study to examine the role of calling for musicians. Their longitudinal study followed 450 high school students for 11 years, examining the impact of a summer music program on the students. One of the goals of the study was to ascertain whether ability leads to calling, and conversely, whether calling leads to ability. Both *perceived* ability and *actual* ability were measured. Perceived ability was measured through a survey asking students to compare themselves to peers, as well as directly asking "how talented are you?" This self-assessment approach highlights a recurrent theme in this book, namely the importance of self-knowledge as an important factor in career pursuit. However, self-assessment was not used to measure actual ability. Rather, they used expert judges, receipt of competition awards, and other external measures. Ultimately, they found that ability is related to calling, specifically that "regardless of their actual musical ability, people with stronger early callings were likely to perceive their abilities more favorably several years later and consequently, were more likely to pursue music professionally."[13] In other words, in their study of musicians strong calling was more persuasive than actual ability in career choice.

Passion: Source or Calling?

Is passion a source of calling, or is passion the substance of calling? Dobrow Riza and Tosti-Kharas tell us that the definition of calling includes the element of passion.[14] What kind of passion rises to the level of calling, and how does it look? The experiences of some of the profiled dualists from Chapter 3 offer insight. The following examples illustrate passion for both sides of A/A/D. None of my questions asked about calling directly. I hoped it would surface on its own. It did.

I asked Chuck Harmony to share his earliest recollection of a performance or creative musical experience.

> *My earliest recollection, and I do not remember how old I was; I know I was in elementary school… I auditioned to be… in the Christmas play, and I made it. 'Cause I always thought I could sing, you understand? So even as a little kid I was a super-performer-singer kind of little guy. And I'll never forget it was the first rehearsal. I*

heard, what's the song? "Fall on your knees, O hear the angel voices?"… O Holy Night. That was the first song we learned and the teacher taught the harmony parts. And when I heard that harmony together, I was like, what is this? I remember that feeling of that "fall on your knees…" It was… intense. I was just like, why does this feel so good? Like, why does nobody else feel like I'm feeling? Like, it was that harmony. And to this day that song, and when I hear a proper performance of that song, it still gives me chills. But that was the first time, like, that I had a surreal experience that I'll never forget. And it was not the song. It was literally when that harmony fell, when that "fall on your knees, O hear the angels voices." I fell in love with music at that point.

I asked David Smith what led to becoming a songwriter.

It was just catching that bug once you put a song together. The first one was called "Story about Myself." And a girl I was dating was like "tell me a little bit about yourself" and I was like "I don't know, I hadn't really thought about that before." I'm like 20. I didn't have anything put together. So I went to my room and I was like "how can I tell her about myself?" So I wrote all these things down in rhyme and wrote my first song called "Story about Myself." And I played it out and people loved it. They memorized the lyrics. It's probably still the most requested song, especially if I go back home. They're like "play Story about Myself" and sad thing is I really don't really remember it actually anymore. But it was just that feeling of having people react and respond and they liked it. I was like wow, this is a really powerful thing. And I wanted to write more that made people feel that way. So, once you catch that bug and you know that you have a tool and a gift to use, you have to use it. I can't ignore that anymore. It's gotta be there, in my life.

I asked Ben Hubbird to describe his primary vocational pursuit. Like Gina, his passion is helping someone else find theirs. It is not working as a music industry creative.

I would really like to build structures that can more powerfully enable artists to create their best and most dangerous work, most exciting work. Anything I can do to insulate an artist from the worry about how they're gonna pay rent and let them take risks artistically I feel like is a small success. I'm not a very ambitious person personally, but if I can broaden that work or further that work in organizations and institutions that do support artists, I consider that success.

And it is possible to have passion for both sides of your A/A/D. I say to Loren Mulraine "You've had your moment of music," referring to his movement from music industry creative to working analytically as a lawyer and professor in the midst of continuing to work in music. His response:

It's not like "what if?" And now looking at it, having gone through that and being where I am now and kind of building what I do musically to the point where I'm proud of it, I realize that man, I really enjoy the different pieces. Last night I was talking to my wife; I had a client that I was doing something for. I had to look at his contract real quick and evaluate something, and I said, "You know what? This gives me a rush." I enjoy this just as much as I enjoy that [music]. I think God creates us all in unique ways. The people who I think struggle the most with the inner happiness thing are those who never lock into what makes them special. If you really lock into what makes you special, then I think you reach a point of really kind of a contentment.

Passion, the "rush" of calling, can be powerful. But you say, "I don't feel that way about a particular activity!" A broadened view of calling leads us to see its many facets and reminds us that you can decide the focus of your passion, which may not be a particular activity. It could be that broader definition of calling which is to a more generalized sense of purpose and seeing vocation as purposeful, meaningful. This broader perspective is a calling to derive meaning and purpose from whatever you do, rather than calling to a specific activity.

You may have your own experiential point of reference concerning calling that may resonate with a spiritual framework, a sense of a more ethereal orientation to your work. Or you may have a consuming passion toward the music industry that is undeniable and insistent. You may hear a clear call that seems almost audible, at times. However, others may be reading this book because you are searching for clarity about your calling, wondering if you really have one, where it is, and experiencing a challenge in discovering it. You recognize that you possess both analytical propensity and artistic drive (A/A/D) and are in the midst of discerning whether one or both deserves your attention. Or you may not believe the idea of calling is central to career decision making at all and are working through career choices in your own way. Wherever you fall along the spectrum, Dobrow Riza and Heller acknowledge that the concept of calling can have both positive and negative implications.[15] The following sections examine challenges and benefits of calling.

Challenges of Calling

Somewhere in the world at this very moment someone is hungry, or unsafe, or without shelter, wrongly imprisoned or otherwise violated, or without means of financial support. Others are depressed, hospitalized, grieving a loss – whether financial or relational – or oppressed because of discriminatory practices, or battling serious illness. What role do these harsh realities of life play when it comes to contemplating calling? Is contemplating calling an appropriate priority if these are your realities? Researchers Hall and Chandler have observed that socio-economic factors can either help or hinder pursuit of a calling and could therefore color its importance to you.[16] You do not have to live in an undeveloped country to have basic financial or other needs trump the importance of pursuing a calling. Even if you live in a developed country, there are populations who share the same needs as those in undeveloped countries, for whom calling is a foreign preoccupation. Ryan D. Duffy and William E. Sedlacek highlight the work of theorists who are paying more attention to the role of limiting forces on career choice.[17] David L. Blustein examined the role of public policy on work and identified "work volition" as an important factor, describing the fact that career is not a matter of choice at all for a majority of workers in the United States because of factors like poverty, discrimination, and lack of education.[18] Getting beyond seeing calling as a low societal priority is foundational. Therefore, the following list of challenges associated with calling begins with what I have labeled "calling guilt."

Calling Guilt 1: Social and Personal Relevance of Calling

The pressing needs of the world cause you to wonder if focusing on calling is of real significance in the grand scheme of things, under the umbrella of "what really matters." Yet if you regularly hear the world's heartbeat, you may actually be hearing the sound of your own calling. To make that sound more audible, the first challenge is to clear away the noise of guilt about contemplating calling at all, creating the freedom to imagine solutions that put your passions to work. This is not a matter of turning a blind eye or deaf ear to the very real and important need for issues like social justice, which is something I am becoming more passionate about with each passing day. To the contrary, perhaps your calling will involve addressing world hunger through artistic endeavors. Without pausing to contemplate career and life pursuits, that kind of quest might never come to pass. Therefore, it is acceptable, and sometimes it is even necessary, to take the time to discover our vocational needs, opportunities, and interests. By reading this book you have begun to embark on that journey, and the journey is a valuable one. Since volitional work and career contemplation are more likely to be contemplated by residents of developed countries, it is all the more important to stay connected to what really matters in life. In this regard it may actually be inappropriate *not* to contemplate calling.

Calling Guilt 2: Obligatory Work

When calling is associated with an ability or talent you have, you may feel obligated to work in the area of your ability. You may experience a sense of duty to your talent, of not wanting to waste it, a sense of obligation that has been so integral, so much a part of you that you have cultivated it, like the students in the Dobrow Riza and Heller study. A similar perspective arises when one feels obligated to work in the area in which a degree was earned. That sense of obligation may feel like calling, and perhaps it is. Therefore, this is not problematic unless you are acting solely from the sense of obligation, rather than from the deeper motivation that calling can engender. The sense of obligation may interfere with fulfilling the calling in a satisfying way or may interfere with the search for calling if the obligation obscures what you really *want* to do, versus what you feel you *ought* to do.

Callings Are Vulnerable to Shifting Influences

Since calling is defined as a passion toward a particular domain, it has an emotional component and is therefore subject to the fluctuations of emotion. This year you *feel* called to work on the business side of the entertainment industry, then next year you do not. Because calling is subjective and often internal, it is easy to second guess it, particularly if obstacles arise, as happens with every career path, or if you receive inputs that alter your perceptions of your calling. For example, research shows that encouragement from family and friends positively affects calling. Likewise, negative feedback could have a negative influence on how you perceive career choice. This does not mean that calling is bad, but that its "soft" nature is influenceable.

Preoccupation with a Called Future, or with Perfection

It is possible to be so preoccupied with seeking a future in which one is living called that today's opportunities may be overlooked. Additionally, believing that you are called to one, and only one, particular occupation can leave you constantly questioning whether you have found it. What if you get it "wrong?" A potential underlying belief that could develop is the nagging suspicion that there is something wrong, either with you or with your life, if you have not, cannot, and do not identify your one true calling. Some will find constant dissatisfaction with their current vocation because, rather than finding the good in your present occupation, you are ever looking for that singular calling that fits you perfectly and resolves all your work unhappiness. We may be led to believe that reaching a career destiny will deliver a brand of fulfillment that will blot out the imperfections of the workplace. However, every job has its challenges; it is simply the nature of work. Some musicians love rehearsals, some hate it. Some love being on the stage but dislike being on the road for months out of a year, unable to see their families or friends for long stretches of time and unable to form a sense of community. Some of us who work on the analytical, business side of the entertainment industry deeply miss the world of artistic performance, but also find genuine satisfaction through expressing the side of ourselves that is analytical. I personally have a love-hate relationship with being in the recording studio. The singing part is fun, but there's the waiting around part for finding the right microphone, or tweaking one part of a song multiple times, or re-recording instrumental tracks. All work is work, even that which has meaning, purpose, and nourishes us. We can miss the joy of today's opportunity searching for tomorrow's perfect calling.

Calling Can Be Difficult to Discern

For many, it is not easy to understand or know your calling, or to know it with certainty, particularly depending on the definition of calling you are working with, e.g., one that requires you to hit the nail of your calling squarely on its specific head. This is true whether you are 18 or whether you are 45 years old, because the self can question the call at any point in life.

Calling is not an ideal that exists in a vacuum. Therefore, these challenges are cited as a practical acknowledgment of that fact, rather than as arguments against calling. Perhaps it is a list that reflects some of your own inner dialogues about it, as it reflects some of mine. Examining calling's challenges also provides the opportunity to consider its benefits.

Benefits of Calling

Calling has become an increasingly popular topic, particularly in the past decade.[19] That is not so surprising, really. Consider: calling is a concept that permits us to see the potential for finding meaning and purpose in our work, and that has real appeal for most of us. We all know people who dread heading off to work each day, who dream of the day they can retire from its demands. Maybe you are, or have been, one of those people. Perhaps it is because part of what we hope to leave behind is the sense of mandates on how we work, why we work, and for whom.

According to the U.S. Department of Labor's Bureau of Labor Statistics, Americans employed on a full-time job in 2016 spent an average of 8.56 hours at work each day.[20] This amounts to approximately 90,000 hours over a lifetime. Many employees routinely work far more hours than their weekly schedule requires, plus time spent commuting to and from work. The same study reported that part-time workers averaged 5.35 hours per day. Multiple job holders averaged 8.45 hours per day, essentially the same as those employed full time. This statistic is particularly relevant for arts and entertainment professionals who often work multiple jobs. It may now be cliché, though patently true, to state that we likely see our co-workers for more hours each day than we see our families. Given the stark reality behind these statistics, it is natural to contemplate what it all means, this matter of contributing a lifetime of hours to causes, purposes, and organizations that may mean little to us, or to whom we mean little. Money is decidedly important as the dominating purpose for maintaining a livelihood. This is clearly an important consideration. Yet once compensation is removed as a controlling factor – either because we have adequate compensation options or because our basic needs have been met – other considerations arise and calling becomes a formidable factor in deciding not only how to spend time, but how to view work. One perspective is to be wholly devoted to it. Sometimes this takes the form of viewing commitments and relationships outside of work as "getting in the way" of our careers: "having" to leave work to spend time with your children, "having" to make time for your spouse or partner, almost as an afterthought, "making" time for self-care so that you are energized for work, rather than for yourself. Or you are so exhausted by work that escapism to television, surfing the internet, or to any pastime that will take your mind off work can dominate how time is spent outside of it.

Living out one's calling, however noble and worthwhile it may be, is not a justification for neglecting other important facets of life. Yet a balanced view of calling can yield certain benefits according to the research. The following summaries represent benefits identified through research on calling. These summaries are not intended to fully describe the research methods, limitations, or findings, rather to highlight some of the results.

Calling Generates and Feeds Inspiration

Calling represents a different way to look at *why* we work. Research by Samuel E. Kaminsky and Tara S. Behrend suggests that calling helps to explain inspiration as a motivational factor. People choose careers they identify with and that inspire them.[21] Working from inspiration is one of the benefits of the presence of calling. If I am inspired to get out of bed each morning because I identify with something meaningful in my work, this certainly surpasses working from an attitude of drudgery. Even if you are not compelled to seek a specific calling as defined by being drawn to work within a particular domain, like the entertainment industry, an alternative that is akin to that definition of calling is the idea of seeing work as having the potential for greater good. That, too, is inspiring. And it does not require the kind of certitude that being called to a particular position, work, or industry carries with it.

Calling Is a Vehicle for Inspired Career Decision Making

Not just decision making, but *inspired* decision making. Calling as an influence on career decision making has been well researched and studied. Kaminsky and Behrend's study, building on the work of Ryan D. Duffy and William E. Sedlacek, found that inspiration was a motivational factor indicating the exercise of career choice. Kaminsky and Behrend found that these decisions have an inspirational component. Prior research on career decision making found that the belief that you can manage your career, known as self-efficacy, as well as logic, or rationality, did not explain all career decisions, like inspiration. Rather, inspiration is not explained except through a concept like calling. According to Kaminsky and Behrend, calling also helps explain how people make career decisions.[22]

Calling Produces More Positive Career Expectations

The research of Duffy and Sedlacek is based on a study of 3,091 freshmen. Students were assessed to determine whether they were in the process of searching for a calling or indicated the presence of a calling. The study showed that respondents who had a calling present or search for calling were more comfortable with their career choices.[23]

Calling Produces Positive Career Experiences

Research shows students who emotionally identify with a field are more apt to work harder at it and have positive experiences with it.[24]

Calling Affects Career Management

Research shows a relationship between calling and self-confidence, whereby they can reinforce each other and contribute to career and psychological success.[25]

Calling Can Contribute to Greater Work Satisfaction

In a study surveying 196 workers in administrative and professional positions about their views of their work, Wrzesniewski et al. found that those who viewed their work as a calling had greater career and life satisfaction. Wrzesniewski et al. found that this satisfaction is connected to perspective.[26] If you view your work as a career wherein achieving status, titles, or advancement is the primary motivator for work, it is not difficult to understand why satisfaction would be diminished or short-lived. As soon as you obtain one promotion, this motivation would compel you to begin looking for the next one, and the next one. Even if you obtain the promotion, only brief satisfaction ensues. If you do not obtain the promotion, dissatisfaction occurs. This is not to suggest that seeking advancement is inappropriate. The meaningful revelation from the research is that advancement alone does not provide satisfaction. Rather, what you *think* about your career is associated with satisfaction. If you believe that your work is worthwhile in spite of promotion, awards, status, or other recognitions typically believed to be beneficial, the meaningfulness that accompanies calling can serve as its own reward.

Calling Yields a Measure of Control over Your Career

You have some control over what compels you, what draws you in, what calls you hear. You can determine how much attention to give to a call, and can generally decide what career means to you, and what beliefs and cognitions you will develop as a result. You may not have ultimate control over how many fans attend your concerts, but you can control the excellence with which you deliver the performance and develop a repertoire that sends a meaningful message to both you and your audience. You may not control the starting salary an entertainment company offers you to work as a social media consultant, even if you negotiate (and negotiation is almost always a good idea). However, you have the power to choose what you believe about your worth, not by placing a monetary value on your worth to the organization, but by valuing yourself and the work you do in intangible terms, knowing that you bring unique skills and contributions, and knowing what the work itself means to you. Eventually, working in this called way may yield monetary rewards as well. But even if it does not, there is the internal reward of working from a place of empowerment and conviction.

Living Called Can Be Socially Beneficial

When calling motivates us to view our work as contributing to the public or greater good, we are more likely to make that a goal and to make such contributions. Once we overcome the challenge of guilt concerning looking for personal meaning in work through calling, we are free to contribute to the greater good in our own unique, called way – to create social entrepreneurships within the music industry, to host that fundraising concert that raises both money for and awareness of someone else's need, to make plans to give back in ways that speak to living called.

Feeling Successful Is Associated with Calling

Hall and Chandler assert that experiencing work as a calling provides "one of the deepest forms of satisfaction or psychological success."[27]

Being aware of research about calling provides the opportunity to consider its place in our lives. However, to manufacture a calling is not the goal. Rather, the goal here is to understand that if there are voices of inspiration, passion, talent, or A/A/D that are, in fact, calling to you, you may choose to listen to them, and doing so may be beneficial both personally and beyond.

Searching for Calling

Calling is a concept I admit I have often romanticized. *Oh, to be one of the called ones*, I have thought. *To choose my calling and be chosen by it.* To be able to say, as I have heard so many others say *"I know that this is exactly what I am supposed to be doing with my life."* An unmistakable encounter with calling is the kind of experience many of us want, expect, and associate with calling. Chuck Harmony had such an experience, described above. Yet this will not be true for everyone. Hall and Chandler tell us that "having a sense of calling is a highly individual, subjective experience."[28] Therefore, we should not require our "sense of calling" to mirror anyone else's. A tractable, open view of calling allows for acknowledgment of its challenges and benefits, and even more fundamentally, facilitates a practical perspective that makes searching for calling *less of a hunt and more of a decision; less of a mystery and more of a license to choose* and to see yourself as fully capable of "getting" calling. If calling is a matter of sensing, and feeling drawn, and passion, then the answers you seek are in the palm of your own hand. If you can sense what you want, feel drawn to a purpose, and identify a passion, you can discern a call. This is a journey to you. This is an empowered view of calling. This is a "search" that is doable for a calling that is discernible.

Discernment

But wait, there's more! Suggesting that the search for calling is knowable does not mean that no work is required to ascertain it. As with anything worth knowing or doing, an investment of time and effort is necessary. Douglas T. Hall's description of calling is "seeing one's work as an invitation to which one must respond and involves discernment (deep reflection or prayer) to find the right career path."[29]

Deep reflection is a means of understanding yourself better. It is a process which involves contemplation, thinking about what you want most, and what is most important to you. Engaging in reflection that is "deep" involves more than surface-level contemplation. It involves being honest with yourself in a way that is not always easy. It means digging deep enough to not only identify your passions, but to count the costs of what it means to fulfill them and then assess whether those same passions still hold up under that kind of scrutiny. For example, if money matters to you – and on some level it matters to all of us because of its practical value – how much does it matter? Because vocation involves compensation, we might imagine that money is the biggest driver for our decisions. It can be, but may not necessarily drive us in the direction we anticipate. Justin Longerbeam knows that working as a music industry logician is right for him, but making money actually muddies the waters for him concerning calling: He recognizes that "The deeper that I get into it, the pursuit of profit has clouded the messaging and principles of why I'm doing this to begin with, which is why I'm trying to figure out how to transition into a non-profit."

There are other drivers besides money that are compelling. Wrzesniewski et al. found that "most people see their work as either a Job (focus on financial rewards and necessity rather than pleasure or fulfillment; not a major positive part of life), a Career (focus on advancement), or a Calling (focus on enjoyment of fulfilling, socially useful work)."[30] Accordingly, fulfillment, socially useful work, promotions, title, influence, status, prestige, fame, notoriety, and other intangibles are all potential drivers that compete with money for our attention, that call out to us. In interviews with profiled dualists concerning what impacted their choice of primary vocation, acquiring achievement or status ranked lowest, with an average ranking of 2.3 out of 7. Eight out of the 13 dualists gave it a ranking of either 1 or 2. That surprised me. My surprise is due, in part, to my own observations of organizational dynamics. In my experience, striving for advancement is a driver that can create intense rivalries, strong competition, sabotage, and criticism of the organization's procedures and of the organization itself. Of course, this is not always the case and we need not assume this is the normative organizational work environment. Those who work on the business side of the industry are more likely to work within organizations. However, the nature of employment tied to gigs rather than organizations (referred to in the research as boundaryless careers) on the creative side of the music business may account for the dearth of advancement as a primary driver. Nevertheless, although the idea of promotion is more connected to organizations, achievement and status apply across contexts. So, when one of the profiled dualists said of achievement/status, "It doesn't drive me, it doesn't overwhelm me, it doesn't control me, but I think about it," it struck me as honest, the kind of honesty that is needed for effective discernment that aids in the search for calling.

The work of deep discernment is self-defined, wherein you are the one deciding what the questions are and posing them to yourself. You are also the one with the answers. This raises the question of the role of advisors, parents, and friends. Calling is a highly individual, personal matter discerned through a process of self-exploration. This does not mean you should not involve the people you trust, who know you well and have your best interests at heart in your process of exploration. And many people do. However, who has more knowledge of you than you? If you choose to seek input, Hall and Chandler suggest that one way to do it is to first make your own initial calling decision. After you identify what you believe to be your calling, then discuss it with others.[31] This balances out the desire for input with the need for independence. It also provides the opportunity to practice recognizing what we want, to hear our own voices.[32]

Prayer

Hall's definition of discernment included "deep reflection or prayer." Hearing one's own voice as a source of discernment stands in contrast to hearing from God. For some, like me, it is an integral part of any decision-making process. Some of the profiled dualists – Gina Miller, Jesse Bobick, Loren Mulraine – also mentioned the importance of hearing from God for guiding their career paths. Like the search for calling, whether you pray, how, to whom, and why are all highly personal decisions. If prayer is normative for you, it will feel inauthentic for you to exclude it from your search for calling.

Tests and Assessments

There are a number of instruments that have been developed to aid in the search for calling. For example, personality tests, assessments of skills and abilities, etc. If we are drawn toward activities that use our strengths,[33] then we need to know what they are. Or maybe you already know what they are, and that is why you are pulled toward careers that use them. Knowing where your A/A/D fits and placing yourself in one of the Duality Exploration Grid quadrants to try out that fit requires and enhances self-knowledge. And self-knowledge is key, as Loren Mulraine points out:

> Know who you are, not who the world says… no offense, because I get the value of… occupational testing, and I think it's legitimate, but I don't think you should look at yourself based on what the test says. Use the test to understand why you are what you are. It is more important for you to know in your heart what feels right… Whatever that thing is, you've gotta do that.

Fuel for Discernment

In addition to doing the work of deep reflection that comes from practices like journaling, inquiry, and meditation, you can bolster your search through action. Experimenting with jobs and hobbies, expanding your skills, familiarizing yourself with causes you deem worthwhile and serving or otherwise supporting them, taking classes or attending talks, reading about specific career paths, talking with an advisor or career coach, taking a risk to walk down a career path that interests you but that you have never considered or dreamed might be within your reach – these are all practices that fuel the reflective process and can invigorate your search. On the other hand, don't stop at doing these activities; combine them with active discernment to ascertain whether you sense being drawn in a particular direction. Likewise, don't stop at journaling or meditation, fuel those reflective processes with your chosen activities.

Confirmation

Sometimes we believe that confirmation that we are moving in the "right" direction or confirming our calling is a matter of measured success: money made, records sold, concert venues filled, artists signed, publishing deals acquired, Billboard chart positioning, plays on Spotify, etc. There is the common belief that if you are following your passion, success will come. To the extent that your calling is authentic, there is a connection between authenticity and success, discussed in Chapters 7 and 9. For the moment, discernment of calling is a matter of comprehending what it is you want to do, simply identifying your passion or main interest. Those external indicators may be sources of encouragement to keep you doing it, but only you can identify the passion, as well as what success looks like for you. Additionally, some of the external indicators of success require an investment of time, even years, before showing up. If your sole means for confirmation of calling is those indicators, you may be misled. Be flexible about what the "right" direction is and stay open to the possibility of more than one "right." Let patience (recall Palmer Parker's journey) and self-knowledge – of what you need and want – be your guides.

Alternatives to Calling

Justin M. Berg, Adam M. Grant, and Victoria Johnson found that some do not view their occupations as a calling.[34] Therefore, I want to speak to the person who is wondering about the applicability of this chapter because you are not sure you accept calling as a valid career decision-making tool, at least, as a valid tool for you. Your A/A/D may account for part of the reason you're ambivalent. Your analytical propensity may be telling you that the way to make career decisions is to make a careful assessment of your options and then to select the most logical choice, maybe a choice based on the pragmatic and practical nature of making a living. Or your artistic drive may direct you to just go with the flow of artistic opportunities that arrive on your doorstep. Or perhaps you had not really considered calling in any conscious way and are not quite sure what you think. If you fall into this latter category, I encourage you to do the exercises found at the end of this chapter. The objective of completing any of the exercises is not necessarily to identify with certainty your calling or a particular career decision at the end of reading this book. Rather, the goal is to engage oneself in the process of reflection and discovery, to be intentional about career exploration, to take the journey. Another goal is to empower yourself around career choices, no matter where those choices lead. Therefore, the option to discard the notion of calling altogether is yours as well. If this is your decision, here are a few questions and propositions on which to reflect before proceeding to Chapter 5.

1. What if you actually do accept the idea of calling but reject the terminology? In other words, if you have a leaning towards a particular career path, as a practical matter that is a type of calling. Having a strong interest in a particular area is a streamlined way of thinking about calling.
2. Kaminsky and Behrend suggest that theorists used to see the concept of self-efficacy as a means of understanding and predicting how prepared someone would be for a career. However, they now recognize that one component that self-efficacy misses is inspiration, the part of us that wants to choose our careers based on its appeal to us, or wants it to mean something.[35] Calling fills that gap.
3. Ultimately, you will need to decide which path to take in your career decision making. If calling does not inform your orientation to work, what does?

Calling is the directional axis of vocation and has been found by career researchers and theorists to offer significant benefits. Therefore, an important part of a vocational journey involves moving toward or considering the presence of calling. Establishing that presence begins with the "search" for calling, which is ultimately characterized by a decision one reaches through discernment and self-knowledge. Finding calling involves *less of a hunt and more of a decision; less of a mystery and more of a license to choose*. The exercises at the end of this chapter will help you begin the process of establishing a baseline calling. *Baseline calling* here refers to a reference point for your initial identification of your calling. As a reference point it serves as a stake in the ground. Yet it is a stake that can be pulled up, reshaped, and replanted if necessary. We need this flexibility since the winds of time and change – changes in your skills, desires, opportunities, goals, the economy, advances in technology, unforeseeable events, and changes in the music industry – may sweep across that stake. Considering the impact of such forces on calling is our next contemplation in Chapter 5.

Discussion Questions

1. Define calling. What accounts for variations in the definitions?
2. Identify the challenges and benefits of calling.
3. Discuss your perspectives on the opening quote from Claude Kelly on the first page of the chapter.

EXERCISE SET 4: CALLING CONTEMPLATION

The objective of this exercise is to contemplate your calling through practicing discernment. Some of these questions lend themselves to meditation, prayer, and quiet reflection. Give yourself the space and permission to incorporate that into this process.

1. Parker Palmer said that teaching was "his natural way of being in the world." What do you believe is your natural way of being in the world?
2. How important is it to you to discover your calling?
3. Journal your insights on calling. First, identify one thing you learned from the chapter; ideally narrow this down to one or at most the two most important things that you learned, as pertains to *you*.
4. Thinking about your search for calling:

    a   Review your reflections from Exercise Set 2 at the end of Chapter 2. Based on those responses, write down whether you are more inclined toward analytical propensity or artistic drive, or both.

    b   List the abilities and skills you have that you want to refine and use within the music industry, either as a creative or as a logician.

    c   Contemplate the purposes you want to serve, contribution you want to make, and/or role you want to play in the music industry. Who benefits? Where are you? What are you doing? How do you imagine that feels?

    d   What work do you *want* to do or have a "consuming passion" about? Be bold, creative. Dream. Write it down. How drawn are you to what you wrote?

    e   Where are you leaning? Write it down. Don't wait for a feeling of certainty. When combined with your response to (d) above, this is your baseline calling.

    f   Do you sense a dual call to work on both sides of the industry using your A/A/D?

    g   Have you been authentic with yourself in answering the foregoing questions? If not, why not? If you have been authentic, you are practicing helpful discernment. If you had difficulty answering the questions from a place of authenticity, start over with another assessment, if you need to.

5. What will it cost you – in time, opportunities, relationships, money, or anything else you deem valuable – to live out your baseline calling? Is it worth it? What would it cost you to *not* live your baseline calling?

6. If you are not ready to explore calling:

   a What is holding you back? If you are not sure, identify a series of questions, things you want to know. Review this chapter again to see if it contains some of the answers. Or are they questions that only you can answer?

   b Answer the questions shown under "Alternatives to Calling." Take a moment to write down your answers if you didn't do so when you read that section.

   c What journey are you ready to take?

Notes

1 Shoshana Dobrow Riza and Jennifer Tosti-Kharas, "Calling: The Development of a Scale Measure," Personnel Psychology 64 (2011): 1001–49: 1005.
2 Amy Wrzesniewski, Clark McCauley, Paul Rozin, and Barry Schwartz, "Jobs, Careers, and Callings: People's Relations to Their Work," *Journal of Research in Personality* 31 (1997): 21.
3 Bryan J. Dik and Ryan D. Duffy, "Calling and Vocation at Work: Definitions and Prospects for Research and Practice," Counseling Psychologist 37, no. 3 (April 2009): 427.
4 Tamara Hagmaier and Andrea E. Abele, "When Reality Meets Ideal: Investigating the Relation Between Calling and Life Satisfaction," Journal of Career Assessment 23, no. 3 (2015): 367.
5 Parker Palmer, Let Your Life Speak (San Francisco, CA: Josey-Bass, 2000).
6 Exodus 3:4; 28:1.
7 Genesis 6:14–22.
8 Jonah 1:1–2. This scriptural reference is the first of God's calls to Jonah.
9 Samuel 3:10.
10 Amy Wrzesniewski et al., "Jobs, Careers, and Callings," 21.
11 Robert B. McKenna, Juliann Matson, Deanna M. Haney, Olivia Becker, McKendree J. Hickory, Diana L. Ecker, and Tanya N. Boyd, "Calling, the Caller, and Being Called: A Qualitative Study of Transcendent Calling," Journal of Psychology and Christianity 34, No. 4 (2015): 295.
12 Shoshana Dobrow Riza and Daniel Heller, "Follow Your Heart or Your Head? A Longitudinal Study of the Facilitating Role of Calling and Ability in the Pursuit of a Challenging Career," Journal of Applied Psychology 100, no. 3 (2015): 696.
13 Dobrow Riza and Heller, "Follow Your Heart or Your Head?" 706.
14 Dobrow Riza and Tosti-Kharas, "Calling," 1005.
15 Dobrow Riza and Heller, "Follow Your Heart or Your Head?" 696.
16 Douglas T. Hall and Dawn E. Chandler, "Psychological Success: When the Career Is a Calling," Journal of Organizational Behavior 26 (2005): 167.
17 Ryan D. Duffy and William E. Sedlacek, "The Presence of and Search for a Calling: Connections to Career Development," Journal of Vocational Behavior 70 (2007): 591.

18 David L. Blustein, "The Psychology of Working: A New Perspective for Career Development," *Career Planning and Adult Development Journal* 33, no. 2 (2017): 60.

19 Jacob A. Galles and Janet G. Lenz, "Relationships among Career Thoughts, Vocational Identity, and Calling: Implications for Practice," *Career Development Quarterly* 61, no. 3 (September 2013): 241.

20 American Time Use Survey, "Average Hours Employed People Spent Working on Days Worked by Day of Week," Bureau of Labor Statistics, U.S. Department of Labor, www.bls.gov/charts/american-time-use/emp-by-ftpt-job-edu-h.htm.

21 Kaminsky and Behrend, "Career Choice and Calling: Integrating Calling and Social Cognitive Career Theory," *Journal of Career Assessment* 23, no. 3 (2015): 394.

22 Kaminsky and Behrend, "Career Choice and Calling," 385, 393. Explains how people make decisions concerning careers.

23 Duffy and Sedlacek, "The Presence of and Search for a Calling," 596.

24 Kaminsky and Behrend, "Career Choice and Calling," 388.

25 Hall and Chandler, "Psychological Success," 171.

26 Amy Wrzesniewski et al., "Jobs, Careers, and Callings," 31.

27 Hall and Chandler, "Psychological Success," 160.

28 Hall and Chandler, "Psychological Success," 161.

29 Douglas T. Hall, "The Protean Career: A Quarter-Century Journey," *Journal of Vocational Behavior* 65 (2004): 9.

30 Wrzesniewski et al., "Jobs, Careers, and Callings," 21.

31 Hall and Chandler, "Psychological Success," 162.

32 Hall and Chandler, "Psychological Success," 163.

33 Hall and Chandler, "Psychological Success," 164.

34 Justin M. Berg, Adam M. Grant, and Victoria Johnson, "When Callings Are Calling: Crafting Work and Leisure in Pursuit of Unanswered Occupational Callings," *Organization Science* 21, no. 5 (September–October 2010): 978.

35 Kaminsky and Behrend, "Career Choice and Calling," 384.

5

THE CASE FOR CONTEXTUAL CALLING

Calling from the Outside In

Calling has two components. The beckoning, that summons to walk toward a particular vocational domain, is the first component (described in Chapter 4). The domain to which you are drawn is the second component. That domain is the context in which calling and duality are expressed and lived. Richard T. Mowday and Robert I. Sutton define context as "stimuli and phenomena that surround and thus exist in the environment external to the individual."[1] Context has been studied because of what it can tell us about how factors outside an individual shape behavior, particularly in the workplace. For example, research has shown that the creative output and behavior of employees with creative personalities is affected by how much supervisory support they receive and the complexity of their jobs.[2] An understanding of context also yields important insight for identifying constraints on or opportunities for behavior.[3] The music industry, as the particular focus of this book, is an external context influenced by a number of stimuli and phenomena that define and shape its operation. Technological change, the economy, the competitive nature of the business, and even sociopolitical factors can shape its volatility and existence. If you are called to work within the music industry, you are subject to all of the factors that influence it, including the inevitable changes visited upon every industry over time.

The calling research of Shoshana Dobrow Riza and Daniel Heller suggests that while calling provides intrinsic direction for career decision making, extrinsic factors, like the economy, can influence calling.[4] As such, there is a symbiotic relationship between you and the domain to which you are called. The dynamic nature of the music industry can impact calling, and the way you live out your calling can affect the music industry. Moreover, being a dualist positions you to have a unique and important impact on the industry. This chapter discusses the ways in which the nature of the music industry, with its frameworks and inputs, impact calling, potentially shaping the way your analytical propensity + artistic drive (A/A/D) looks, feels, or functions. The chapter begins with an overview of influences that act on the industry and shape its fluidity, explores what happens to calling when an industry changes, and ends with a discussion of the impact you can have on the industry.

An Evolving Industry

The music industry is dynamic, a living, breathing entity. A comprehensive guide to changes in the music industry is outside the scope of this book. That would constitute a book in itself, and many texts and articles analyzing those changes have been written about it, particularly over the past 20 years. Rather, the goal here is to examine and provide background information about some of the inputs that contribute to the changing context of the music industry.

Sociopolitical Changes

First, there was music. Before there was streaming or downloading or recording there was just music. Before there were instruments to play it on, or sophisticated theories about how to compose it, or sing it, or play it. Some would say it has always existed within us and we have found ways to express it that evolve continually, as music itself has evolved. New expressions in the form of fresh genres – from pre-classical, to blues and jazz, to hip-hop, world dance music, disco, neo-soul – reflect not only new ways to frame music, but new reasons to express it and new messages reflecting social needs and desires. Consequently, music reflects social change, and social changes are reflected in new music. There are always new reasons to sing and play. Messages to get out. Music has long contained social and political commentary, and implicating the "danger" of new forms of music to serve as such commentary dates back to Plato:

> *This is the point to which, above all, the attention of our rulers should be directed, that music and gymnastic be preserved in their original form, and no innovation made. They must do their utmost to maintain them intact. And when anyone says that mankind most regard, "The newest song which the singers have," they will be afraid that he may be praising, not new songs, but a new kind of song; and this ought not to be praised, or conceived to be the meaning of the poet; for any musical innovation is full of danger to the whole State, and ought to be prohibited. So Damon tells me, and I can quite believe him; he says that when modes of music change, of the State always change with them.*[5]

Plato's words anticipated the folk songs of Joan Baez; Bob Dylan's *Blowing in the Wind*; jazz melodies written expressly for the civil rights movement, like jazz drummer Max Roach's *We Insist, Freedom Now!* suite; Bruce Springsteen's iconic *Born in the USA*; the unapologetic voice of hip-hop music with its racial, gender, social, and economic commentaries; internationally, Hugh Masekela's *Bring Him Back Home*, advocating for the release of South African Nelson Mandela from prison. The messages in the music remind us of music's importance, its purpose, its meaning, its power. These musical outputs were created in response to the times in which they were written, and the industry impact: change. Hip-Hop, as just one example, has absolutely dominated Billboard charts and is overwhelmingly profitable. It is a genre that is changing the industry, even down to language. For example, Hip-hop artist Drake's mixtapes and "playlist projects" have upended the industry language concerning what an album should be called.[6] The nomenclature matters to us because the undeniable reach and power of hip-hop to transform an industry matters.

Technological Changes

We talk about the impact of technology on the music industry a lot. It is the subject of blogs, podcasts, books, articles, classes, conferences, and legislation enacted to keep the law in synch with the change. It is an important topic. Every industry has been disrupted by technology for as long as technology has existed. The horse and buggy industry was disrupted by the auto industry. The auto industry was disrupted by robotics, displacing workers who used to perform manual labor in car factories. The publishing industry was disrupted by the printing press, then by photocopiers with piracy potential, and now by digital technology and the blogosphere and podcasting. Consumer products like ovens and televisions have been disrupted too. Microwave technology has changed food preparation. And televisions have changed in scope and purpose; not only are they no longer tubes that once resided in large wooden cabinets, they are slowly being replaced by different types of viewing screens like computers and mobile devices. Services like Uber and Lyft have disrupted the taxi and ride-hailing sector of the transportation industry. Medical technology has changed the way doctors diagnose illnesses and service patients. Lawyers now compete with artificial intelligence services that can mediate disputes online. No industry is "safe" from the disruption of technology, and music is no different.

If the Industrial Revolution opened the beginning of the twentieth century, the century closed with a new revolution – digital technology – which has changed everything about the music and entertainment industries. Digital instrumentation delivers strings, wind instruments, alterations of voice, and entire orchestras that can be contained and replicated with key strokes; not perfectly, but revolutionarily. Changes in recording technology: digital. Though we now recognize the internet as a way of life, its impact on the music industry has been nothing short of astounding. Now anyone, not just a mega record label, can produce a high-quality recording. And broadcast it through streaming. And advertise and promote it through social media and online retail outlets. And sell it through internet downloads, or make it available through subscription services.

The way we hear music has also evolved. It was once the pride of an opera singer to sing with such volume as to be heard all over the opera house without the aid of amplification devices, originally because such devices did not exist. Now, acoustical architecture and microphones make it possible for live performances to broadcast heightened volumes and quality of sound never before experienced. This has not changed the need for quality in operatic singing, but has certainly changed singing generally for all genres and has altered the listener's experience. Who has not left a night club or concert in an amphitheater with ears ringing? I doubt that ever happened to Plato or Socrates.

Listening to Detroit jazz station 105.9 FM, WJZZ (branded "the jazzy one") was my go-to radio station in high school. I could sit for hours listening to Herbie Hancock, the Jazz Crusaders, or Jean Carne. Today that station no longer exists, and with the advent of digital streaming and internet phenomena like Spotify and Pandora, listening to radio as we know it has changed forever. Broadcasting has also expanded to include webcasting and podcasting.

Recording music has evolved over time. From gramophones, record players, vinyl, shellac, compact discs, reel-to-reel tape recorders, and analog technology to digital recording devices. Not all of these terms are readily recognized by some readers of this book because the technology associated with some of these words is now obsolete, eclipsed by something new with expanded capability.

The way we listen to music, as impacted by technology, can even signify affluence. When I went to college the more expensive your sound system was – with its big speakers and brand name receivers – and the louder your music could be played in your dorm room and throughout the dorm's hallways, the more affluent you might be considered. Today's listener can still purchase the best technology has to offer, but smaller, more private listening devices make those wealth distinctions less obvious since listening to music has become a more privatized experience than it was 30 years ago because of technology.

The distribution of music has shifted from brick-and-mortar retail outlets to the online marketplace. Record stores of all stripes once dotted many cityscapes. There was the small, specialized store that sold only classical music and jazz, but whose selection was deep and wide, like An Die Musik in Baltimore, Maryland.[7] Then came the mega, multilocation record stores like Tower Records that closed in 2006. They succumbed to big box stores like Wal-Mart and even a specialty store like Barnes and Noble. But, alas, why drive to a store with a limited inventory when you could more conveniently access the largest catalogs in the world from your bedroom via the internet? Therefore, distribution of music has also changed dramatically within the last 20 years. Again, technology.

The live music experience has also changed. Live concerts can be streamed and recorded, then posted to and re-experienced on YouTube. Virtual reality combines the visual with the musical experience. Hologram concerts are no longer an idea but a reality. A concert featuring the late Roy Orbison on stage with a live orchestra, made possible through hologram technology, began touring Europe in spring of 2018 and moved on to the United States (U.S.) and Canada.[8] Japanese pop star Hatsune Miku is an anime artist who began a series of holographic tours in 2016.[9] Concert goers watch 10-foot Hatsune sing and dance in much the same way one would go to experience a human performance, but not. The holographic concert offers a different kind of "live" performance experience where a deceased performer is resurrected and animated characters are given life. Who would have thought it possible? Creators of hologram technology.

These changes are inspiring and encouraging to many artists and creators. Change signifies freedom to be new and different, to infiltrate new markets and ventures, to be entrepreneurial. Once dependent on the major labels to notice, affirm, and support their careers, artists are stepping up and stepping out to claim the opportunities the digital entertainment world affords, opportunities to capitalize on being independent. Whole sub-industries supportive of that indie vibe have emerged like TuneCore and CDBaby. Sometimes these businesses are created by dualists with strong analytical propensity, who have both ushered in and helped artists embrace industry change. Shawn Carter, known as famous rap industry mogul Jay-Z, started out as an independent artist seeking opportunities from major labels. When they were not interested he started his own label and grew to be a dominant force as an independent and then as head of one of the kinds of companies who had rejected him. Moreover, his establishment of music-streaming company Tidal was a forward-thinking business move, an expression of a creative's analytical propensity. Jay-Z's duality has served him well in a changing industry, and in turn he has helped shape it. Chancellor "Chance the Rapper" Bennett is another example of an artist who has been inspired by the changing industry. Bennett's Grammy award-winning *Coloring Book* album made history when it became the first to debut on the Billboard 200 based solely on streams, rather than on units sold. Both Jay-Z and Chance the Rapper, whose successes now seem larger than life, started as independent artists who could see indie status as an advantage. For example, in response to questions raised in the media about the nature of Bennett's streaming deal with Apple Music, he tweeted "I think artist[s] can gain a lot from the streaming wars as long as they remain in control of their own product."[10] Both Bennett and Jay-Z clearly recognize the importance of paying attention to the business of things. These opportunities in response to a changing industry are available to all. I am an independent artist. So are many of you. I embrace the new reality that I can produce my own recordings with quality and at reasonable expense. Being inspired is a positive response to change.

On the other hand, the revolutionized music industry has also been threatening to some of the companies who dominated it for years. Conferences and think-tanks have been devoted in recent years to figuring out how to tame the "new" music industry. Technology has often been framed as an enemy because of its heightened potential for new and more pervasive forms of piracy. Piracy is, indeed, real. Yet technology's constraints and limitations also offer new opportunities: new ways to think about what consumers are willing to pay for, what pirates cannot pirate, even new interpretations of the law to support a changing environment. These opportunities are available to the multinational corporation and music industry entrepreneur alike. As the music business continues to evolve, so do opportunities to exercise both artistic drive and analytical propensity to discern and strategize ways to capitalize on novelty. Music industry creatives will evolve with it, and so will music industry logicians. Using your A/A/D strategically is as important and as possible as ever.

The Econosphere

Consumer Demand

It is tempting to assert that changes in technology account for most of the industry's vicissitudes, and it has clearly been the primary driver. But there are technologies that fall flat and lack impact, for example, Google Glass smart glasses that debuted in 2012. They seemed like a good idea at the time, but ultimately, Google Glass proved too expensive for most consumers and had other challenges. The technology itself had virtuous qualities, but insufficient consumer demand. Like Google Glass, Napster appears on *Time* magazine's list of "20 Most Successful Technology Failures of All Time."[11] Napster facilitated the exchange of MP3 music files between users of the website. You could send a song on MP3 to me, and I could send one to you, obviating the need for purchase of any music exchanged through the website itself; the site was the technology that facilitated the exchange. Ultimately, courts ruled that such file-sharing services infringed the copyrights of the songs' copyright owners and Napster was effectively shut down.[12] Before its shutdown in 2001 Napster had 80 million registered users. It is listed as one of *Time*'s most *successful* tech failures, a failure that resulted from a lack of support from the legal system, not a lack of support from consumers. But why was the service so popular? Because Napster did not start the revolution, it started long before then. Consumers were ready for a Napster. Consumers had tired of paying full price for an album with ten songs to obtain the one or two songs that they really wanted. Napster permitted access to one song at a time, a model that the music industry has reclaimed with the advent of Apple iTunes and streaming services. Additionally, once the internet became a source for obtaining music, Napster made music easy to find by creating a centralized interface. And, of course, the convenience and seemingly inexhaustible supply of inventory on the internet is undeniable. By pointing this out, I am by no means suggesting that accessing music without paying for it is legal or acceptable. As an entertainment and intellectual property attorney I fully understand the legalities involved and do not condone copyright infringement. However, the salient observation is that at the time Napster came along the record industry was simply not keeping up with the times and providing a legal option for its consumers. That was a market mistake. Additionally, despite providing legal online alternatives, they sued consumers, albeit lawfully and legitimately under copyright law, for attempting to obtain music in ways that were more convenient and, of course, cost free. The cost-free part was illegal, but the convenience of the internet is now a marketplace necessity that has disrupted every industry and has forced every enterprise to rethink its business model. Napster helped magnify a longstanding marketplace reality that if you do not meet consumer demand, someone else will. It should be met with legal, legitimate supply. Therefore, those with the legal right to offer music benefit themselves and their customers when they respond to demand. Additionally, music piracy is not new. It has existed with every form of technology. Unfortunately, as long as there are ways to circumvent the law and those who are willing to do it, piracy may never die, as new ways to obtain music illegally may continue to evolve along with the industry. Yet what Napster, iTunes, and a host of other online services have taught us is that new markets and ways to serve them exist. Consumers want change. And the desire for this change is ultimately an economic one in terms of supply versus demand. Technology makes change possible, but consumer demand is the economic engine that fuels technology's overall use, prevalence, and the extent of that change.

Making a Living, or Shaping a Career?

Music industry professionals must find ways to execute strategies that respond to a changing industry context in order to direct and manage their careers. In addition to industry changes, the nature of careers has also changed over time. Much of the research on careers was once based on a workplace centered around organizations, typically companies, that hired employees and were the orbit for career advancement. But theories that recognize the changing role of organizations in shaping careers have emerged over the past 20 to 30 years.

This freedom and need to craft a career is referred to by organizational behavior researchers as boundaryless and protean careers. Specifically, the boundaryless career is shaped by departing from traditional notions of dependence on long-term employment within a single organization, i.e., it represents a career that transcends organizational boundaries. Shifting economic forces – not just within the entertainment industry but generally – have occasioned a shift in the ability of organizations to provide life-long employment that once characterized the job market. The number of employers who offer such employment opportunities has been decreasing worldwide. As a result, employees can no longer depend on a single job with a single lifetime employer. Career researchers studying these trends recognized that the way we conceptualize, study, and talk about careers needed to be updated to match the growing reality and coined the phrase "boundaryless career."[13] That reality is that workers need to adapt to these economic changes and learn to operate outside the boundaries of conventional organizations. This mindset has often characterized artists, since identifying long-term artistic opportunities is generally challenging. Songwriters, for example, may be signed to a music publishing deal that fosters a relationship with a specific publishing company, but these work-for-hire or other contractually stipulated arrangements are often short term in the traditional sense. However, the boundaries of the boundaryless career are both physical and psychological. Therefore, while fewer music business creatives may have long-term employment relationships with *physical* organizations, they may develop a *psychological* dependence rooted in the contractual arrangement. Protean career theory focuses workers on meeting the psychic challenges of vocation, managing one's career instead of being merely managed by an organization, creating new career frontiers that are values-driven and self-directed.[14]

Recognizing boundaryless and protean career theories provides knowledge to create freedom from having a purely reactive response to the industry changes previously described, freeing you to shape your career in ways that you want, including ways that match your interests and calling. Though industry changes are inevitable, as the music industry illustrates, is it possible to adapt to changes without compromising calling? If adaptation is desirable, what happens to A/A/D? What happens to calling when an industry changes?

Calling in a Context of Change

Even if the music industry stayed frozen in time it would be a challenging context in which to earn a living, particularly on the creative side. Yet when industry changes are introduced, the context can become even more challenging since access to the conventional path to artistic success is changing. Opportunities to use analytical propensity on the business side are changing as well. Kevin Bruener has lived those changes both as a music industry creative and as a logician. He observes:

> *The industry's always going through changes and trends especially trends with music, so sometimes there's things that are popular that you just feel like there's no good music anymore. So you experience that a lot when you're in the industry.*

One option is to be adaptable, and calling helps facilitate this. Douglas T. Hall and Dawn E. Chandler examined psychological success, including how success looks when the work environment changes, as change is a workplace reality that visits every industry. Hall and Chandler assert that calling facilitates adaptation when it is necessary to learn new skills or to grow in a different direction. They propose that "when the person sees her career as a calling, she will have a strong focus on goals that reflect her purpose. As a result of this goal clarity, she will exert the effort needed to succeed and carry out the calling."[15] Knowing what impact you want to have and recognizing that change is imminent helps with adaptation. Claude Kelly understood the importance of adapting to change.

I certainly wasn't one of those cautionary tales of being cheated in the business. I just recognized that the business was changing. Things as they were weren't gonna work anymore, so I'd better start paying attention to what's happening so I can find my legacy in this changing business, which led to Louis York and Weirdo Workshop.

A number of researchers suggest that calling produces positive outcomes when changes arise. For example, in addition to adaptation, a different option would be to take the career path that provides the most financial stability at the time, and put calling aside. However, Shoshana Dobrow Riza and Daniel Heller found that "people with strong callings will prioritize the intrinsic benefits of their careers over the extrinsic," particularly for challenging career paths.[16] Calling represents a type of intrinsic benefit, and money and status represent extrinsic benefits. When employment opportunities are scarce is when there is the greatest tension between intrinsic and extrinsic rewards. And that tension definitely characterizes the music industry. Dobrow Riza and Heller would agree. Their findings were derived from their study of musicians, wherein their objective was to examine music as a challenging career context.

Samuel E. Kaminsky and Tara S. Behrend conducted a study to examine the relationship between calling and career choice attitudes. The measure they used to assess calling was developed by Shoshana Dobrow Riza and Jennifer Tosti-Kharas which contained 12 items, including the statements "I am passionate about" and "I would continue being a ___ even in the face of severe obstacles."[17] Kaminsky and Behrend assert that calling ignites passion about career, even in the face of obstacles.[18] Lastly, Hall and Chandler's research found that people with a sense of calling were better able to adjust to the inevitable and often challenging times that are attendant to every career.[19]

Calling can serve as a powerful management strategy in the face of change. The gig economy presents another framework for examining how calling can be affected by a changing context.

The Gig Economy

What happens when you cross changes in technology with changing economic tensions? The result is the "new" gig economy. Gigs are not new, particularly to the music industry. Yet an econometric change that has become a focal point in the music industry is the role of the gig economy, particularly in the context of career options and planning. The growing dialogue in the creative community has encouraged artists, songwriters, filmmakers, and other creatives to ride the waves of change by casting aside any requirement or expectation of an ongoing commitment from a single employer, like an orchestra, and be prepared to pursue gig-by-gig opportunities. This employment approach is new nomenclature for a familiar phenomenon, particularly for artists in the music industry. The term gig has long been associated with the music industry, believed to have originated with African American jazz artists, though the stories of origin vary slightly – from gig as the name of the carriages they played from (when excluded from playing regular venues) to an abbreviation for "God Is Good," a reaction to the rare occurrence of being paid for performances.[20] Despite the variations in the details of the term's origins, attribution to jazz musicians is a consistent theme. Freelancing, a similar arrangement, is often used synonymously and has been a way of life for many writers of literature for hundreds of years. But in the twenty-first-century gig economy, both freelancing and gigging have a slightly different face. What is new is the way in which workers are finding the gigs, through websites or mobile apps that facilitate the connections. For example, transportation services like Uber and Lyft, and personal services platform Taskrabbit, make it possible for suppliers of the services to earn income, revolutionizing not only the consumption of transportation and personal services, but also dispatching and financially supporting millions of freelancers all over the world. The multiple job holding reported by Neil O. Alper and Gregory H. Wassall[21] now has a digital platform engine that helps drive it. This means that creatives now have improved access to alternative means of support, at least theoretically.

Even though the pervasiveness of the gig economy has increasingly become a focal point for discussions about careers, accurately measuring participation is elusive and dated, according to the U.S. Bureau of Labor Statistics (BLS). As of 2005, BLS estimated that 2 to 4 percent of all employees in the U.S. are "contingent" workers, those without ongoing contractual or other commitments from employers. And "about 7 percent of workers were independent contractors, the most common alternative employment arrangement" for the same time period. U.S. census data also provide statistics, indicating that "between 2003 and 2013, all industry sectors experienced growth in non-employer (self-employed) businesses."[22] The gig economy is not limited to the entertainment industry and includes a range of occupations, from health care to transportation and warehousing.

As with any employment outlook, working in the gig economy carries both advantages and disadvantages. Unpredictability and a lack of security are expected short-term disadvantages. But analysts are also recognizing the more long-term disadvantages, like the absence of clear retirement planning options, and the need to address and provide for one's own health-care coverage, ordinarily offered by most employers as an employee benefit. There are still questions concerning how to classify gig work, either as employment in the traditional sense or not. Some companies are reluctant to accord workers the status of employee and the benefits that go along with that status. This question is being considered in both legislatures and lawsuits, and the outcomes vary by country. For example, Uber has not had the success in China that it has had in the U.S. because the gig economy has not been as well received there. Even though China is considered the world's largest ride-hailing market, local regulations in China precluded Uber's operations there.[23] Although Europe has not banned Uber, in early 2017 the European Court of Justice ruled that Uber is a transportation service subject to regulation like other transportation services. This ruling that affects European Union countries restricts the way Uber can operate and curtails some of its offerings in those countries. For example, the ruling precludes Uber from offering UberPop (like UberX in the U.S.) and requires compliance with regulations imposed on taxi services.[24]

Economists in the U.S. have voiced concerns about the exploitation factor in the gig economy, pointing out the absence of traditional work benefits. Monique Morrissey, an economist at the Economic Policy Institute in Washington, DC, testified in a 2018 congressional hearing about the gig economy and the adverse impact of the non-standard workforce on retirement savings.[25] Morrissey's testimony highlighted the fact that self-employed musicians have always been participants in a gig economy, and prefers use of the term "non-standard workers" as a catch-all term to include independent contractors, contingent workers, and the self-employed. The objective of her testimony was to urge Congress to act to protect workers who are part of the gig economy, particularly with respect to retirement savings. Since the U.S. has the most developed gig economy,[26] the absence or existence of regulatory frameworks (like those in China) that may incorporate protections for workers is likely to have broad impact on those working within it. In addition to the legislature, the legal system also serves as a vehicle for examining and challenging the safety of an economic context. Accordingly, courts are rethinking long-accepted definitions of what classifies someone as an independent contractor and considering whether a determining factor should be how dependent the worker is on the company, or how dependent the company is on the worker. These contemplations come in the wake of a number of lawsuits against Uber and other online platforms that supply the digital gig economy with workers who are often classified as independent contractors, rather than as employees, and thereby do not always receive the advantages that usually come with designation as an employee.

Despite financial disadvantages associated with working in the current gig economy, it is still appealing to many because of its non-financial advantages, like flexibility and variety, and this can help creatives maximize opportunities that do not always occur on a weekday or typical 9-to-5 schedule. Another advantage is the opportunity to shape your career by experimenting with different jobs without having to commit to the organization for which you work. Yet participation in the gig economy is just one way of thinking about how to contextualize calling.

Being Who an Industry Needs

One of the exciting things about a changing context like the music industry is the opportunity to shape and innovate its future. The current narrative surrounding the gig economy is that you should participate in it to maintain a place of economic relevance, i.e., it is a narrative that tells you that you need the gig economy. And for some, there is an element of truth in that narrative, depending on where you are in your career. Yet there is another narrative to recognize and declare. This greater narrative is true for all of us, and it is this: *the music industry needs you*. It doesn't really need another individual looking for a job in which to express analytical propensity, or looking for their next big hit, or looking to become the next "it" artist – though those ambitions are legitimate and appropriate. But its real need is people who can speak into the void of an unknown future through their uniqueness. Your industry context – with its uncertain and shifting boundaries – is calling to your calling. That's what happens to calling when an industry changes. This is a unique time, with an opportunity to be uniquely you in a business that needs your uniqueness, that needs you to live your calling.

How will you do that? A central message of this book is that your duality positions you to be an integral and effective player in the industry, whether on the artistic side, business side, or both. When I spoke with seasoned and highly successful industry veteran Claude Kelly, he shared his perspective about involvement on both sides of the industry:

> *If there is a death to the music industry, which I don't believe, but if there is a killer, a cancer to the music business the cancer is a lack of creative professionals who are sitting behind desks, or creative professionals who haven't decided to split their time healthily between still being creative and doing their business. They were musicians before, they don't sing anymore. Or they don't play. Even if it's gigging on the weekends. I go to record labels sometimes and I hear no music playing. None. I mean, dentist offices have music playing. And you're like, is this Wall Street? Or is it the music business? And it requires you loving music all day to think about business correctly for music that you love all day.*

Dualists are uniquely qualified to "think about business correctly," as Claude puts it, not only because of your A/A/D, but because being part of the music industry may be part of your calling to the industry, part of a calling to duality, or for some, it is part of a calling to Career Duality. As a prolific artist, vice president of marketing for CDBaby, and as a Career Dualist, Kevin Bruener highlights the value of being a music industry professional who can authentically speak the language of both business and art.

> *I wouldn't have had this job had it not been for the music side. I mean, one thing that I've always found fascinating, astonishing, surprising, is that the majority of the people working in the business on the business side have no idea what it's like to be an artist. And that's what has, I think partly, what has made me do so well in this position and help our brand in that way where our client is the artist. Our client is not any executive at another music business company. So we need to be able to speak to and understand the artist community. And I've just in all my years in the music business in lots of conversations with lots of different people, if you've never written a song you don't know what it's like to write a song. If you've never been out on tour or just the*

whole creative process and what's going through the artist's mind, I think it's just surprising how many people on the business side don't understand that world that the artist is living in when they're creating art and trying to get something out that they want to say or feel. So that's something where... me as a musician has made it so much easier for me to work with a brand like CDBaby that speaks directly to musicians because I'm one of them. I know what it's like and I'm in it still. I'm not talking about the good old days, I'm still doing and trying just as much as anybody.

The message? As a changing context the industry needs creative-minded business professionals, and business-minded creatives – dualists. It needs *you*. And it needs you as much as you need it.

Win–Win

There is mutual benefit to contributing to the industry's health, an added benefit to being called to an industry. Maintaining a base of knowledge about the music business provides benefits to you in three areas: satisfaction, protection, and independence.

Satisfaction

Using his business knowledge on his employer's behalf is Kevin Bruener's job, and through it he is influencing the industry. But he finds satisfaction in also applying that knowledge to his own creative endeavors.

I'm pretty close to the pulse of what's really going on at the musician level, not necessarily the corporate level of what the president of [names some large entertainment companies] are doing. I'm not in that world, and frankly, I don't care. But really what's happening with the pulse of artists and the opportunities... on the business side, I think having a better understanding – because it's my job – of how these platforms are evolving and changing, and things like Spotify, understanding that if you use these platforms properly you have a much better chance of success. And here's how you can use it. And these kinds of things probably will lead to more positive results. So just being in there has made me really excited about releasing more and more music and working with our band... and so that excites me.

Protection

Claude Kelly's admonition about working on both sides of the business also addresses the benefit to creatives in terms of guarding and protecting your business interests. You may have heard horror stories about artists who signed away their rights, underestimated their worth, or otherwise negotiated bad deals for themselves. These are not just stories. They are real. Therefore, there is practical, self-interested value to understanding the business and contributing to how it operates.

Independence

Justin Longerbeam's calling as both a music industry logician and audio engineering creative is to support and empower artists. Knowledge can yield independence, which is a type of industry power.

> *I think that there is a lot of room in the non-profit sector to empower artists to reach their potential without being indebted to a corporation maybe. And the ability to access grants and those sorts of things I think is more interesting to me and maybe speaks to artists a little more closely than corporate interests. So my goals right now are to figure out how I can, within this community, create a non-profit organization that supports the artists… to empower artists to own their work and work for themselves… providing resources that artists aren't indebted to.*

When joined with calling, satisfaction, protection of interests, and independence are apt motivators for working knowledgeably within the music business and positively contributing to its existence. The future of the industry needs meaningful, substantive influence from its participants to advance in progressive new directions, to survive as a forward-looking industry context, and to renew itself in continuously fresh and innovative ways.

Some have suggested that music industry creatives have no choice concerning maintaining a base of business knowledge, that you must do so in order to survive in a gig economy. The benefits of understanding the business of music are clear, as described in this section. But understanding the business for practical reasons does not negate the role of calling. The music industry needs both creatives and logicians. This book makes a distinction between (1) knowing the business as a creative, but working primarily as a creative (because that is your calling); (2) knowing the business to work as a music industry logician (because that is your calling); and (3) knowing the business to work on both sides of the business as a Career Dualist (again, calling). There is a bigger discussion to be had that includes the gig economy but extends beyond it. Moreover, aspects of the current narrative concerning the gig economy are disturbing. The narrative seems to suggest that you are essentially a tool of the music industry, kind of like a pencil and a sheet of paper, or a hammer and nail. You are not, unless you choose to think of yourself that way. Therefore, I reiterate an underlying message of this chapter: the relationship between you and the industry is a symbiotic one, you need the industry, and the industry needs you.

Entrepreneurship, Leadership, and Innovation

Justin's vision of independent, empowered artists who are equipped to work for themselves is consistent with a growing narrative in the entertainment industry, particularly within the context of the "new" gig economy, where freelance arrangements constitute that employment model. The dictionary defines freelance as "a person who acts independently without being affiliated with or authorized by an organization."[27] It is a term that is sometimes used interchangeably with entrepreneur, but the definitions are different. An entrepreneur is "one who organizes, manages, and assumes the risks of a business or enterprise."[28] As a legal practitioner I was an entrepreneur attorney who started and maintained my own law practice, and sometimes contracted with freelance attorneys and administrative staff as needed. Both freelancers and entrepreneurs engage an ethos of self-sufficiency and self-determination, and the music industry needs both. Freelancers have the flexibility to support a gig economy – ideally, one that provides fair and adequate compensation and benefits – and support the fluid nature of a rapidly and constantly changing industry. Entrepreneurs create new entities, identities, and ventures or find new ways to revamp familiar enterprises.

The industry also needs thought leaders and innovators. Despite the evolving landscape of the music industry, in some ways it has not changed enough. For example, the role of women and persons of color in positions of influence on the business side of the industry has improved markedly, but there is still a lot of room for progress. Disputes sometimes land in court in order to challenge conventional ways of doing things, and such litigation will probably always be with us. There will always be areas in which innovation is needed. Claude Kelly provides insight from years of experience in the business where he has had a front-row seat to the absence of innovation, witnessing places where imagination and ingenuity do not always exist, but could, and in his view, should.

> *Money, we felt, was being left on the table because people were all chasing the same avenues… Even going to a show in itself as a format has predictability to it. So you know when you go to a show, take for example for your favorite artist… and before you even get there because you know the music you can kind of surmise what the set list is gonna be. You know they're gonna do their hit at the end. Then they're gonna do that encore and you're not really supposed to leave and you have to wait and you clap. The whole thing has become so run of the mill that even if you love the artist there's still no element of surprise. We talked a lot about Black entertainment and how pigeon-holed it is and how we wanted to break out of some of those boxes and how Black artists weren't given the same chances that white artists were given and… the platform I've had as a songwriter and producer, I should use some of that strength to defy some of those labels and boxes. So with all that in mind, again, it felt necessary to not just throw stuff up against the wall and see what stuck, but really talk about the different ways that things weren't being done smart. And on a whole, on a whole, what drove me the most, what scared me – because we're paying out of pocket, investing in ourselves, and also like in business in general – is just how much money gets wasted. And… neither one of us wanted to just spend, give our money away aimlessly. But just the idea that we have this business where very few artists do well. And that's a fact. But they sign thousands. One year we saw the number and it was like 4,500 artists were signed that year and I think maybe under 20 or 30 had proven to even break even. And we scratched our heads and what other industry would*

you be selling a product, and at the end of the year you take stock… If we're Nike, and we're selling a specific sneaker. And at the beginning [of the year] we say we're gonna sell 4,500 different styles of sneaker. At the end of the year only 10 or 20 are working, and then you turn over the next year and you don't decide to pull the ones that don't work, or to really work on improving some of the ones that could almost work. December comes around and everyone talks about how the industry's failing, everyone takes a long vacation until around the end of January when it's time for the Grammys, and they just do the same thing again. And it's nonsensical. It doesn't really make sense in the real world of anything, any other product… and we said we just can't do that. Especially you can't afford to do it when you're independent. And so those are the conversations that forced us to be savvy. And we're not perfect. We're guessing 'cause everyone's guessing. But that business mind was more important than us just keeping our head in the music. We knew we could write could songs. And actually, I think everyone knows already walking into this that, oh, Claude can write good songs, he has a history of that. What else can he do? And so the challenge became, let's show them how well we can bring these good songs to the world. And let's show them how lean we can be, but how colorful we can be at the same time and express it, and develop our artists. And when things are not working, take stock and stop early as opposed to spending, spending, spending, spending, spending in the hope that a miracle will happen. Some of the things that maybe the big labels… can't afford to do because the machine's already moving but they really don't make sense. So that's equally as much a passion for us. Even in the creative process when we're writing we're saying alright so when we write this, is it for a soundtrack? Will this lead to another avenue besides just the radio? Will this lead to us being on Broadway? Will it lead to synch work and commercials? Will they take this little tiny piece? Sometimes Chuck [Harmony] will say – and I think it's brilliant – he'll say "we're creating new sample-able music" because everything's been sampled. So let's create new things that in 20 years they'll have new string lines to borrow from or new drumbeats to take. Those kinds of things are where people are leaving money on the table, are actually more of our focus, rather than "can we write a song." Because I know we can write music.

Claude's words evidence a type of boldness and thought leadership that can impact the industry. It comes from a place of dual calling: calling as a creative, and calling as a logician. Everyone will be differently called, and everyone will have their role to play. Part of your calling to this industry context may include manifesting leadership of your own. "I can't control the industry," you may be thinking. Perhaps not. But you can impact it. You can impact it on at least two levels: (1) *why* you work – if you are called to particular work to serve a community that is this industry context, you can serve it from that place of calling and purpose; (2) you can also impact the industry by *how* you work. If you accept gigs for free when that's not beneficial; if you don't understand how the business works; if you do not persevere to do the work that calls you – all of these individual actions and attitudes have impact. You cannot be Indie Arie, or Tim Westergren, or L.A. Reid, or Derek Sivers, or Lauryn Hill, or Adele, or Mike Curb, or any of the profiled dualists featured in this book. Fortunately, you do not need to be. You can and must be you.

Because *you* are who the industry needs. It needs Career Explorers who are in the midst of deciding where to best plant their vocational stake. It needs Artistic Explorers who work as creatives, compelled by the calling of artistic drive that influences their career choices. It needs Dualist Explorers who support the business side of the industry, working primarily as non-artists whose calling is to express analytical propensity but whose artistic drive keeps them connected to the industry in the most real and relevant ways. And it needs Career Dualists, whose affinity to the industry is demonstrated by their even split to working within it. They may be the most adept at utilizing their A/A/D for future changes.

No matter how your A/A/D quadrants you, today's career environment, not just the entertainment industry, is fraught with uncertainty. At any time, you may choose to transition from one quadrant or from one occupation to another. So, it pays to learn new capabilities and to hear the voice of your calling to navigate and contribute to the often complex career terrain of industry context.

Discussion Questions

1. What is context?
2. How can context impact calling, or can it?
3. Describe boundaryless and protean careers.
4. Discuss the relationship between the gig economy and industry context.
5. Identify correlations between freelancing, entrepreneurship, leadership, and innovation. How do they relate to independence?

EXERCISE SET 5: CUSTOMIZING CONTEXT

The objective of this exercise is to consider the implications of calling being impacted by industry change.

1. Would you continue to be [*insert your baseline calling from the Chapter 4 exercises*] in the face of challenges created by contextual change?
2. If you needed to make adaptations to your skills or knowledge, what are some adaptations that would best fit you? What if you need wholly new skills?
3. The impact I want to have on the music industry today is: _____.
4. The best way for me to be who the music industry needs is by/through: _____.

Notes

1 Richard T. Mowday and Robert I. Sutton, "Organizational Behavior: Linking Individuals and Groups to Organizational Contexts," *Annual Review of Psychology* 44 (1993): 198.
2 Greg R. Oldham and Anne Cummings, "Employee Creativity: Personal and Contextual Factors at Work," *Academy of Management Journal* 39, no. 3 (June 1996): 607.
3 Gary Johns, "In Praise of Context," *Journal of Organizational Behavior* 22 (2001): 32.
4 Shoshana Dobrow Riza and Daniel Heller, "Follow Your Heart or Your Head? A Longitudinal Study of the Facilitating Role of Calling and Ability in the Pursuit of a Challenging Career," *Journal of Applied Psychology* 100, no. 3 (2015): 695–6.
5 Plato, "Book IV," *The Republic*, translated by Benjamin Jowett, https://en.wikisource.org/wiki/The_Republic/Book_IV (italics added).
6 Hugh McIntyre, "Hip-Hop Artists Are Changing What the Industry Calls an 'Album'," *Forbes*, June 16, 2017, www.forbes.com/sites/hughmcintyre/2017/06/16/hip-hop-artists-are-changing-what-the-music-industry-calls-an-album/#2751d57f3ad6.
7 Once a specialty music store, now a live music venue: http://andiemusiklive.com/.
8 Daniel Kreps, "Roy Orbison Hologram Tour Sets North America Dates," *Rolling Stone*, July 10, 2018, www.rollingstone.com/music/music-news/roy-orbison-hologram-tour-sets-north-american-dates-694945/ and https://basehologram.com/news.
9 Sam Machkovech, "Review: Japanese Hologram Pop Star Hatsune Miku Tours North America," *Ars Technica*, April 28, 2016,
      https://arstechnica.com/gaming/2016/04/waving-glow-sticks-at-hologram-anime-pop-stars-our-night-with-hatsune-miku/.
10 Carl Lamarre, "Here's How Much Chance the Rapper Says He Was Paid for 'Coloring Book' Release on Apple Music," *Billboard*, March 17, 2017, www.billboard.com/articles/columns/hip-hop/7728589/chance-the-rapper-apple-music-coloring-book-tweets.
11 Lisa Eadicicco, Matt Peckham, John Patrick Pullen, and Alex Fitzpatrick, "The 20 Most Successful Technology Failures of All Time," *Time*, April 3, 2017, http://time.com/4704250/most-successful-technology-tech-failures-gadgets-flops-bombs-fails/.
12 It resurfaced as a legal website through a series of transactions described at https://en.wikipedia.org/wiki/Napster.
13 For the history of precisely how the term was coined, see Note 1 of "Introduction" in Michael B. Arthur and Denise M. Rousseau, *The Boundaryless Career* (New York: Oxford University Press, 1996).
14 Philip H. Mirvis and Douglas T. Hall, "Psychological Success and the Boundaryless Career," *Journal of Organizational Behavior* 15 (1994): 369.
15 Douglas T. Hall and Dawn E. Chandler, "Psychological Success: When the Career Is a Calling," *Journal of Organizational Behavior* 26 (2005): 165.
16 Dobrow Riza and Heller, "Follow Your Heart or Your Head?" 706.
17 Shoshana Dobrow Riza and Jennifer Tosti-Kharas, "Calling: The Development of a Scale Measure," *Personnel Psychology* 64 (2011): 1048.
18 Samuel E. Kaminsky and Tara S. Behrend, "Career Choice and Calling: Integrating Calling and Social Cognitive Career Theory," *Journal of Career Assessment* 23, no. 3 (2015): 385.
19 Hall and Chandler, "Psychological Success," 165.
20 "Why Did Jazz Musicians Start Referring to an Engagement as a Gig?" https://english.stackexchange.com/questions/129577/why-did-jazz-musicians-start-referring-to-an-engagement-as-a-gig.
21 Neil O. Alper and Gregory H. Wassall, *More than Once in a Blue Moon: Multiple Jobholdings by American Artists*, Research Division Report #40 (Santa Ana, CA: Seven Locks Press, National Endowment for the Arts, 2000).
22 Elka Torpey and Andrew Hogan, "Working in a Gig Economy," U.S. Bureau of Labor Statistics, May 2016, www.bls.gov/careeroutlook/2016/article.

23 Chris F. Wright, Nick Wailes, Greg J. Bamber, and Russell D. Lansbury, "Beyond National Systems, Towards a 'Gig Economy'? A Research Agenda for International and Comparative Employment Relations," *Employee Responsibilities and Rights Journal* 29 (2017): 254.

24 Hamza Shaban, "Could Europe's Uber Ruling Affect the Future of the Gig Economy?" *Washington Post*, December 21, 2017; *Academic OneFile*, http://link.galegroup.com/apps/doc/A519780334/AONE?u=tel_a_belmont&sid=AONE&xid=4ff03975.

25 *Hearing on "Exploring the 'Gig Economy' and the Future of Retirement Savings,"* statement of Monique Morrissey, Economic Policy Institute, February 6, 2018.

26 Wright et al., *Beyond National Systems*, 254.

27 *Merriam-Webster's Collegiate Dictionary*, 10th edition (Springfield, MA: Merriam-Webster, 1993).

28 *Merriam-Webster's Collegiate Dictionary*, 10th edition.

6

CALL AND RESPONSE

Elementary school was where I first learned that Alexander Graham Bell invented the telephone. Though there were actually many inventors involved in bringing us the invention that has revolutionized communication, Bell was the first to receive a patent for the device in the United States in 1876. Telephone technology has undergone lots of modifications since then, yet the basic concept of the call and response remains unchanged. The analogy of vocational calling to telephonic calling is a natural one, particularly in terms of a response to a call. One component of the technology that remains a constant is the requirement of a notification that permits you to know that someone is calling. These audibles began as thumps, then ringing bells and buzzers. The digital age has yielded additional options: a chirp, a song, a ringtone. Whatever the signal – whether chirp, bell, or ring – that summons lets you know that a call has arrived. Whether you choose to ignore or respond to the call, and irrespective of who is on the other end, a call requires a response. Researchers agree.

According to Douglas T. Hall and Dawn E. Chandler, career success does not emanate simply from being called or even from knowing what one's calling is. They assert a calling model of career success that assumes that you must actually respond to the calling. Douglas T. Hall's description of calling denotes seeing your work as "an invitation to which you choose to respond" and is based on a decision that involves "discernment (listening, deep reflection, prayer) to find the right path."[1] If you adopt Hall's description of calling and choose to see it as an invitation, not a mandate, following the call to see where it leads is a logical next step. You may sense the intangible pull in a particular vocational direction, whether you have stopped to examine and label it as a calling or not. Or you may be interested in going deeper in contemplating a search for calling, so that you will know which path to follow. This chapter invites you to consider how you will respond to calling in your life.

Tuning into the Presence of Calling

Contemplating a response to calling rests on two preliminary presumptions: that there is a call to respond to, and a reason or desire to respond to it. By reading this book you are tuning into the potential presence of calling. You may have begun the search that is introduced in Chapter 4 and, hopefully, have completed the exercises found at the end of the chapter. You have begun to see some patterns emerge, from identifying yourself in one of the quadrants in the Duality Exploration Grid, to identifying a leaning that serves as a baseline calling from the Chapter 4 exercises. Some of the puzzle pieces are beginning to fit together. You have been engaging in the process of reflection and are excited to contemplate the presence of your calling (or callings). Even if you do not feel certain of the direction in which your calling is pointing you, it is the process of inquiry that is essential. As long as you engage in the inquiry, it is possible to contemplate calling's presence. The research of Ryan D. Duffy and William E. Sedlacek studied the presence of calling to determine its relationship to career development. They surveyed 3,091 first-year college students using an instrument created by Michael F. Steger and Brian J. Dik developed to measure how students viewed their callings. The assessment contained two items, answerable via a five-point Likert scale that ranged from "not at all true of me" to "totally true of me." The items students responded to were "I have a calling to a particular kind of work" and "I have a good understanding of my calling as it applies to my career."[2] Items or questions about the source of the calling were purposely omitted. This assessment placed the presence of calling in the eye of the beholder, as viewed from the perspective of the one who is called. Like the students in that study, you can determine the presence of calling for you, and that discernment is preliminary to a response to it.

Therefore, now is a good time to consider this: if you have not completed the Chapter 4 exercises that tackle searching for calling, return to that chapter and do them. Don't worry about perfect or final answers; the goal is the journey. This chapter, which focuses on responding to a call, will be more meaningful and useful once you have established a baseline for the presence of calling since it is not possible to answer a call that does not exist. As the Duffy and Sedlacek instrument for assessing the presence of calling suggests, you can embrace the presence of your own calling by first acknowledging it. That is a key place to begin. Recall (from Chapter 4) that calling need not be thought of as mysterious or unknowable. It can unfold incrementally, a piece at a time through self-knowledge and self-identification with the call. You choose not only the call but how you will respond to it. What will motivate or direct your response? You.

Hurdles, Hitches, and Hindrances

Keeping the Lines Open

In the early days of cell phones, when use was first becoming popular and ubiquitous, dropped calls seemed the norm. Right in the middle of a riveting conversation you might suddenly realize there was no one on the other end of the call. No response. Dead air. Verizon's now famous ads asking the question "can you hear me now?" showed an actor testing the reliability of their network, suggesting that even in the most remote locations a call could be received or heard. The trademarked slogan became a familiar refrain, symbolizing the importance of problem-free, uninterrupted communication. The analogy holds when it comes to vocational calling. You cannot respond to your calling if you cannot hear it. Like audio signals in a phone call, if there are voices present they must be audible. Even after you've identified a calling, it will be difficult to make progress toward living called if you are hampered by internal distortion. Responding means resolving the issues that hamper signal flow. Avoiding dropped calls. Keeping the call clear, free from noise. Noise is "any sound that is undesired or interferes with one's hearing of something."[3] Interference causes distraction, and distraction takes your attention and focus from your calling and redirects it away from hearing or living it. Let's consider distractions that can affect your response to calling.

Economic Tradeoffs

The role of compensation is naturally a part of any discussion on vocation. We think of money not as a mere distraction from calling but as a necessity; as previous chapters have discussed, economic factors influence career decision making. However, this chapter asks a question about money that is particularly salient concerning responding to calling. The question is one of economic *perspective*: how important is compensation to *you*? Each of us perceives its role a little differently, individually. How you answer the question, i.e., how you view where money fits in guiding your career decisions, can impact your response to calling.

Working from a perspective driven by calling competes with working solely for money, as suggested by the research of Throsby and Hollister who found that the two dominating factors influencing the progress of an artistic career are financial problems and time constraints, leading to secondary employment that is time consuming but often necessary.[4] Dobrow Riza and Heller highlight these two factors – time and money – as tradeoffs creating a type of career dilemma for creatives that differs from the dilemma represented by the Career Duality dilemma (CD/Di). CD/Di is the quandary created from analytical propensity + artistic drive (A/A/D), concerning whether one's artistic drive or analytical propensity (or both) should direct one's career decisions. Dobrow Riza and Heller point to a related but additional decisional dilemma: that of choosing between a career that provides financial security and one which engages a passion related to calling.[5]

Money can be construed as a measure of success that is a chief motivator for career decisions. In the case of the profiled dualists, money was an important factor in directing analytical propensity and artistic drive, as indicated by their responses to some of the interview questions.[6] Consider these excerpted responses to "Why did you decide not to become a full-time musician?"

I really wish that musicians made a lot more money.

(Kim Lannear)

I think you have to sort of concede certain lifestyles by being a professional musician for a long time. Specifically… money isn't consistent. Not to say that I don't think that it can be, but…

(Justin Longerbeam)

Because I was pursuing being a touring musician – our goal was always six months a year of touring – I just got poor and just really poor, and more poor. And we were all very young and I was the only one in the band with a credit card… I understood what a credit card was but I didn't understand how finance like that works. I didn't realize how much damage I was really causing myself in the long run. And CDBaby was my job on the weekends when I was touring, so they just supported me… It was a financial decision that made the most sense because I was just so poor – to just stop touring, stop pursuing that. Then also love, and wanting to have a house for my partner and she was in school at the time right around the same time that I was touring. And bills got real… and then also I was delivering pizzas for a while during this time and I was like "money sucks" or it's really difficult to figure out as a starving musician.

(Joel Andrew)

Responses to the question "Would you switch careers entirely to music/ entertainment?" also revealed issues related to money with respect to what it would mean to work full time as a creative.

Yeah. I totally would. That's really what I want to do. If I had the time to do it and not have to worry about money and if there were more viable ways to make money in music then I would do it… just something to sustain me and be relatively comfortable, I would do it. Honestly, another reason why I'm doing Scripturally Sound was so that I can have income to just feed my passion in music. That was definitely another reason why I went into it. 'Cause I was thinking about how can I make money.

(Kim Lannear)

Kim was not the only dualist who would consider a full-time music career, if money wasn't an issue. When asked how being analytical affects artistic drive, specifically when I asked whether being vice president of marketing at CDBaby positively or negatively affected his music, Kevin Bruener talked about being creative as the impetus for making music, not money.

It's easy to get yourself just out of that pure space of creating in that place of why you wanted to do it in the first place. Because I don't know many musicians, if any, that the reason they wanted to get into music was because of the money. I'm sure there are some but usually you don't pick up a guitar because you want cash to come out of it. You pick it up to do something else.

David Smith's decision not to make music full time because of money can be heard in his response to a similar question. His response reveals how money affected his current career path when asked why he decided to become vice president of music entertainment at his bank.

So, the idea for that was never in my plan. I wasn't smart enough to think of something like that at the time or aware that that was even out there. I just knew that I had to pay the bills, and music wasn't doing it at the time. There was a friend who would come to my shows and she was very supportive of my music and she knew I was struggling financially, 'cause I went to her as a banker and asked, I gotta get a plan together here, I'm struggling paying my bills. So, she was kind of helping me manage money but my money was so sporadic: show here, show there. I mean I was dependent on booking a gig to pay for rent... And she was like, well they're hiring at the bank, you could be a part-time teller, have a little bit of a consistent income while you pursue your music. I thought well, I guess that's interesting. Maybe I could explore that.

Music is profitable for some creatives. Is it a coincidence that Chuck Harmony's success as a Grammy-nominated and multiple award-winning producer reflects an unmitigated confidence that he would be financially successful as a producer? In his words, "I knew I could put music together so it's a no brainer that I could make money from that."

But his financial success as a producer does not match what he views as his calling. Hall and Chandler point us to the research of Everett Hughes, an early career theorist who emphasized the importance of perspective. Hughes made a distinction between how you view your career success – which he called the subjective career – versus how society views your career – which Hughes called the objective career.[7] Chuck's objective success was clear: financial achievement and industry recognition as a music industry leader who has worked as a producer and songwriter with some of the biggest and most objectively successful artists in the country. Yet Chuck's subjective measure of success was low, as his ultimate calling in the industry is to be an artist and music industry logician, rather than a producer.

While meeting financial needs is tied to vocation, research suggests that having a calling perspective that looks beyond financial gain yields a number of benefits, including career and general well-being.[8] Therefore, if one chooses a response to calling that focuses on money, there is a tradeoff between the money and satisfaction, to some extent. There is also a tradeoff in terms of how you spend your time. Saying "yes" to performing gigs regularly may mean saying "no" to a promotion at your day job (if you have one) so that you can be freer to travel for concerts. This is a tradeoff that is sometimes worth it. And at other times it comes at a price that seems high. It depends on how much performing means to you. Is the calling important enough to move you to make the trade?

Objective measures of success like money or status point to what you have attained, but the deeper fulfillment occurs when there is congruence between objective accomplishments and subjective ones, like sense of purpose. Hall and Chandler summed it up by observing that "true success is not just getting what you want in life—it's liking what you get."[9]

Survival of the Fittest

Compensation is not the only potential distraction that can affect your response to calling. What if the nature of the calling itself poses hurdles to attaining your goals? Another challenge that is related to economic realities but presents its own dynamics is competition. Television programs like *American Idol, X Factor,* and *The Voice* are contests that award a prize to the vocalist who emerges as the one and only singer that bests all other contestants. Such high-stakes contests are designed to be competitive, partly for entertainment purposes. Yet they offer a peek inside the kind of untelevised rivalry musicians routinely face: live auditions, video or audio recordings that serve as demonstrations of your ability, having to prove yourself and your ability over and over again in an occupation filled with others as talented or sometimes more talented than you. If you are called to music as a creative, could the prospect of constant competition affect your response to the call? Is it even possible to always be the best? Is being "the best" implicit in the call? Is this a driver that moves some to leave music entirely, or to continue to work within it but on the business side of the industry instead?

Scarcity is at the root of the competitive challenges associated with the music industry. Coveted seats in orchestras, theatrical roles, venue gigs – lucrative or otherwise – and record and publishing deals are scarce. These shortages can cause a musician to ask this question: if this calling is so impractical, should I follow it? Kevin Bruener expressed his own experience with that challenge.

> *I think on the negative side something I would add is that when you're really close to the industry I think it's easy to get jaded towards certain aspects of it. You know, it's something that all people face the further they get into the industry. If you're this band in some town, you're doing great, and the label gets interested then you get brought into this world where there's a lot of people making judgments about whether or not you're good enough. All those kinds of things come into play, and I think for an artist it can have very negative impact. I saw it in Nashville all the time. People would just freak out and leave. Because it's tough. So much talent and there's a lot of people that are making just judgments about you and your music and whether or not you're "good enough" and that can really be a challenge to navigate. And so, when you're in the music business you can see that side of it and as an artist it can make you feel like sometimes I should just give up. Why do I keep doing this? I'm not as good as that person, so how can I even possibly keep kidding myself that there's gonna be some kind of career here?*

Chuck Harmony anticipated the judgment Bruener mentions, and it drove his decision to work as a producer for many years, rather than as an artist.

> *And I never say this but it's so true, like in all honesty my music-producing career was me taking the safe route… as a music producer and trying to get into the music business I spent so much time putting artists on a pedestal, and it really stunted my growth a lot. I guess you have this ideal of what an artist is, and so how dare you even consider yourself that kind of person, especially if you have insecurities, if you're coming from a point where you didn't get the encouragement so you're kind of just feeling your way through, trying to figure stuff out. I knew at an early age that I could've definitely been an artist and I prevented myself from that because I didn't want the heartache of it and I didn't want the rejection of it.*

Chuck's confidence in his ability to be a successful producer helped insulate him from the competitive sting of working as an artist. The competition he believed he would face as an artist distracted him from the call. Shoshana Dobrow Riza and Daniel Heller explored the relationship between calling and ability, and the impact of calling on career pursuit. They examined which influence in your life will dominate if there is conflict between extrinsic factors, like money, and intrinsic factors, like calling, in terms of career pursuit. Their findings are particularly relevant since they specifically examined the conflict within the context of the music industry. Dobrow Riza and Heller cite the U.S. Department of Labor statistics that serve as indicators of the "difficult nature" of this career path.[10] If you have personally felt the pressure of that competition, you now know that there are researchers that recognize it too! That characterization reflects how few musicians typically obtain jobs as musicians. For example, a 2004 study for the *New York Times* by Daniel J. Wakin showed that only 10–15 percent of students graduating from Juilliard found full-time employment in music. The difficulty of finding such employment has driven some to leave the profession altogether, as Wakin reports.[11]

Yet the Dobrow Riza and Heller study found that your response to heightened competition depends on the strength of your calling; the stronger the calling, the more likely you are to "make it" in the music industry. Their study examined career decision making amongst musicians seeking to work as musicians, not musicians who may wish to work on the business side of the industry. Nevertheless, music industry logicians can benefit from their findings as well. According to their research, a strong calling will influence you to focus on your own beliefs about your ability. A strong calling causes you to work toward fulfilling the calling, including working hard at your musical skills. This results in a higher perception of ability, which causes diminished concern about competition or other external influences like making money. Consequently, they found that *the belief that you will be one of the few musicians to beat the odds of fierce competition* is key, and this belief is inspired by strong calling.[12] Their longitudinal study examined musicians who experienced early calling in adolescence and tests the correlation between early calling and adult career pursuit of music. They examined what kind of career decision you make when there's a conflict between intangible internal rewards – doing what you love – and measurable external rewards – good salary or status. Ultimately, they found that strong calling, which enhanced belief in musical ability, contributed to increased success. Those with strong callings were much more likely to be employed as professional musicians or to earn a degree in music than those with lower callings. "Whereas these individuals demonstrate extraordinary levels of persistence about this pursuit, those with weaker callings typically take themselves out or are taken out of the running in such challenging labor contexts."[13]

Interestingly, according to the Dobrow Riza and Heller study, even if strong calling leads you to respond positively and earnestly to the call, this does not inevitably lead to a happily-ever-after ending if viewed from a financial stand-point. The low number of available opportunities to work as a professional musician in the classical music context means you are more likely to work freelance and part-time and earn $12,000/year less than those not professionally involved in music.[14] However, they posited that those who "make it" have been so persistent that they may "be able to achieve positive intrinsic and extrinsic outcomes."[15]

If you are at that precipice, standing at a crossroads that A/A/D or another summons could lead you to, and are concluding that a career as a full-time musician or creative is too arduous a calling to respond to, the vocational path of the music industry logician may be no easier. Though researchers like Dobrow Riza and Heller rightly characterize the musician's career path as par-ticularly challenging, working on the business side of the entertainment industry is also challenging in part because of changes taking place in the music industry (detailed more fully in Chapter 5). For example, the internet and the advent of digital technology have disrupted every industry, and the music industry is no exception. Mobile devices – tablets, smartphones, and laptops – make it possible to consume music on the go, rather than via the stationery equipment that was traditionally used for playing CDs. Consequently, new delivery platforms remove the need to sell physical products like CDs and have shifted the business model for the consumption and delivery of music. Consumers can access single songs rather than entire albums when they purchase music. And purchases are another matter altogether, as consumers look to platforms like Spotify, Pandora, Tidal, YouTube, and Apple Music for musical experiences that involve streaming music which provides a more radio-like experience that does not currently require any purchase at all. How do you continue to monetize an industry that no longer has the same products to sell, to different buyers, who consume and purchase music much differently than in the past? If you want to work as a music industry logician, your challenge is to contemplate solutions to address these and other questions. In the absence of clear answers, the industry adjusts the best way it can. For example, record labels that were once at the center of the traditional business model are evolving out of existence or morphing into more multifaceted entities. Many have adjusted to a changing landscape by laying off large numbers of employees who supported the older business model while creatives and retailers adjust to shrinking revenues. Therefore, those who aspire to positions as record company executives, artist managers, agents, publicists, retailers, and other roles supporting the business of music face competition for coveted business roles, just as artists do. If you are called to express your analytical propensity through this behind-the-scenes business career, the challenge to respond to the call or to seek a less competitive career exists just as it does for those seeking to express artistic drive as creatives.

Moreover, notions of success and achievement for music industry logicians rival that of creatives. For example, let's compare the goal commercial musicians typically set for themselves to a comparable goal for music industry logicians. Musicians often identify the achievement of superstardom or rock star status as evidence of having "made it" and have that goal in mind when defining success. Achieving Beyoncé or Taylor Swift status on the artistic side of the industry would be comparable to becoming CEO of a multimillion- or multibillion-dollar entertainment company on the business side.

The CEO career path is not an easy one in any industry, nor one achieved quickly. It represents the broadest scope of responsibility and is the highest and most prestigious position you can attain in the corporate world. Progressing upward on any organizational ladder is often a competitive pursuit. The stories of CEOs are filled with angst, uncertainty, and tough times. Leaders are criticized and held accountable for every declining profit and not quickly applauded for a company's successes. Moreover, if you are a woman or a person of color, reaching the CEO ranks is as rare as becoming an entertainment superstar. The number of females and executives of color is markedly smaller, which indicates that such a path may be even more arduous for those individuals. There were 32 women CEOs in *Fortune* 500 companies in 2017, an increase of 50 percent from the previous year.[16] Whereas, in 2017 the *Atlantic* reported the presence of only four African American CEOs in *Fortune* 500 companies, and that number is expected to decrease with the retirement of Ken Chenault from American Express in 2018.[17] These statistics for *Fortune* 500 companies are not specific to the entertainment industry. Rather this list is offered to support the comparison to superstardom, since the *Fortune* 500 is comprised of superstar companies, i.e., those that "represent two-thirds of the U.S. GDP with $12 trillion in revenues, $890 billion in profits, $19 trillion in market value, and employ 28.2 million people worldwide."[18] It's the big time in terms of corporate superstardom. There are also entertainment companies on the *Fortune* 500 list, including Apple, Comcast, Disney, Time Warner, Twenty-First Century Fox, CBS, Loews, Viacom, Netflix, LiveNation Entertainment, and GameStop.

However, the entertainment industry is not the only industry that is competitive. According to the 2017 Jobvite benchmark recruiting report, consumer internet, education, and media have the highest job-to-applicant ratios. In other words, for every one position available in the consumer internet industry (Google, Amazon, eBay, etc.), there are 66.6 applicants vying for the job. For education and media, the numbers of applicants competing for a single position are 53 and 52, respectively. The report cites leisure and hospitality industries – which includes the arts and entertainment sector – as actually slightly *less* competitive according to the report, with 50.1 applicants applying for a single position.[19]

Whatever the pursuit, profession, discipline, or industry – strength of passion, commitment, and determination are needed to reach your goals. This is a reality to be borne in mind in contemplating a response to calling. Therefore, the research of Dobrow Riza and Heller is helpful in pointing out that a strong calling can help to resolve the career decision dilemma, and can redirect you from the distraction of competition.

Who Is Calling?

In the days before digital technology, telephones notified you that a call was coming in but lacked the capacity to alert you concerning who was on the other end until you answered the call. Caller-identification technology has essentially erased that anonymity so pervasively that it is now difficult to imagine a time when there was a risk associated with answering a call. It was probably inevitable that inventors would seek out a means to screen calls, since knowing the source of a call better helps us to prepare our response: whether to answer the call, fear it, anticipate it, ignore it – all connected to the who behind the call. We all have screens and filters through which we see others, opportunities, and ourselves. The source of a calling can act as such a filter. To examine the source of calling is to ask: *who or what is calling*? Peer pressure? Family? A sense of duty to your abilities? This inquiry is related to discerning the call itself, therefore sources of calling are discussed in Chapter 4. However, a calling's source influences how you respond. Let's acknowledge that who is calling matters. Just as with receipt of a phone call, your response is tied to whomever shows up on your caller identification. For example, if your talent or ability is the source of your calling, you may feel an obligation to respond. Likewise, if the source of your summons is a transcendent one, it can be rather tough to say "no" to God! For those interested in God as a transcendent source of calling, the research of Robert McKenna et al. undertakes that exploration.[20] It can also be tough to say "no" to other transcendent callers, like a sense of purpose to serve a needy population.

On the other hand, if your parents ignited and are essential to keeping your calling aflame, your response may not actually be to the call, but to them. If they stop fanning the flames of "your" passion, it could die altogether, ultimately eliminating the need for any response from you at all.

The source of the calling may facilitate or hamper your response to it. An empowered perspective on calling suggests that your response can and should be less dependent on the source of the call and more influenced by the call itself. (If you hold to the view of God as the caller, this perspective is still an empowered one, if your belief supports God as a powerful being and/or source of power.) Since calling is defined as a strong passion or interest, your response to it can be kept alive if you stay connected that to the passion component, no matter what source gave it birth.

Unanswered, Missed, and Unrealized Callings

Not answering a calling is an option. It has to be. Life is not perfect. There are distortions, those things in life that can get in the way of answering the call, like the issues identified in this chapter. But is not answering the call a *good* option? Researchers have studied what happens when a call is unrealized, missed, or unanswered. Tamara Hagmaier and Andrea E. Abele examined unrealized callings, while Justin M. Berg, Adam M. Grant, and Victoria Johnson studied missed and unanswered callings. Because calling is something you identify with as a part of you, an unanswered calling could result in a lifetime of regretting the decisions that have led you to a career which has nothing to do with the call. Likewise, trying to answer multiple callings could lead to an inability to answer all of the calls.

Berg, Grant, and Johnson define an unanswered calling as an occupation you feel drawn to, i.e., that meets the parameters of a calling, and is a "central part of his or her identity," but is an occupation in which you do not work. As they put it, "it is not part of one's formal occupational role."[21] They examined the implications of choosing not to answer a calling. In introducing their study they cite the growth in narratives for young people, specifically for Generations X and Y, to follow your dreams and to believe that you can do anything.[22] Therefore, they explored "how individuals experience and respond to unanswered callings."[23] The following description of their study is an abbreviated summary and not intended to describe all aspects of the study, data analysis, or findings.

They interviewed 49 individuals from various occupations. Stage 1 of the research focused on 20 participants who were educators: ten from elementary schools and ten from university settings. The selection of educators for closer study was based on the researchers' belief that educators would be passionate and therefore drawn to many different interests. The interview questions were divided into four phases. Questions in phase 1 inquired about the respondents' current work, e.g., one of the questions in that stage was "What is a typical day like in your job?" Phase 2 asked interviewees to outline their career path and identify any unanswered callings. Phase 3 asked participants to reflect on their process for responding to unanswered callings and saw the emergence of "job crafting" in responses (more on job crafting in stage 2). Phase 4 asked them to discuss their experiences with unanswered callings. For example, this stage specifically asked study participants if they ever think about what it would have been like to have pursued a different occupation.[24]

Stage 2 of the study focused on 29 participants from other occupations: 13 from a non-profit political advocacy organization that advocated for women's economic advancement, and 16 from a leading for-profit personal products manufacturing company. Participants from both organizations represented a range of positions from employees occupying lower-level jobs to senior professionals. This part of their data collection included both an interview and a survey. The interview protocol was designed to hone in on both job crafting and unanswered callings. Job crafting is a term coined by Wrzesniewski and Dutton that they defined as "the physical and cognitive changes individuals make in the task or relational boundaries of their work."[25] Some of the ways employees enact these changes include changing the scope or number of tasks they perform at work, changing the way they interact with others in their workplace, and changing the way they think about their jobs and the meaning they attach to their work. The objective of job crafting is to change your experience and identity at work.[26] Stage 2 of the study incorporated questions that investigated job crafting. For example, one question in this stage of the study asked "Do you have a dream occupation other than your own, or another occupation that you feel drawn to pursue?" A follow-up question for respondents who identified a dream job asked whether the respondent has incorporated aspects of the dream occupation into the respondent's current job. Incorporating new tasks from a dream occupation would be a form of job crafting. After compiling the list of occupations elicited from these questions, the researchers identified the dream occupations as potential unanswered callings. Several participants identified unanswered callings in the realm of the creative industries. Specifically, music was cited five times, as well as creative callings like photography, novel writing, and creative directing. However, others cited analytical unanswered callings like law and business management. Eight non-profit and eight for-profit participants who mentioned dream jobs were then asked to complete an online survey to rate those occupations on a seven-point scale. The results from stages 1 and 2 were combined and analyzed.

Their findings led to several propositions about responses to unanswered callings. They offer nine propositions that help describe their findings. Not all nine are included here, but the following are of particular interest for CD: (1) Job crafting is a positive way to address unanswered callings, as it contributes to "experiencing enjoyment and meaning at work."[27] (2) Individuals who do not see job crafting as an option, because of the restrictive nature of their jobs, pursue unanswered calling through leisure crafting.[28] Leisure crafting involves pursuit of an unanswered calling outside of work either vicariously, through others' experiences, or through pursuit of a hobby. Respondents in their study used leisure crafting not just for enjoyment, but to respond to the unanswered calling. (3) Leisure crafting "increases the likelihood of experiencing enjoyment and meaning outside of work."[29]

In addition to identifying and defining unanswered callings their study also identified "missed" callings, which they define as working in an occupation that you do not consider to be a calling, plus you have at least one unanswered calling. They found that job crafting and leisure crafting were utilized by individuals with missed callings too, but utilized for the purpose of making up "for forgone fulfillment of their unanswered callings."[30] Therefore, they also found that (4) responding to unanswered callings can cause not only positive experiences, but can also cause regret and stress if carrying out either of the crafting techniques is difficult.

Lastly, they also found that some participants identified what they refer to as additional callings. Additional callings involve viewing "your current occupation as a calling and having one or more unanswered callings."[31] In contrast to individuals with missed callings who are making up for lost opportunities, those with additional callings look to supplement the calling they are already pursuing. As a result, individuals with additional callings do experience regret, but it is more short term. Additionally, the type of stress experienced for those with additional callings is connected to a sense of being overwhelmed, burdened through attempting to balance their multiple callings.

What If versus What Is

Researchers Hagmaier and Abele build on the distinctions of Duffy and Sedlacek between the search for calling, its presence, and its realization. Like Berg, Grant, and Johnson, Hagmaier and Abele focused on the realization phase and therefore set out to explore what happens when you perceive an inability to fulfill, or realize, your calling. The goal of their research was to ascertain the correlation between realizing your calling and life satisfaction. The following description of the study is intended as a brief synopsis.

They tested four hypotheses related to realization of calling. Their investigation consisted of two studies, one examining the short-term relationship between calling and life satisfaction and the second study examining the long-term relationship between calling and life satisfaction. In study 1 they surveyed 235 German professionals in business, economic, health, and education sectors. The survey assessed calling, life satisfaction, self-congruence (when personal ideals are in harmony with your actual self), and engagement orientation (how absorbed in or challenged by your work you are). Measuring calling was based on their belief that "living one's calling is equally or even more important than knowing one's calling."[32] This idea is an underlying premise of this chapter. Their findings suggested that satisfaction is directly connected to realizing your calling through self-congruence and engagement orientations. In study 2 they tested whether the findings from study 1 were long lasting, and tested whether self-congruence and engagement orientations were important to the study 1 findings. Study 2 consisted of 248 nurses identified through the German Association of Nurses. The results of study 2 confirmed the study 1 results, i.e., that satisfaction is directly related to realizing your calling, specifically through self-congruence and engagement. Moreover, the second study confirmed that such satisfaction is long lasting, specifically 16 weeks later, when the participants repeated the survey after two successive eight-week periods.

An aspect of the study involved speaking with respondents who felt limited in their ability to fulfill their callings. As might be expected, one of the limitations respondents related was compensation. They felt limited to pursue their calling when they had to choose between the calling and making money. Other limitations they cited included hostile work environment, a country's economic conditions, and physical ability.

However, one of the recommendations from the Hagmaier and Abele study is that limitations can be overcome through expanding the available options. They recommended job crafting, citing the work of Berg, Grant, and Johnson.[33] Responding to calling through job crafting is an empowered way to think about options for answering a call. It is borne of sheer determination to not be limited by compensation, competition, or anything else that might get in the way of living called.

Living called right where you are may not only be a response to calling, but also a response to forestalling the temptation of regret. In fact, one of the survey questions in Hagmaier and Abele's assessment of life satisfaction asked participants to respond to the statement "If I could live my life over I would change almost nothing."[34] There have certainly been moments when I have contemplated the past. What would have happened if that year I took off law school to explore a singing career would have lasted longer and the exploration would have dug deeper? Asking the "what if I had" question is like looking through a rearview mirror, a kind of wishing in reverse. Wishing you had dared more, dreamed more, sometimes wishing you had lived a more called life. Therefore, it is fine to ask the *what if* question in advance rather than in the reverse, i.e., to ask "what if I do *not* respond to this calling to see where it leads?" Contemplate it. If the answer that surfaces evidences any form of potential regret, the next step is to pose a *what is* question: what is the best way to fulfill this calling? Channel your artistic drive to work on your behalf to lead you to creative possibilities.

Belief, Relevance, and Necessity

Identify your calling, then follow the path and see where it leads. Game over, response rendered, drop the microphone, right? Yet career pursuits are rarely so simple. The concept of calling is a foreign one to many. Not because they have never heard of it, but because they may not have contemplated how it applies to them. This is your moment for contemplation, and to do so with the insight empirical research and hearing others' experiences can provide. Once you have invested in your moment(s) of contemplation, you are in a position to effectuate a conscious, empowered response to calling. Remember, a call is an invitation, not a mandate.

Discussion Questions

1. Identify the distractions from calling discussed in the chapter.
2. What do the research of Hagmaier and Abele and Berg, Grant, and Johnson examine?
3. Explain the practical value of the Dobrow Riza and Heller research.

EXERCISE SET 6: RESPONSE TO CALLING

The objective of this exercise is to contemplate your response to your calling.

1. Have you responded to what you have identified as your calling? (If you have not identified a calling, return to Chapter 4 and complete those exercises before proceeding.)

    a   If yes, journal how you have responded and how it feels to have done so, whether the call seems "right."
    b   If not, why not? What are the distractions that are impeding your response?

2. Take a moment to contemplate what it would mean to miss, not answer, or not realize your calling. Where are you? What do you see? How do you feel? Journal the answers to these questions.

Notes

1 Douglas T. Hall, "The Protean Career: A Quarter-Century Journey," *Journal of Vocational Behavior* 65 (2004): 9.
2 Ryan D. Duffy and William E. Sedlacek, "The Presence of and Search for a Calling: Connections to Career Development," *Journal of Vocational Behavior* 70 (2007): 594
3 *Merriam-Webster's Collegiate Dictionary*, 10th edition (Springfield, MA: Merriam-Webster, 1993).
4 David Throsby and Virginia Hollister, *Don't Give Up Your Day Job: An Economic Study of Professional Artists in Australia* (Sydney: Australia Council, 2003): 36.
5 Shoshana Dobrow Riza and Daniel Heller, "Follow Your Heart or Your Head? A Longitudinal Study of the Facilitating Role of Calling and Ability in the Pursuit of a Challenging Career," *Journal of Applied Psychology* 100, no. 3 (2015): 695.
6 Some of these excerpts from the interviews are also found in Chapter 3 with the entire interview response.
7 Everett C. Hughes, *Men and Their Work* (Glencoe, IL: Free Press, 1958), quoted in Douglas T. Hall and Dawn E. Chandler, "Psychological Success: When the Career Is a Calling," *Journal of Organizational Behavior* 26 (2005): 155.
8 Bryan J. Dik, Ryan D. Duffy, and Brandy M. Eldridge, "Calling and Vocation in Career Counseling: Recommendations for Promoting Meaningful Work," *Professional Psychology: Research and Practice* 40, no. 6 (2009): 626.
9 Hall and Chandler, "Psychological Success," 173.

10 Dobrow Riza and Heller, "Follow Your Heart or Your Head?" 697.

11 Daniel J. Wakin, "The Juilliard Effect: Ten Years Later," *New York Times*, December 12, 2004, p. AR1. *Academic OneFile*, http://link.galegroup.com/apps/doc/A126052253/AONE?u=tel_a_belmont&sid=AONE&xid=9dd9e287.

12 Dobrow Riza and Heller, "Follow Your Heart or Your Head?" 698–9.

13 Dobrow Riza and Heller, "Follow Your Heart or Your Head?" 708.

14 Dobrow Riza and Heller, "Follow Your Heart or Your Head?" 708. Classical music performance was the context of the Dobrow study, therefore incomes for artists working in the non-classical realm of commercial music may be higher.

15 Dobrow Riza and Heller, "Follow Your Heart or Your Head?" 708.

16 Valentina Zarya, "The 2017 *Fortune* 500 Includes a Record Number of Women CEOs," *Fortune*, June 7, 2017, http://fortune.com/2017/06/07/fortune-women-ceos/.

17 Gillian B. White, "There Are Currently Four Black CEOs in the *Fortune* 500," *Atlantic*, October 26, 2016. www.theatlantic.com/business/archive/2017/10/black-ceos-fortune-500/543960/.

18 http://fortune.com/fortune500/.

19 "New Year, New Job: What Job Seekers Need to Know in 2017," p. 3, www.jobvite.com/wp-content/uploads/2017/01/Jobvite-New-Year-New-Job-Data-Report-2017.pdf. The leisure and hospitality sector includes the arts and entertainment sector, according to the U.S. Government's Bureau of Labor Statistics.

20 Robert B. McKenna, Juliann Matson, Deanna M. Haney, Olivia Becker, McKendree J. Hickory, Diana L. Ecker, and Tanya N. Boyd, "Calling, the Caller, and Being Called: A Qualitative Study of Transcendent Calling," *Journal of Psychology and Christianity* 34, No. 4 (2015): 294–303.

21 Justin M. Berg, Adam M. Grant, and Victoria Johnson, "When Callings Are Calling: Crafting Work and Leisure in Pursuit of Unanswered Occupational Callings," *Organization Science* 21, no. 5 (September–October 2010): 974.

22 At the time their study was published in 2010, Generations X and Y were the focus as the next generation. At the time of the publication of this book, the comparable group would be millennials and their successors, Generation Z.

23 Berg et al., "When Callings Are Calling," 975.

24 Berg et al., "When Callings Are Calling," 992.

25 Amy Wrzesniewski and Jane E. Dutton, "Crafting a Job: Revisioning Employees as Active Crafters of Their Work," *Academy of Management Review* 28, no. 2 (2001): 179.

26 Berg et al., "When Callings Are Calling," 979.

27 Berg et al., "When Callings Are Calling," 982.

28 Berg et al., "When Callings Are Calling," 983.

29 Berg et al., "When Callings Are Calling," 984.

30 Berg et al., "When Callings Are Calling," 985.

31 Berg et al., "When Callings Are Calling," 985.

32 Tamara Hagmaier and Andrea E. Abele, "When Reality Meets Ideal: Investigating the Relation Between Calling and Life Satisfaction," *Journal of Career Assessment* 23, no. 3 (2015): 371.

33 Hagmaier and Abele, "When Reality Meets Ideal," 378.

34 Hagmaier and Abele, "When Reality Meets Ideal," 371.

PART III

The Impact of Career Duality: Synthesizing Possibility

7

AUTHENTICITY

The final tier of the Career Duality model connects calling to authenticity. Specifically, the model suggests that responding to calling yields authenticity. Recognizing the importance of authenticity in career decision making lays a foundation for shaping a career that is yours – chosen by you for you – representing contributions to the world that only you can make, that are as unique as you are. No two people have the same fingerprints. Even identical twins are not exactly identical. Each of us comes into the world as an original, completely distinctive and uncopied. Authentic. Yet when we overlook, take for granted, or disregard that kernel of truth that is you or me, that "thing" that separates us from every other creature that has ever existed, it becomes obscured and we can spend our whole lives searching for what makes us ourselves. There is something captivating about the idea of casting aside restraint and pretention, resisting the temptation to live as someone other than who we believe we are, thereby escaping the clutches of what I call the "ought-to world." The ought-to world is created by internal counsel that tells you what you should and should not do, but its primary dictates concern things you *should* do. In the context of career, there are any number of oughts that seek to influence our decision making.

- You ought to work in the field in which you earned your college degree(s).
- You ought to make as much money as you can.
- You ought to select a career that is practical.
- You ought to do what you do best.
- You ought to do what your family wants you to do.
- You ought to do what you feel.
- You ought to follow your dreams.

- You ought to follow your calling.
- You ought to follow both sides of your A/A/D.
- You ought to follow only one side of your A/A/D!

The list of directives could go on, with each ought potentially contradicting another. Sometimes the ought-to's scream so loudly that you cannot hear the sound of your own voice, your sincere want-to's, your calling. Calling and the uncomplicated career desires of your heart whisper timidly, unsure if they dare question the ought. And why would you question some of them? It is not as if some oughts are not legitimate career issues to consider. After all, there is nothing particularly sinister about pondering money or other practical work considerations. However, the challenge of the ought-to world in the context of career choices is that too much attention to any given ought can yield a sense of duty that interferes with sound decision making and feels disruptive to that desire to live life on our own terms or consistent with calling. There must be a way to tune in to a different channel, a framework that facilitates making career decisions that acknowledges any legitimate oughts yet honors your genuine wants, preserving your unique career self. This chapter discusses the role of authenticity as such a framework for making and living our career choices, with a view toward crafting a type of success that is nurtured without undue regard to the opinions or judgments of others.

Defining and Recognizing Authenticity

According to Merriam-Webster, that which is authentic is that which is "not false or imitation." Likewise, authenticity is the state of "being actually and exactly what is claimed."[1] For example, counterfeit paintings or currency deceive us into thinking they are something that they are not; they present themselves as originals with all of the social value associated with originality, usurping fact, honesty, accuracy, and truth. The research of Alex M. Wood et al. examines authenticity in the context of the authentic personality, which involves how much consistency or inconsistency – known as congruence or incongruence – there is between a true self and one that is influenced by other factors. Building on prior research supporting a person-centered approach to defining authenticity they identified three factors as the basis for examining congruence: self-alienation, authentic living, and accepting external influence. Self-alienation occurs when there is a discrepancy between your conscious awareness and actual experience. An aspect of self-alienation is "not knowing oneself, or feeling out of touch with the true self." Authentic living involves "being true to oneself in most situations and living in accordance with one's values and beliefs."[2] The third factor has to do with the extent to which you believe you must conform to others' expectations. According to Wood et al., this tripod of factors forms the basis for personal authenticity.

One True Self or True to Self?

Researchers who examine authenticity within the contexts of self-concept and identity have debated the idea of an unchangeable, and therefore singular, self. Hazel Markus and Ziva Kunda examined the idea of a true self by exploring whether the self-concept is rooted and stable versus changeable. If changeable, then there is reason to question the idea of a singular "true" self. It is not too difficult to contemplate the complexity of the self. We all are the products of many variables with as many expressions: private yet public, spiritual yet earth-bound, intellectual yet emotional. Moreover, we operate within a variety of social realms: work, family, romantic, religious, cultural, gendered, ethnic, racial, etc. The idea that each of these contexts brings out something different in us, yielding a kind of multiself, is a reasonable conclusion. On the other hand, the concept of a core self that is an ever present nucleus that presides over our reactions to all contexts resonates as well. Accordingly, Markus and Kunda undertook their study to address the debate within the research community. Is it possible to know oneself? Is the self really knowable if malleable, or is that what we have been schooled to believe?

Markus and Kunda make reference to the self-concept as a non-unitary self that is comprised of a wide variety of selves, including an "ought" self, consistent with my ought-to world concept. Since the self is capable of changing to reflect this variety, Markus and Kunda term this compilation of selves at a particular moment the "working self-concept," i.e., the concept of self we have on a given day, or in a particular situation.[3] These terms suggest that the self is not a personal fixture, but a reactive, transitioning personage. That's good news! Because even if you absolutely love who you are, who among us cannot learn new things that may affect who we are in positive ways that also bode well for those around us, and for our careers? Or, if a particular career path seems to define us in a manner that seems foreign or detrimental, it is helpful to understand research-based reasons that desired change can appear on the horizon. In fact, included in the array of selves Markus and Kunda identify are hoped-for selves, ideal selves, and possible selves.

They theorize that malleability of self occurs subtly and therefore conducted a study of the working self-concept to examine what prompts the self to change. They tested this through a study with 40 female undergraduate students, in which they created conditions for a challenging event to ascertain whether the event would prompt the participants to change their self-concepts in response to the challenge. The event involved word associations and tasks that challenged their self-concepts. Ultimately, the study indicated that the self is *both* stable and changeable, i.e., that one's core self-concept can be temporarily changed in response to a particular situation. That core self distinguishes you from me, and can thankfully adapt, grow, and change as needed or desired. Therefore, misconceptions of authenticity that revolve around the one true self conceptualization can be misleading if they do not allow for this kind of variation.

A related misconception is that unfiltered transparency equates to authenticity. The notion that saying or doing whatever one wants or feels under the justification of authenticity is a misguided way of understanding or living the principle. There is the risk that valuing a misinterpretation of authenticity – similar to valuing unbridled, disrespectful, or unkind candor under the pretense of honesty – can become one big excuse for behaving irresponsibly and then claiming one is simply being authentic. This brand of "authenticity" serves neither self nor society.

Herminia Ibarra, a distinguished researcher at Harvard in the field of identity, calls attention to "the authenticity paradox." Ibarra studied authenticity in the context of leadership transitions, noting the challenges individuals faced when attempting to be authentic in transitioning into a leadership role. She found that new leaders sometimes experienced ineffectiveness if they were "true-to-selfers," persons who expressed their true thoughts even when situationally inappropriate. Likewise, leaders she refers to as chameleons are willing to change to fit situations, but may also be ineffective if perceived as disingenuous, even if being chameleon-like is authentic for that individual. She suggests that authenticity does not involve a never-changing "true self" in the quest for effective leadership. Her observation from her research is that leaders should consider an "adaptively authentic" perspective that experiments with different leadership styles.[4] That guidance for leaders has broader application and extends to anyone seeking to better understand the nature of authenticity.

Being true to oneself is not the same as having one true self. Questioning the singular true self concept may ring particularly true for those of us who are partly analytical and partly creative, whose analytical propensity + artistic drive (A/A/D) causes us to regularly grapple with which "true self" to bring to a given situation. During the writing of this book I had an unexpected yet enlightening conversation with a friend of mine who is a well-connected Grammy-winning producer. I mentioned to him that there are times when I feel less connected to the local music scene when I attend events. He said,

> I think that's because you don't know which you to bring to those events. You feel you have to bring the Associate Dean/Lawyer you. You should also bring the artist you. It wasn't until I listened to your music that I really got who you are. You should let them [the Nashville entertainment community] see the artist you more often, then they will know you understand who they are.

That struck me as profound. Maybe you can relate to his words, as I did. I then shared with him that I am writing this book about the split of analytical and artistic selves. Even though I am keenly aware of my own A/A/D on many levels, as writing this book illustrates, in that moment I felt understood and even freer to express *both* selves in the context of my industry interactions. His words build on Ibarra's observations, i.e., being adaptive in our authenticity may mean showing others more than one true self.

His encouragement also points to another potential misconception about the interplay between authenticity and receiving feedback from others. Misinterpreting authenticity could lead us to devalue seeking or listening to advice or counsel, for fear that doing so may taint our connection to what a true self would want. Yet we recognize that the self can be negatively influenced by internal directives like narcissism, greed, misuse of power, and other nefarious motives, or can be undermined by self-doubt or low self-esteem. Conversely, external influences like family, teachers, advisors, friends, or books of wisdom can offer helpful and meaningful insights. Therefore, authenticity can serve as a litmus test or filter for ascertaining whether the advice is pertinent; specifically, whether the advice is pertinent for *you*. Agreeing with all input that comes your way would be an extreme way to receive external influence. Likewise, rejecting all advice would be the opposite extreme. Hearing advice and taking it are two different things, and you are empowered to decide when rejecting it is appropriate. Having the three-part inner rudder of authenticity that Wood et al. described can empower you to filter advice through knowing yourself, knowing your core values and beliefs, and knowing that you do not have to conform to others' expectations, whether you choose to accept their advice or not. An important aspect of authenticity is having the freedom to choose what you want to do and who you want to be.[5]

In summarizing the debate about one true self versus being true to self, the research propels us to embrace both concepts to see how the self-concept relates to authenticity. While the idea of having one true self seems a reasonable anchor for authenticity, isolating that conceptualization can obscure the totality of self and actually work against living authentically unless we define it carefully. Being true to self encourages us to establish core values and beliefs that we use as a foundation for guiding our career decisions and lives. We can label that core set of beliefs "one true self," so long as we recognize its many situation-specific identities, which frees us to express it in authentic ways.

A hypothetical example helps sum up these ideas. Let's suppose that you decide to follow your artistic drive and pursue a career as a performer. Let's also suppose that your core self and natural inclination are to be quiet and reserved, yet you value your audience and believe that connecting with them requires an energetic stage presence. You struggle with whether it is authentic to be a different person on stage than you are off stage. Would pursuit of the performance vocation be an inauthentic career decision? The incongruence you might experience comes from focusing on the one true self philosophy. In this instance, that philosophy suggests that cultivating skills and behaviors that feel unnatural is inauthentic. However, if your goal is to be a performer, not just for self-expression but to also entertain and relate to an audience, adopting a strong stage presence is congruent with your desire to reach others, is being true to yourself, and is therefore authentic. Many are now familiar with Beyoncé's adoption of her Sasha Fierce alter-ego; it allows her to be the dynamic entertainer her fans have grown to love and even expect. Not only does she have an on-stage persona, she has given her a name and identity! Making a conscious decision to have an on-stage image actually empowers her to maintain an authentic self off stage, while being authentic during a performance. It would be inauthentic for *you* to endeavor to be Sasha Fierce on stage, since that is not who you are. But merely adopting an on-stage presence need not be inauthentic, nor is making a career decision that requires you to do so, if your core values lead you in that direction. There is room for both: a core self that is true to its core values.

Let's also examine a different hypothetical for career decisions that engage analytical propensity rather than artistic drive. In this hypothetical, you learn of an opening to work on the business side of the music industry for an organization that promotes music festivals. You believe your strong organizational skills, creative marketing ideas, and value orientation toward learning new things make you perfect for the job. There's only one potential problem: the position requires regular public speaking to potential advertisers, as well as for the organization's senior management officials. As in the first hypothetical, your natural inclination is to be low key and quiet, and you see having to do regular public speaking as being out front, in the spotlight in a way that you had hoped to avoid by working on the business side. On the one hand, there is a requirement of your core self to cultivate new skills and make a psychological adjustment. However, to the extent that you value learning new things, taking this position would still permit you to be true to self.

It is helpful to have a framework that helps us make meaningful distinctions between authenticity and misconceptions about it, and to guide our thinking about what is beneficial about authenticity. The hoped-for selves, ideal selves, and possible selves identified by Markus and Kunda are all manifestations of a core, true self.

Does Authenticity Matter?

Personal Impact

In the abstract, being authentically true to one's self is an uncompromising expression of who we are, a worthy career aspiration. But what impact does it have, if any, on us? Wood et al. set out to explore the question of authenticity by creating a tool for measuring it and examining whether there is a connection between authenticity and well-being, which the researchers identify as having two dimensions: subjective well-being and psychological well-being. Subjective well-being has to do with having high life satisfaction and low anxiety and stress. Psychological well-being involves personal growth, positive relations with others, self-acceptance, and purpose in life.

They conducted a two-part study. Study 1 developed a 25-item Authenticity Scale with items representing each of the three factors (previously referenced) of authenticity. For example, statements like "I feel out of touch with the real me," represented self-alienation. Statements like "I always stand by what I believe in" represented authentic living, and statements like "Other people influence me greatly" represented accepting external influence. Two hundred undergraduate students participated in study 1. They then measured the anxiety, stress, and happiness of the participants. Study 2 more closely examined the validity of the Authenticity Scale, for example, to confirm usefulness of the tripod of authenticity factors across gender and ethnic groups and to identify correlations with the Big Five personality traits (the Big Five are discussed in Chapter 2), among other things. Accordingly, the second study was comprised of four different samples, including an ethnically diverse sample (180 working adults in northern England), two college samples (one of 158 undergraduate students, the other 213 second-year psychology students), and a community sample (104 participants).

Some of their findings: (1) They found their Authenticity Scale to be a valid measure of authenticity; (2) the scale related to the Big Five personality traits "with more authentic people being more extroverted, agreeable, conscientious, open, and less neurotic";[6] and (3) authenticity is an important predictor of well-being. In fact, they report that authenticity is one of the strongest predictors of well-being, which is consistent with findings from prior research. (4) Authenticity is linked to self-esteem, a finding that also confirms prior research.[7]

Though being in touch with ourselves, standing by what we believe in, and not being overly influenced by others is not always easy, the Wood et al. research suggests that it is rewarding. The promise of well-being makes authenticity an appropriate framework for sorting through the ought-to's of vocational choices to find not only that vocation which will contribute to your well-being, but that which will be intrinsically *yours*. It is a framework that can help verify if we are walking down a path that is right for us or expose if the path is really better for someone else. Parker Palmer said that authentic vocation comes from our true selves. He eloquently suggests that "Discovering vocation does not mean scrambling toward some prize just beyond my reach but accepting the treasure of true self I already possess."[8] Though input from others can be helpful, we need not rely on parental, societal, or other injunctions to find our way. If we are discerning enough to know ourselves, and bold enough to trust that knowing, vocational authenticity is waiting. Moreover, it carries with it the benefit of general well-being and self-esteem. And that is huge for our personal development. But how socially valued or valuable is authenticity?

Cultural Impact

I took my first class on Impressionism after I completed my undergraduate degree. Though the class was offered by a prominent university in Atlanta, my enrollment in the class was not driven by a desire to receive credit or anything more than a simple interest in learning more about art. Little did I know I would actually gain so much more. To this day that class experience lives in my memory as an academic exploration that yielded not only a deeper interest in art, but an appreciation for the social purposes of art and for the artists that produce it. The class taught me a history of artists that birthed a new movement by defying the artistic norms of the day with respect to light, color, form, and subject matter. Impressionism is so widely revered today and the knowledge of its radical history is now so well known that it is easy to dismiss the truly defiant and authentic spirit from which it originated. By the end of the nineteenth century proof of its impact could be seen by the following that the movement had amassed, and by "the impatience of a younger generation in France to break new ground."[9] It is an example of authenticity inspiring authenticity. Hundreds of years later, millions like me over these past centuries since the movement started would come to value this art form both personally and socially. So recognized is its legacy that it may now be cliché to state that Impressionism represents a movement, not just a way of painting. Nevertheless, it must be said. It was a movement that dared to question art, taste, culture, beauty, and societal norms, and to speak out in new ways with new messages. For example, on the surface the work of Degas depicts the grace and beauty of the ballerina, yet his depictions are decidedly of women at work: a woman trimming a hat, another yawning over an ironing board.[10] These were new ways to "speak" about women and work. These are fruits of creative authenticity.

Artistic movements move us. They connect with something personal within us and wind up saying something that crosses generations globally. Whether we agree with a particular movement's messages or not, the impact of an authentic movement cannot be denied. "New" genres like hip-hop and rap music exemplify today's Impressionism. These contemporary artists have a key motivation in common with Monet and Manet: the desire to express themselves in unconventional new ways with bold, controversial messages and styles of expression. Consequently, like Impressionism's impact on the world of visual art, the cultural impact of rap and hip-hop on music is unmistakable.

Michael Gibson has studied the correlation between hip-hop music and authenticity. He found that "street credibility," a type of industry authenticity, is an important marker for success for those working in the genre.[11] Hip-hop and rap music express specific types of personal experiences ranging from living in "the hood" to being African American and having the race-based experiences associated with being Black in the United States (U.S.). Given the urban and Black American origins of hip-hop and rap, these experiences provide a certain credibility, without which you may not be perceived as an authentic hip-hop artist, which may ultimately impact your cultural influence. In illustrating the importance of authenticity to the genre, Gibson's synopsis of his research recounts the story of Vanilla Ice, who lost credibility as a rapper when he falsified his biography to state that he had an urban upbringing. As a white rapper, Ice may have felt it necessary to establish authenticity through a more urban identity but wound up doing just the opposite. Gibson found that not all hip-hop artists approach or define artistic authenticity in the same ways, which is particularly relevant for artists who want to work in the genre but are white, or who do not fit conventional images of mainstream hip-hop culture. Gibson's study identified three types of hip-hop authenticity tied to specific time periods: (1) hip-hop of the past: an old-school style associated with the late 1990s, "the period when the genre began approaching assimilation into the mainstream;"[12] (2) modern rap that emulates conventional styles but stays relevant and willing to innovate;[13] and (3) authenticity based on exploring innovative hip-hop styles that may define the future, rather than relying and resting on convention of the past.[14]

His study examined how authenticity was expressed in the careers of 35 hip-hop artists in a midwestern state in the U.S. The study sample included 23 Black males, ten white males, and two Black females, a sample he found to be representative of the hip-hop music scene in that state. Most of the artists in the sample could be categorized in one of the three groups described above, formed around commonalities that included not only their style similarities and perspectives about authenticity, but demographic similarities as well. For example, most artists who are part of group 1 (old-school rap) are white, and according to Gibson "do not fit the traditional image of the young, black, MC from the inner city – an image which has been perpetuated by artists, labels and fans alike over the genre's history."[15] Whereas, group 2 (modern rap) was comprised primarily of young, Black men who live in the inner city and some Black women. The third group (innovative hip-hop) was diversified in terms of race, age, and class but only one member of the group was female. Members of both groups 1 and 2 prized a type of artistic authenticity that downplays the importance of economic benefit, i.e., they create because of a love for the art with much less regard for whether they become commercially successful and had a preference for cultural capital like being trendy and hip.

Some artists possess either the economic freedom to pursue artistic authenticity or are willing to make sacrifices for the art and become the prototypical starving artist. They prize authenticity and do not want to be seen as being more concerned with commercial success than with preserving the authenticity of the art. They want to avoid becoming or being labeled as "sellouts."

Selling Out

When asked what genre of music I sing, I usually respond "it's a jazzy style, kind of sprinkled with R&B and both secular and sacred messaging." *A jazzy style.* In the past I have been hesitant to refer to myself as a jazz artist. Having interacted with the genre through research, teaching, and consumption, I am aware of some of its defining distinctions, often promulgated by jazz artists and critics, and have wondered if I dare claim to belong to an art form with such particularities of structure that require special mastery. Deviations from performing an art form in the "purest" sense may appear inauthentic, particularly if digressions are invented to increase commercial appeal. When it comes to commercial achievement, Kenneth "Kenny G" Gorelick is a jazz musician who has been enormously successful. He has been cited as "the highest-selling instrumental musician in modern times and one of the best-selling artists of all time, with over 75 million records sold."[16] Yet an internet search on Kenny G yields a few results with headers like "Why is Kenny G so hated by jazz purists?" There have been some jazz artists and critics who have been critical of his musicianship, but that does not fully capture the nature of the criticism he has received, which also seems to include whether he plays "real" jazz. For example, in a *Jazztimes* article written by George Varga in 1999, Gorelick indicated that he wanted to expand his repertoire to include some "classic instrumental songs, like maybe a Louis Armstrong song."[17] Shortly after the article was published Gorelick released an album that, indeed, featured Armstrong's "What a Wonderful World." Nevertheless, some critics took issue with his foray into what Varga referred to as him doing "real" jazz, as opposed to the smooth jazz style for which he is best known. The requirement to produce music that conforms to the requisites of "real" jazz can impose a standard of authenticity that could conflict with an individual musician's sense of authenticity, even if your goal is, as Kenny G said, to "find the right songs and do them in a way that won't compromise their integrity, while letting me be true to myself,"[18] versus selling more records, which Gorelick specifically said he was not trying to do, according to the Varga article. The reason for the criticism is unclear, as are the criteria that might erase it.

Not only does jazz have structural requirements for musicians, it can be mystifying to listeners, particularly some of the Avant Garde sub-genres of jazz. Like perceptions of classical music that the art is best understood through study or a specific kind of listening, jazz has an elitist air despite stereotypical associations with it as having a grittiness, those old images of performances in dark, smoky basements by drug-addicted artists that once characterized descriptions of it. When composer Aaron Copland wrote *What to Listen for in Music*, published in 1939, one of his goals was to help the listening public develop a keener sense of music appreciation, wherein he pointed to the building blocks of music like harmony, melody, form, and structure. Copland contended that if you want to maximize your appreciation for music, you need to know how to listen to it. Some would say the same is true for jazz, which many see as a type of indigenous American classical music.

Although we may not think of hip-hop as requiring a guidebook to lead us in how to listen to it, like classical music or jazz, Jay-Z asserts that one of the problems with the controversiality of hip-hop is that people don't know how to listen to it. In his autobiography, *Decoded*, he says as much: "The problem isn't in the rap or the rapper or the culture. The problem is that so many people don't even know how to listen to the music."[19] In fact, the book's title hints at the insights that might lie between its covers, not only about Jay-Z, but about decoding the culture and nature of the hip-hop and rap music industry, getting to the authenticity that resides not just within a genre, but within its artists.

There can certainly be a tension between making art for art's sake – e.g., honoring a genre's structural integrity – and making art for the sake of making money, particularly if the commercial objective appears to compromise the art. When the latter is perceived to occur an artist is not really applauded for legitimately meeting her financial needs; rather, such an artist may be labeled a "sellout," which is regarded as a form of inauthenticity. What is shaping this tension? What does it mean to "compromise" an art form? Where does the pressure to sell art in its "purest," most authentic form come from? How do we know what is authentic art? Does cultural capital negate economic capital?

In general, capital refers to resources and advantages that provide some form of empowerment. Economic capital includes currency and resources like cash and property that yield financial independence and economic empowerment. The term "cultural capital" was coined by Pierre Bourdieu, who was a French professor of sociology at the Collège de France. Bourdieu wrote over 20 books and hundreds of articles analyzing the relationship between art, literature, and culture from an interdisciplinary perspective and examining the impact of art and literature on society. His concept of cultural capital acknowledges that just as there is social and economic capital, cultural capital is a type of knowledge that empowers members of society to "accurately" interpret the meaning of art and literature, a type of cultural competence. Since the core of Bourdieu's writings focus on cultural production, cultural capital also refers to the type of knowledge that deems some art legitimate and other cultural products illegitimate. How does one distinguish between the two? By possessing the kind of knowledge – cultural capital – that helps one to discern that which is aesthetically valid, i.e., authentic. Consumers and music critics possess cultural capital. If either group does not like your work, they can impact its commercial success if they choose not to buy it or to encourage others to consume it. Therein lies the tension for artists: *should* you produce jazz, country, hip-hop, pop music, or other music to align with evidence of consumer expectations, for example, through top positions on charts like *Billboard*, or number of plays on Spotify, YouTube, or radio? Or *should* you create music based on standards of excellence and authenticity that align with the genre's form – for example, producing "real" jazz – and esteem consumer reactions as secondary? Or are there other inquiries within us that replace "should" (often a red flag concerning authenticity) with a different interrogation?

Living authentically usually comes at a cost, literally. Some impressionists like Monet and other visual artists like Van Gogh and Gaugin lived in poverty, personifying the paradigm of the starving artist. You may recall reading Ben Hubbird's response when I asked him why he chose not to become a full-time artist; he specifically mentioned the tension between art and commerce.

I grew up in the punk rock ethos where expecting to make a living from your art was almost frowned upon or at least the commercialization of art was very suspect. And I still think that the most interesting art isn't made for those reasons. The premise that artists have to starve to make good work is obviously flawed, but I think there is a lot to be said for art that isn't made with the intention of financial gain. There's a tendency towards predictability I guess when you have a built-in financial incentive to make art that will sell. Part of the value of that ethos is that it removes that incentive. "Just make art, we're not trying to make money."

But do you have to choose between art and money in order to be authentic? Hip-hop has challenged that perception. In 2017 Nielsen reported that for the first time ever, hip-hop overtook rock to become the dominant genre in album and streaming consumption in the U.S.[20] That consumption translates into wealth for artists who are at the top of those charts. For example, *Forbes* magazine reported that Jay-Z, Diddy, and Dre are the richest musicians of any genre. How rich? According to *Forbes*, Jay-Z's fortunes grew from $810 million to $900 million over the preceding year.[21] As of October 2017, *Forbes* estimated his wealth at $5.8 billion.[22] Some of these artists' incomes, like Jay-Z's, are not based solely on music. But the origins of the music are about saying what the artists felt authentically needed to be said. As Jay-Z observes in his book, "the great hip-hop writers don't really discriminate. They take whatever's at hand and churn it into their work. Whatever feeling demands a release at a given moment finds its way out in the songs."[23] That sounds like it would meet the tripod of Wood et al. for authenticity: knowing and being in touch with self, being true to self, and not basing actions on the expectations of others. That certainly fits hip-hop!

One of the participants in Gibson's hip-hop study observed, "You want to keep what you do genuine, but at the same time you have to be smart if you want to survive."[24] The survival he mentions speaks of maintaining both economic and cultural capital. Therefore, this perspective reflects a degree of balance and practicality. Gibson says aesthetic legitimacy is marketable, which is a pathway to financial success and fame, and there is nothing wrong with making music for money within the confines of the law. In fact, the history and nature of U.S. copyright law – the law that protects creative products – were designed to afford the kind of protection that facilitates profiting from your creative work. Copyright law has a built-in incentive for authenticity in that it requires that creative works possess a level of originality to be protected. The legal structure of creative works is built on a foundation intended to foster innovation, supporting authenticity. And if authenticity is the thread that is woven throughout the fabric of the creative industries, living authentically is vital for music business creatives and logicians alike.

Living Authentically

Authenticity and Calling

The Career Duality model's proposition that authenticity and calling are synergistically tied to each other is supported by career theorists. For example, K.B. Homan suggested that calling relates to a quest for authentic existence.[25] Richard J. Leider and David A. Shapiro asserted that "Until we heed our calling, we're not living authentically; we're adopting someone else's model for who we should be."[26] While authenticity represents the "ought to" world, calling – as discussed in prior chapters – is the passion that represents our innermost desires, the "want to" world. Each has its rightful place in career decision making. Inauthenticity impedes calling, but authenticity supports and leads back to it.

The Anti-Authenticity Trap: Who Are You Trying to Please?

I began working on my first studio music project around the same time that I started my law practice as a full-time endeavor. Though I began practicing entertainment law in 1994, I had done so on a part-time basis on the side, with written permission from my employer, for several years. I launched it as my sole source of income in 2003, thereby resigning from my day job. I was excited about building my practice and often shared my enthusiasm with my circle of friends and professional acquaintances whenever they asked what I was working on. Some would ask, "but what are you doing with your music?" Not impressed by my lawyering activities. So, I ramped up my songwriting and worked all the more earnestly on recording my album. I was excited about my music project and often shared that enthusiasm with friends and acquaintances. Some responded "that's nice, but I want to hear about what's happening with your law practice." Not impressed with my music activities either. I think you get the picture. Perhaps they weren't such nice people. Or maybe it was an unrealistic expectation to think that everyone or anyone should share my enthusiasm for these pursuits that were so important to me. But wait, that's the point: to whom were my activities important? Fact: you cannot please everyone. Fiction: you should try to please as many people as you can. I didn't seem to be pleasing anyone at the time. Question: *Who are you trying to please?* While input from external sources can be helpful, it is important to remain in touch with ourselves and our values, authentically ascertaining our motives for processing that input.

Therefore, authenticity is a helpful device for avoiding the anti-authenticity trap of making career decisions aimed at obtaining someone else's approval. That is a no-win proposition, a trap from which there is no escape, except to make your own authentically driven decisions. A math analogy offers a practical way of thinking about how to practice authenticity for making decisions in connection with calling. In elementary school you learned that the way to check your subtraction was through addition. For example, in calculating 3,000 minus 2,000, if the answer you calculated (known as the "difference") was 1,000, you would add the difference to 2,000 to check your math, and if that answer added up to 3,000, you would know your subtraction was correct. 3000 represents where you started, and if you wound up back there, then you knew that your calculations led you to the right place and the right answer. Calling is the place we want to get back to for authentic living. Here's how an authenticity equation looks:

Authenticity Equation: Calling minus external input = Authenticity

Want to check your "math?" Add authenticity (using the definitions and discussion in this chapter) to any external input you have received. Does the external input override, negate, or eviscerate your calling, or does it lead back to it? If the input does not lead back to your calling, then it is feedback that may lead instead to inauthenticity and may warrant being set aside. If your calling is still in the formation stages, i.e., you are searching for or verifying its presence, you may be inclined to accept feedback as a way of figuring out your calling. However, you need an anchoring point of some kind, or the input you receive will have you tossed about like a wave on a sea. Authenticity – that combination of personal values and beliefs that comprise your unique self – is the guidepost that can help to identify or verify your calling. Likewise, responding to calling yields authenticity.

Branding for Personal and Cultural Impact

Branding has been a popular and relevant but sometimes stale topic for entertainment professionals over the past 20 years. Music industry creatives and logicians alike are encouraged to identify a personal brand and to communicate it clearly and often. Yet the whole idea of branding can come off looking unoriginal, overworked, and smack of that trying-too-hard feel, if your underlying motive is to be remembered like a hackneyed television commercial. While a comprehensive discussion of branding is outside the scope of this book, taking a moment to address it briefly within a discussion of authenticity makes sense. And the thought is simply this: authenticity first. The first order of business with respect to branding – before identifying a brand, before even deciding what that might look like or mean for you – is to identify your core values, beliefs, and preferences. Once you have that in mind, branding will be more a matter of simply sharing the real you than displaying a marketing persona that is a cheap imitation of who you really are. Once you lay the foundation of authenticity, you will be on your way to having the personal and cultural impact that is the ultimate goal of effective branding.

Success

We are taught to believe in happy endings. Even if we were not taught it, we would want them; it's just our human way. Generally speaking, we want Cinderella to wind up with Prince Charming. We want Mulan – an animated character rather different from Cinderella – to defeat her country's enemies, save both her family's and country's honor, and still wind up with the prince. We want happy endings in the realm of career too. We want success. For many, career success means attaining fairy tale-like endings. Yet when we are authentic, as David Smith's words attest, that is often when success – the kind of success that we define for ourselves – can result.

> *And I can kind of elaborate on something here. So, after I had kind of dropped pursuing music, and nothing was working out, I'm obviously getting a little Nashville bitter, the Nashville blues, whatever they call it when things aren't going your way musically. I said, I'm done with writing with people, I'm not liking these country songs anyway, they're not what I like to write, because I was more R&B, hip-hop, and I'm writing this what I thought was cheesy country stuff. So I stopped booking co-writes, and kind of got just sick of music for a little bit, a little bitter when I got into banking. But after a while I'm like I'm just gonna write by myself. And writing by myself got me back to enjoying music again and being authentic and real to myself and who I am as a writer. And during that time, I think I grew the most as a writer. Because I was writing for me, I was writing my experiences, my style, it really gave me a voice in the room. So when people started hearing those songs my calendar started booking up with co-writes like crazy. And I had a better voice in the room... But I had the freedom to explore that because of my business life, because it was paying the bills. So now I don't have to get that Luke Bryan cut, I don't have to try to be that guy in the room now. I can write what speaks to me and what speaks to you is more than likely going to speak to more people than just trying to get this cut.*

Discussion Questions

1. What is the Wood et al. authenticity model? Define each of its components.
2. How is cultural capital different from economic capital?
3. What is the connection between impressionism and hip-hop music? How does that connection relate to authenticity?
4. What do authenticity and calling have in common? How are they connected?

EXERCISE SET 7: AUTHENTICITY MAPPING

The objective of this exercise is to inventory and reflect on your own authenticity. Create an authenticity map (Figure 7.1) by answering the questions below.

1. *Inventory:* What are your core values, beliefs and preferences?
2. *Self-knowledge:* On the artistic side, my messaging is jazz hymns and sacred music. What messaging is uniquely yours, from your experiences and connected to your core values and beliefs?
3. *Authenticity:* (a) Whom are you trying to please? (b) What would it take to get you to answer the question with "me"?
4. *Personal impact:* Both authenticity and calling are linked with well-being. Reflect on the state of your well-being today. If you want to work on it, how might being authentic contribute to improving it?
5. *Cultural impact:* What do you want your cultural impact to be? Does it lead back to calling?

FIGURE 7.1 Authenticity map

Notes

1 *Merriam-Webster's Collegiate Dictionary*, 10th edition (Springfield, MA: Merriam-Webster, 1993).
2 Alex M. Wood, P. Alex Linley, John Maltby, Michael Baliousis, and Stephen Joseph. "The Authentic Personality: A Theoretical and Empirical Conceptualization and the Development of the Authenticity Scale," *Journal of Counseling Psychology* 55, no. 3 (2008): 386.
3 Hazel Markus and Ziva Kunda, "Stability and Malleability of the Self-Concept," *Journal of Personality and Social Psychology* 51, no. 4 (1986): 859.
4 Herminia Ibarra, "The Authenticity Paradox: Why Feeling Like a Fake Can Be a Sign of Growth," *Harvard Business Review* (January–February 2015): 58.
5 Silviya Svejenova, "The Path with the Heart: Creating the Authentic Career," *Journal of Management Studies* 42, no. 5 (July 2005): 951.
6 Wood et al., "The Authentic Personality," 395.
7 Wood, et al., "The Authentic Personality," 396.
8 Parker Palmer, *Let Your Life Speak: Listening for the Voice of Vocation* (San Francisco, CA: Jossey-Bass, 2000): 10.

 9 William Gaunt, *The Impressionists* (Singapore: Barnes & Noble, 1995): 44.
10 Gaunt, *The Impressionists*, 244.
11 Michael Gibson, "'That's Hip-Hop to Me!': Race, Space, and Temporal Logics of Authenticity in Independent Cultural Production," *Poetics* 46 (2014): 39.
12 Gibson, "'That's Hip-Hop to Me!'", 44.
13 Gibson, "'That's Hip-Hop to Me!'", 46.
14 Gibson, "'That's Hip-Hop to Me!'", 49.
15 Gibson, "'That's Hip-Hop to Me!'", 43.
16 Brittany Frederick, "Jazz Saxophonist Kenny G Highest Selling Instrumental Musician in Modern Era," *AXS*, August 16, 2014, www.axs.com/jazz-saxophonist-kenny-g-the-highest-selling-instrumental-musician-in-16894.
17 George Varga, "Kenny G Changes His Tune," *Jazztimes*, May 1, 1999, https://jazztimes.com/features/kenny-g-changes-his-tune/.
18 Varga, "Kenny G Changes His Tune."
19 Shawn Carter, *Decoded* (New York: Spiegel and Grau, 2010), 54.
20 Nielsen Company, "2017 U.S. Music Year-End Report," January 3, 2018, www.nielsen.com/us/en/insights/reports/2018/2017-music-us-year-end-report.html.
21 Zack O'Malley Greenberg, "The *Forbes* Five: Hip-Hop's Wealthiest Artists 2018," *Forbes*, March 1, 2018, www.forbes.com/sites/zackomalleygreenburg/2018/03/01/the-forbes-five-hip-hops-wealthiest-artists-2018/#1761cb5147c1.
22 Luisa Kroll, "*Forbes* 400 2017: Meet the Richest People in America," *Forbes*, October 17, 2017, www.forbes.com/sites/luisakroll/2017/10/17/forbes-400-2017-americas-richest-people-bill-gates-jeff-bezos-mark-zuckerberg-donald-trump/#769a115f5ed5, accessed August 21, 2018.
23 Carter, *Decoded*, 263.
24 Gibson, "'That's Hip-Hop to Me!'" 47.
25 K.B. Homan, "Vocation as the Quest for Authentic Existence," *Career Development Quarterly*, 35 (1986): 15, in Robert B. McKenna, Juliann Matson, Deanna M. Haney, Olivia Becker, McKendree J. Hickory, Diana L. Ecker, and Tanya N. Boyd, "Calling, the Caller, and Being Called: A Qualitative Study of Transcendent Calling," *Journal of Psychology and Christianity* 34, no. 4 (2015): 295.
26 Richard J. Leider and David A. Shapiro, *Whistle While You Work: Heeding Your Life's Calling* (San Francisco, CA: Berrett-Koehler, 2001), in Justin M. Berg, Adam M. Grant, and Victoria Johnson, "When Callings Are Calling: Crafting Work and Leisure in Pursuit of Unanswered Occupational Callings," *Organization Science* 21, no. 5 (September–October 2010): 974.

8

WRITING YOUR OWN TALE

Charting Your Authentic Career

An Authentic Path: Career Duality

A Career Duality dilemma (CD/Di) arises from being at the crossroads that possessing analytical propensity + artistic drive (A/A/D) can instigate. Therefore, the goal of the explorations in this book is not only to resolve that dilemma, but to envision and create a realm of career possibilities. Synthesizing the concepts of calling and authenticity help us to envision what is possible, while CD is a useful construct for living out those possibilities. Accordingly, the purpose of this chapter is to describe the benefits and challenges of CD, to map out specific how-to's and strategies for managing those challenges while fully exploring the possibilities, with a view toward fashioning a career that is personally authentic and responsive to inner callings, as suggested by the CD model.

A Tale of Two Masters

There is an emotional component that accompanies CD/Di. A/A/D palpably *feels* like a dilemma, at times. The dilemma itself is not just a decision-making quandary about how to fully live out our A/A/D. The dilemma is that it can feel like a practical impossibility to live it out in a way that facilitates authenticity, responds to calling, and is manageable, both internally and externally. This manageability component evokes a scriptural principle found in Jesus' words during the sermon on the mount. He said "No one can be loyal to two masters. He is bound to hate one and love the other, or support one and despise the other. You cannot serve God and the power of money at the same time."[1] Whether you believe or reject the biblical teachings of Jesus, the principle described provides a helpful way of thinking about managing A/A/D. The underlying principle represented in His words speaks of knowing what is most important to you and prioritizing it with a recognition that our highest priority is what we will ultimately honor most. The scripture does not suggest that you cannot have two priorities, but that you cannot serve two priorities *equally* at once. All secondary pursuits will be "hated," "not supported," or "despised." In the context of A/A/D, how can you best "serve" both artistic drive and analytical propensity if not equally? And how do you decide whether you will serve *both*?

The Duality Exploration Grid introduced in Chapter 2 illustrates quadrants of duality that reflect priorities based on time commitments. Depending on the amount of time you spend expressing analytical propensity versus time spent pursuing artistic drive, the grid identifies you as either an Artistic Explorer, Career Dualist, Career Explorer, or Dualist Explorer. The categories offered by the grid are helpful for understanding how your current use of your A/A/D fits with CD. It also illustrates what CD requires, particularly in terms of time. However, time is not the only issue to address in identifying dual priorities. Let's suppose that, according to the Duality Exploration Grid, you are considered a Career Dualist – someone who spends a high amount of time on activities that engage both artistic drive and analytical propensity. If this is the quadrant into which you fit, was this a conscious choice that you said "yes" to? How well are you managing its demands? Is it an authentic choice? Does CD respond to your calling(s)?

I pose these questions to suggest that the *how* of prioritization requires making your own career choices, writing your own story. Career decision making and prioritization can be confusing, uncertain, and stressful. Yet if we think of it as an opportunity to create our own story – complete with plot twists and turns that lead to unpredictable discoveries – we can positively anticipate the narrative as it unfolds since we are the authors and thereby empowered to fashion it as we choose. It is not disastrous if the plot shifts unforeseeably. In fact, it would be pretty uninteresting otherwise. Think of your favorite story, whether told via film, novel, or live theatre. Do you really want to know the outcome before you have had a chance to get to know the characters, experience the suspense, laugh at the jokes? When someone else gives us movie details before we have had a chance to see the film, we call those spoilers and most of us don't like them. We want to go on the journey the story represents, rather than simply jumping to the end of it.

The dualists profiled in Chapter 3 and throughout this book have shaped their own tales, and I have shared some of my own. What is yours, and how will you uniquely define it? For example, there is, of course, no requirement to pursue both A/A/D propensities. There are plenty of music industry creatives who believe that their calling, their story, is to be a full-time musician, artist, songwriter, or composer, even if they have the analytical propensity to work as music industry logicians. Those stories unfold with a solitary focus. The clarity of that focus may take time for them to see, but they shape that vision. On the other hand, some dualists feel a pull to invest artistic drive, but lack authenticity or a sense of calling and wind up not choosing the artistic route.

Life stories are written through a series of choices comprised of rewards and tradeoffs. It is a tale spun through recognition that you alone narrate your options. You are empowered to say either "yes" or "no" to CD. The key is in informed choice. Recognizing potential challenges associated with options helps in preparing to meet them if we choose to. Let's begin with examining the extrinsic and intrinsic challenges associated with putting CD in practice. Intrinsic challenges are conditions created by internal thoughts and feelings, whereas extrinsic challenges are challenges that arise because of external conditions outside of us that we do not control.

Intrinsic Challenges of Career Duality

The Two Masters Phenomenon

The mixed blessing of having both artistic drive and analytical propensity is that we may want to use both aptitudes, which can spin us into many different directions. On the artistic side we may play multiple instruments, sing, write and arrange music, produce, and engineer sound. On the analytical side we may have the propensity to develop and execute detailed plans, manage artists, practice law, start a business, and hold leadership positions in a variety of organizations that may or may not be directly related to the entertainment industry. And why shouldn't we use both sides of our A/A/D if we have both? Isn't that what CD is all about?

A familiar saying attached to having multiple areas of expertise is "Jack of all trades, master of none." The adage describes the individual who knows a little about a lot of things, but a lot about nothing, i.e., who is "master of none." Clearly, there is a time challenge that goes with the frenzy of activity spurred on by being a Jack of all trades. There is also the challenge of sometimes *feeling* like a master of none. Mastery takes time, commitment, strategic planning, and effort, whether for realization of artistic drive or for analytical propensity. On the artistic side mastery involves playing or singing the right notes, wowing an audience, and writing songs that command Grammys, or likes, etc. It also means becoming a part of the music industry community. Then there is the matter of mastering knowledge of your fans, gatekeepers, agents, managers, and specific markets. Mastery also involves knowing who you are as an artist, composer, and performer and conveying that identity to others. On the analytical side mastery of law, accounting, finance, entrepreneurship, innovating business models, or managing artists and entertainment companies is what yields success. It takes effort, discipline, and discernment to develop expertise, market and brand your efforts, and establish contacts. Mastery is the antithesis of being a Jack of all trades and master of none.

The following are examples of situations that might leave you feeling like a "master of none" regarding artistic drive:

- You have not played a live gig in six months or more.
- You find out that a friend who started their musical career at about the same time as you has just signed a publishing deal, and you have never been approached.
- You attend a concert and marvel at the featured artist's skills, then reflect on how little time you spend on honing your playing/singing/writing.

These are situations that could leave you feeling like a "master of none" regarding analytical propensity:

- You have been trying to get your startup company off the ground for over a year with almost no progress or anything to show for your ambition.
- You are struggling financially.
- You attend music industry/law/other entertainment business events and recognize that you know few attendees or interact with them infrequently.

You live and move between both the world of the music industry logician and that of the music industry creative. And you feel special because you have the skills, talent, and ambition to do both. But it is a waltz that can leave you feeling like you don't have a regular dance partner, as you move without a singular focus, which can lead to feeling incomplete as you attempt to navigate each world.

I have lived these feelings on both the artistic and analytical sides. Multi-potentialed persons believe they can do just about anything and excel. Whether that is true or not, it leads to trying lots of things, which could lead to mastering nothing – or feeling like you have not really mastered one thing in particular. Winners of Pulitzer, Grammy, Oscar, Tony, Nobel Peace, and other coveted awards are often those who have invested and devoted singular attention to a particular pursuit, usually over a period of many years. Yet when you work between two worlds, there is the possibility that you may never reach a pinnacle in either sphere, which means that you may never receive those extrinsic rewards, and that could be internally costly. How will you feel if you are a good lawyer – with the propensity to be a great lawyer – but never excel to "great" or receive any legal community recognition because you float between the law and the music industry? Or how will you feel if you are a good songwriter but do not excel to "great" or receive any music industry recognition because you float between songwriting and working as the head of a music industry accounting firm?

How you feel depends on what motivates you to do what you do. For example, in 2016 Bob Dylan was awarded the Nobel Prize in literature. The Nobel Prize recognizes mastery. In fact, the Latin inscription on the gold medal given to recipients reads: "Inventas vitam iuvat excoluisse per artes," which loosely translated means "And they who bettered life on earth by their newly found *mastery*" (italics added). Dylan took a while to publicly comment on having received the award, causing some concern amongst at least one member of the

Swedish academy that grants the prize.[2] Others speculated on whether he valued being a recipient. Dylan later stated that he never expected to receive the award.[3] Perhaps this influenced not only his public comment about it but may also be the reason he is the consummate songwriter master: the pursuit of songwriting for him was apparently more about writing songs than winning prizes. If you are moving between both A/A/D worlds, you may lack the singular focus that typically leads to the highest forms of public recognition. Managing this intrinsic challenge is a real one to consider in contemplating CD.

Feeling the Two Masters Phenomenon

Every "yes" to an activity that engages your analytical propensity is a "no" to activities that engage artistic drive. For example, saying "yes" to starting my entertainment law practice was an effective "no" to working on my album at the same time. Starting a practice meant identifying a business model, raising capital, creating an internet presence, marketing, learning the substantive law well (attending seminars and conferences, purchasing and reading reference books, reading statutes and cases), establishing partnerships with other businesses and firms, engaging administrative and legal personnel, purchasing law-related software and office equipment, finding office space, etc. With that choice I was also choosing to make law the "master" I served in terms of time priority. You're thinking "but you could have still worked on your album." You are correct, yet by choosing my practice as the primary "master" the work on the album was not my priority. Indeed, although I did return to working on my album, starting my practice delayed the album for several years because it got the leftovers of any time and attention that was not devoted to my practice. Every decision carries smaller, imbedded decisions. Consequently, giving more time to practicing law was not the only outcome I was creating. The fact is that I was *enjoying* focusing on my practice. This is the essence of what being a true dualist is like. I am genuinely an analytical person who not only possesses analytical propensity, I *enjoy* being analytical. I also enjoy possessing the ability to sing and write music. Yet if you feed your analytical propensity more, particularly if you enjoy it, it may outgrow your artistic drive. It starts to feel more familiar and comfortable to work in that analytical world. And it starts to feel less familiar and comfortable to feed artistic drive. Then an irony developed: choosing to focus on my practice – as enjoyable as that was – reminded me that I was moving further and further away from music. And that created fear because I would never want to move away from music entirely. This is what I mean by *feeling* the two masters phenomenon: fear and enjoyment coexisting together, to sometimes create anxiety and career confusion.

Another two masters phenomenon involves managing feelings associated with being part of multiple communities, yet "master" of none of those communities. I enjoy being part of bar associations, and there are many that I have been part of, from intellectual property and entertainment law associations, to regional ones, to national ones, to those for lawyers of color. Then there are educator associations, administrator associations, music industry associations, entertainment industry associations, and non-profit associations that engage my art-related interests, like jazz and opera. There are also communities for singers and songwriters. Am I part of all of those communities? Or none of them? Realistically, how much a part of all of them can I be? This is a question of not merely how much time to commit to various organizations. This ambivalence is a matter of being part of multiple communities that all mean something to me, yet having to make some tough choices and managing the mindsets and sacrifices that accompany those choices. If you are a person who likes to roll up your sleeves and be an integral part of a community, like me and other dualists, you will have tough choices to make as a Career Dualist and will need to manage this internal challenge. Even if being a part of professional associations is not particularly important to you, being a part of music industry communities has value. Therefore, you will still need to identify which communities best fit with your CD identity; will it be the communities that engage you analytically, or those which hold the most promise for your artistic drive?

Let's take an example outside the realm of law or community affiliation. You have been working hard at your day job as a copyright administrator and your efforts pay off when the company offers you a promotion. The position is at the managerial level and involves an increase not only in salary but in responsibilities, as well as some required travel. You will need to learn the new scope of work and to put in lots of extra time to perform your job well, but because of your analytical propensity you know that you have what it takes to be successful in this new role. You recognize that there will be some sacrifice involved when it comes to your music. Whether you choose to accept the promotion or not, you have feelings of divided loyalties, realizing that you cannot fully serve your music if you accept the promotion. Your loyalties were already divided because your day job was not serving music full time. Now the promotion threatens to move you yet further away from music, as the new "master" you will honor with most of your time will be the managerial position. The two masters phenomenon has an emotional component to manage if CD is the route you choose as your career path.

Overpowered by Empowerment

Self-knowledge that leads to empowerment has been a consistent theme of this book. The good thing about sensing your own power is that you can marshal the courage to act on it. The flip side of the empowerment coin is that you feel empowered to do *everything*, which can lead to the challenge of feeling and being overwhelmed. Some of this anxiety can be addressed through time management, but this goes beyond the need to manage your time. This requires managing yourself. As I write this chapter I am simultaneously planning a concert that will take place in a month and a half, while planning to present at an academic conference next week, and still meeting the demands of my day job as an administrator and professor. The prospect of planning the concert is exciting, but in reality, there is so much to do for it besides singing (engaging musicians, choosing repertoire, writing music, scheduling rehearsals), and when combined with normal daily activities feels like an awful lot. Does it make me question my commitment to include singing in my life, even infrequently? Yes! Surprised at that response? Singing is so worthwhile and feels like an essential part of me. But pursuit of my artistic drive concurrently with my analytical pursuits can be stressful, nonetheless. The power to say "no" to overdoing either analytical or artistic pursuits requires having internal guideposts like calling and authenticity that remind you of where your true priorities and purposes lie. Listening to those guideposts and disciplining your sense of empowerment is an intrinsic challenge to be managed.

Extrinsic Career Duality Challenges

In some ways, the extrinsic challenges of CD are easier to address than the intrinsic ones. This is true because the extrinsic challenges are familiar, expected, and lack the emotional component associated with the intrinsic challenges. Intrinsic challenges arise in part because you are still contemplating what is most authentic for you in a given moment; the internal authenticity dialogue is an ongoing, unfinished one. Managing the intrinsic challenges requires managing yourself. Therefore, managing extrinsic challenges becomes a simpler task once the intrinsic dialogue is settled. The two primary external challenges of CD are time management and managing the expectations of others.

Time Management

The number of books written on time management over the years could probably fill a football stadium, and then some. There are many methods and philosophical approaches to how to manage your time. Some focus heavily on prioritization, some on daily scheduling, some advocate the use of checklists or specific tools like calendars and planning or task-management apps and software. Whatever time-management methodology you choose, time itself is invaluable. Once spent, it cannot be reclaimed, so allocating it meaningfully is worth doing deliberately, with real intention. Additionally, walking the path of CD can be daunting. Each of us has that finite, unchangeable 24 hours in a day, 365 days, or 52 weeks in a year. And CD requires that the time we have does double duty, fitting dual obligations, whereas someone who does not choose CD can devote all 365 days to a single career focus.

Therefore, before recommending any "how's" concerning time management, it is important to reiterate that CD is a choice. As a preliminary matter, you must genuinely buy into the value of pursuing activities that engage both your analytical propensity and artistic drive. Only then can you accept the potential demands on your time and plan strategically how to manage it. Once you reach that point through saying "yes" to CD, the time-management tips discussed below will be relevant and applicable.

Managing External Expectations

The external expectations of others are insidious, subtle threats to authenticity that can pose both an intrinsic and extrinsic challenge. These expectations exist for all industries. For example, if you are tall, thin, have a trendy, unique fashion sense, and are especially good-looking (in that conventionally defined way often depicted in media advertising), chances are that you have been told that you should consider modeling as a career. That societal assumption likely has nothing to do with your sense of calling, abilities, values, ambitions, or interests. It is simply an expectation that others may have for you. If you do not want to be part of the fashion industry or have modeling for a career, you have to fight that external messaging to forge a different career path. Likewise, if you are musically talented, there will be societal, parental, and other external influences that pressure you to choose music as your full-time career. But good-looking people do not have to be models; they have the right to consider other career options. Neither do all singers and musicians have to choose the music industry as a full-time career. You can choose a path that permits you to engage both the artistic and analytical you. But you will need to manage external expectations to effectuate CD.

Career Duality Benefits

Given the challenges associated with CD, why say "yes" to adopting it as a career plan? My mother has a saying that I believe is profound. In her words, "What works *against* you ought to work *for* you." The sentiment behind the saying is that circumstances or conditions that appear to be disadvantages can and should become advantages when we view them that way. The greatest reward of saying yes to CD is fulfillment of both sides of A/A/D, satisfying the dual call. CD has other benefits too, listed below.

1.   Living CD can help minimize or stave off regret. The difference between CD and simply pursuing two things at once is that both artistic drive and analytical propensity are pursued as dual *careers*. CD provides the opportunity and strategic foresight for implementing both. Realistically speaking, the dual pursuit will impact the scope of your contributions in each pursuit and will create different outcomes than pursuing only one path. Nevertheless, CD compels you to make a career-oriented musical or analytical contribution rather than regretting and imagining the career(s) that might have been.

2. CD expands your career options, particularly through goal setting. You are free to set your own customized goals and prioritize them as you see fit. This frees you to dream as big as you want and to believe that your dreams are empowered by your choices. Setting goals opens the door to an entire subset of options:

    - fuller exploration and use of your abilities;
    - a heightened sense of career fulfillment;
    - participating in the music industry on multiple levels;
    - exploration of multiple callings;
    - answering the "why" career questions through action.

3. Pursuing both sides of A/A/D supports following your callings and living authentically. If using the full panoply of your talents is important to you, CD facilitates meeting that goal.

4. Taking a CD approach encourages you to do inner work, specifically, the inner work of:

    - identifying yourself as a dualist;
    - examining the proportionality of what "masters" you are serving (aided through use of the Duality Exploration Grid).

    Both these tasks assess your current duality, which is a precursor to managing it.

5. You may have unconsciously set goals to pursue both your artistic drive and analytical propensity but have not taken specific actions to do so. CD helps shift those goals to the forefront of your thinking and offers an approach for pursuing the dreams that you have identified as important to you.

6. CD permits making art for art's sake with less financial pressure since one of your careers can financially support the other.

7. There may be other interests outside the entertainment industry that you want to fulfill. If you can successfully manage the challenges of CD, you can develop the skills to manage the challenges of pursuing other competing interests as well, if desired.

8. Dual pursuits can double (or more) your financial options while helping you to experiment with new skill sets and shape your career. Justin Longerbeam shared his experience:

    DJ gigs paid a lot of money, so I started throwing events that also paid money. Engineering in my basement for friends' demos started bringing in money. I started getting to work at this music company so then friends wanted me to help them put out their records. All of those things, spreading myself as thin as possible, while also performing and playing in bands sort of led me through to a path where a career started to take shape.

Charting Your Authentic Career

There are strategies that can be employed to maximize the preceding array of CD advantages and manage its challenges. But life has a certain ebb and flow; CD/Di will occasionally rear its head and adjustments will be needed. There will be times when you need to refocus, reimagine, and return to these strategies. Accept and embrace that reality. This is all part of career management. You can do it. And you can do it with deliberateness and attention to this career "map."

Strategy 1

Celebrate your A/A/D as an aspect of authenticity. This is a strategy for staying energized in those times when you wonder why you've chosen to walk down two roads instead of one. Consciously remember that you are uniquely created and qualified to pursue both analytical propensity and artistic drive. It is a gift of multipotentiality.

Strategy 2

Engage in job crafting and leisure crafting. CD is an avocational approach (where avocation is self-defined) to concurrent employment that facilitates fulfillment of A/A/D through career exploration. Job and leisure crafting (described in Chapter 6) are strategies for executing this avocational approach. When I asked the profiled dualists about whether they considered the work that is not their primary vocation as an avocation, I explained that an avocation falls somewhere between a hobby and a full-time career. Almost invariably, they resisted thinking of their part-time work on either the analytical or creative side as a hobby. In fact, Joel Andrew revealed that engaging in the avocational work is tied to his identity. It isn't just "extra" work.

> *It is certainly more than a hobby for me. It's part of my character, it's what my friends would define me as. It's definitely what my partner would define me as. Almost paramount. Maybe it's because I'm a new lawyer, I've been practicing for about a year. And I've been working in the legal music world for 4–5 years compared to how long I've been a musician. But maybe it's kind of like the mirror I put up around my friends, that I see myself in is that I am a musician first and foremost. But I enjoy tinkering with music, I enjoy plunking around with music if I have free time I will put it into that in the same way that I would into other hobbies... but there was a period when I didn't play music because I'd first started in law school and I thought that was like the right thing that I should focus so intently on law and school because I wasn't the best student. But when I did that I lost a sense of myself, lost a little bit of focus and direction and I didn't have that release like I needed. I mean it's my therapy, it's also how I connect to my friends because all my friends are musicians, or many of them are. Many tours, they were vacation times with my friends as much as they were me expressing myself musically. So definitely more than a hobby. I have yet to figure out*

exactly what it means to me though… and I come from an artistic family… I'd be a bit lost if I didn't play music somewhat frequently.

Strategy 3

Channel your creative side to focus not on what you can't do, but on what you *can* do in heeding the CD call. This book was born in part from my desire to work out my own dual call, and to help others with theirs. But it certainly doesn't contain all the answers or advocate a one-size-fits-all approach. What steps can you take to *creatively* work out yours?

Strategy 4

Manage the intrinsic challenges.

- *Use positive language to recall and affirm who you are.* You are a master of duality, not a Jack of all trades. Or think of yourself as a kind of career renaissance man/woman/person. Imagine/create other positive labels, or jettison the labels altogether in favor of regularly reminding yourself that you are living out your dreams and calling.
- *Manage others' expectations through authenticity,* i.e., be true to yourself. Review Chapter 7 as often as needed or desired and repeat the reflective exercises found there. Occasionally reread your journal entries from this book to affirm yourself with your reflections.
- *Manage your own expectations.* You are human. In addition to your career pursuits you need sleep, fun, time with your family, internal renewal, and other activities that help us to thrive. These are not options. We *need* these inputs to achieve balance, to find joy and meaning in our lives. A satisfying career is icing on the cake, but don't forget to bake the cake! This means that you have to make regular and realistic assessments of what you can and cannot do, and more importantly – accept that self-assessment. Self-knowledge empowers you to trust yourself. I know that I can only perform so many live gigs a year because I want them to be good (not perfect since they won't be), meaningful, and enjoyable. And realistically, since I have a full-time job, there is only so much time I can devote to doing so. How much time I choose to devote to music may be very different from how much time you choose. We set ourselves up for defeat if we expect to do more than we reasonably can, or compare ourselves to others. I am satisfied to perform one or two "big" concerts a year plus possibly play smaller gigs about once a month. That would actually be a lot for me, and I am empowered to adjust down or up as I need or want. What would work for you? Will you accept the expectations you set for yourself?
- *Manage anxiety… and yourself.* CD expands what is on your plate as you endeavor to manage dual careers. And the more we have on our plates, the

more likely we are to encounter stress. However, stress is not generated solely by how much we have to do. It also has to do with how we think and feel about what's on our plates. Some people have less to do than others, yet experience more stress. Stress is connected to thoughts and choices. I can choose to repeatedly tell myself "I have so much to do to get ready for this concert!" or I can choose optimism: "I get to perform this weekend!" Cognitive behavioral therapy (CBT), employed by many psychiatrists and other therapists, offers an approach to managing your behavior through managing your thoughts. I highly recommend three books by Dr. David Burns, MD that offer perspectives and how-to's for thought management through CBT: *When Panic Attacks* focuses on dealing with anxiety; *Feeling Good: The New Mood Therapy* deals with broader self-management issues like procrastination, self-esteem, and depression; and *Feeling Good Together* focuses on using cognitive behavioral therapy to manage how you think about your relationships, including family members, significant others, co-workers, and other relationships. He also has a podcast and website that offer additional resources.[4] Dr. Burns has conducted research on the number of patients who have been helped by reading his books and deems them highly effective. However, if stress or anxiety levels feel unmanageable, you should freely seek out a trained medical or mental health professional, without hesitation, and may choose to put CD on the back burner until you receive the help you need. Remember, CD is a choice that you are empowered to "unchoose" and rechoose at will, depending on what is happening in your life.

- In addition to CBT, spiritual practices offer another approach to self-management. I use a combination of CBT and spiritual practices, e.g., I endeavor to ground my thoughts in scriptural principles, to recall memorized scriptures, to pray daily, and to meditate on specific scriptural passages and principles. This is what is most authentic and effective for me.[5] How or whether you engage in spiritual practices is a personal matter for you to decide. The important thing is to have a strategy for self-management that you are comfortable with, that works for you.

Strategy 5

Manage extrinsic challenges. Once you master the intrinsic challenges, managing the extrinsic ones opens the door to creating an action plan for living a CD choice.

- *Manage your time.* In some ways it is the easiest thing we have to do, not because we have so much time to manage, but because we can choose to recognize that it is a finite commodity that we cannot expand but can certainly maximize through planning. The question is, will we?

a. First, let's not overlook the obvious: (a) Do you have an appointment calendar… (b) that you use? If you don't own one, get one today! If you have one but don't use it, start using it today! An obvious no-brainer, you say? Maybe it is for you; I hope so. But this suggestion is inspired by my regular work with college students who want to do a lot, but do not always seem to implement some really easy, simple, practical ways of getting things done and prioritizing what needs doing. So I'm going to say this: Do not overlook the obvious. It is simply poor planning to try to keep all of your appointments in your head. Free up some brain space and automatically short circuit some measure of anxiety by letting a planning device like a calendar do the work for you. Using it means not just placing appointments in it, but referring to it regularly throughout the day. How many of us have been stood up by someone who says they had the meeting on their calendar but forgot they put it there? Using a calendar means *using* it. Just knowing you have made time in your life for the things you value is helpful. Using our calendars also helps us track when we're over-extended and have bitten off more than we can realistically do in a given day, week, or month. It helps manage anxiety.

b. Time management requires creativity, which your A/A/D gives you. I am really good at finding time to do small tasks. Breaking tasks down into bite-sized pieces helps me feel (and be) productive and also helps with anxiety because those tasks come off my plate. My other go-to anxiety and time-saving device is "fastest first." Let's say I have three things to do: I have sized them up and know that two of them will take about an hour each, but the third thing will take an entire day. I get the two one-hour tasks out of the way first instead of delaying those quick hits with a task that I know will take a while. There are lots of other creative ways to manage time, and such a list would probably be really long! Rather, you can find some good techniques on your own through books, podcasts, and other resources.

c. A book I recommend that links self-management and time-management concepts is *The 7 Secrets of the Prolific: The Definitive Guide to Overcoming Procrastination, Perfectionism and Writer's Block*, by Hillary Rettig. Even though the context is writing, it also applies to music industry practices that require discipline on the creative side, like rehearsing, vocalizing or practicing regularly, and songwriting. It also applies to work in the analytical context, like project planning. You may find another book that you prefer. The key is to use what you read. No matter what techniques you hear or read about, simply reading about them will be ineffective. It's kind of like believing you'll become a great tennis player by reading about it but never picking up a racquet. Unless you put time-management principles in practice, they are guaranteed to *not* work for you. You can start small. Get and use a calendar and go from there. Today.

d. Cultivate thinking of time as something to invest, not just spend. This helps us to recognize just how valuable it is.

e. When I interviewed David Smith, a CD ninja who writes songs prolifically, he talked about scheduling creativity. Yes, *scheduling* creativity, instead of simply waiting for inspiration. It really works and is a practice used by some of the most respected, successful songwriters. There is a catch though: you've got to have and use a calendar to do it.

f. Summers, vacations, retreats, weekends, and sabbaticals offer opportunities to maximize your time away from your primary vocation to kick your CD into high career. You can choose specific times of the year to make a CD choice, instead of trying to fit it into your daily schedule. You do not have to wait for these seasons to live your duality. However, they offer concentrated times to implement leisure crafting. Loren Mulraine uses his summers away from working as a university professor to focus on creating music.

g. A related recommendation comes from Kevin Bruener, who says "Know your rhythms." I wrote most of this book at 4:00am every weekday morning before heading off to work. I discovered that for me, morning is the very best time of the day, and the time when I am most productive. However, I know others who are night owls and that is when they come alive. You have your own rhythm. Find it, work with it.

h. Delegate. You do not have to personally oversee every detail of your life. Really, you don't. And in some areas, you actually need someone else's expertise. Personal assistants, agents, managers, attorneys are all potential delegates that help save time. Their services are not free (though most states have volunteer lawyers for the arts organizations for artists who meet the income guidelines). But these are people who can save you time, anxiety, and often money in the long run. When I was a full-time lawyer, it amazed me how much money a musician would spend on new recording equipment or a new instrument but would not spend on an attorney to protect their songs or businesses. Do not assume services are not affordable. Shop around, but do not let a lack of information keep you from a good thing.

i. When Justin Longerbeam talked about how he used time to shape his career (see CD benefits discussion above), he mentioned spreading himself "as thin as possible." But notice he did not say spreading himself *too* thin, as the saying often goes. I interpret this to mean he was not poorly managing his time or overtaxing himself emotionally and physically. Rather, given his outcomes I believe that he managed himself intrinsically by setting his own expectations, gauged what he could do, and managed his time to work at multiple activities as a Dualist Explorer. Nevertheless, not everyone should "spread themselves thin" nor should you model your career choices after someone else's, like endeavoring to walk in Justin's shoes. Find your own path to shape *your* authentic career *your* way.

- Bottom line: if you are not willing to manage your time, CD is not a good career-management approach for you. But if you can manage your time, the payoff can help positively shape your career.
- *Say "no" to external expectations* and demands from others when you need to. And with CD, you will probably need to say "no" a lot. This actually falls under managing both intrinsic and extrinsic challenges. Sometimes, this can be easier said than done. A book I recommend for some helpful ideas and perspectives about this is called *Not Nice: Stop People Pleasing, Staying Silent and Feeling Guilty… and Start Speaking Up, Saying No, Asking Boldly, and Unapologetically Being Yourself*, by Dr. Aziz Gazipura. This is a strategy for freeing yourself in the most empowered and genuine way. But a preliminary step is to identify what is authentic for you in terms of core values and beliefs, so that you will have a rudder for saying "no."

Strategy 6

Practice gratitude. The research tells us that living authentically is a strong predictor of well-being.[6] If your CD choice is an authentic one for you, acknowledge its benefits; don't take them for granted. Journal these reflections from time to time, or share them with others. And every now and then laugh out loud that you've found a measure of career clarity. Purposely reflect on how beneficial living CD may be, as an authentic choice. Doesn't that make you want to yuck it up, or at least sit back and smile?

Strategy 7

Believe that CD is possible. It can be done. The profiled Career Dualists have made CD work for them, and if they can do it, so can you when you chart your own path and write your own tale.

Strategy 8

Stay flexible. If CD is not working for you, either change how you are approaching it, or even stop doing it. There are three other quadrants in the Duality Exploration Grid besides CD that can all engage A/A/D. You are empowered to find your right fit in the grid. Or you may choose to live outside it.

Life without Career Duality: Contemplating a Different Dream

This book proposes CD as an authentic career path for addressing CD/Di based on first understanding and exploring your A/A/D. It is a recommendation suitable for dualists who *want* to express *both* sides of their A/A/D through dual careers, who find their most authentic selves and/or satisfied calling in doing so. In addition to CD, the Duality Exploration Grid offers additional career quadrants of A/A/D to choose from to actualize duality. However, for some dualists, expressing both sides of their A/A/D vocationally is something they will consider, for example, through reading a book like this, yet there is a pull towards living the dream of working as a full-time music business creative. Therefore, this section addresses this issue in brief in relation to contemplating saying "no" to duality.

To which dualists is this section directed? Take this self-assessment:

1. You are not experiencing CD/Di. That's a big one. In other words, your dilemma is not choosing between a vocation that expresses both analytical propensity and artistic drive. Your dilemma is whether to make the leap to full-time creative.
2. When you read the word "dream" just now concerning being a full-time creative, it kind of leapt off the page for you. Something in you may have said, "yeah, that's me."
3. You have worked through the book's chapter exercises and comprehend the CD concepts. Having done so, you do not sense a dual call and base it on having done all of the personal assessments.
4. You believe you have what it takes to make it as a full-time music business creative. This is based on your own self-assessment.
5. You are willing to do the work and withstand the sacrifices it takes to make your dream live.
6. You have done the research needed to assess (5) above, i.e., you understand what work and sacrifices may be required to be a full-time creative.

If you can place a check mark next to most of these statements, CD will probably not feel like a satisfactory path for you. And if so, you owe no explanations or apologies to anyone for choosing what you believe is best for you. Only you know whether the music business creative route is the path for you, and whether it will yield your idea of success. Determining what "making it big" means will be different for everyone; this gets back to the discussion in Chapter 7 of what constitutes authentic success for you.

There are also some practical realities to consider. According to Next Big Sound, a company that analyzes data trends in the music industry, over 90 percent of the artists in their analytics system "have less than 3% of the total fans and plays" on YouTube, Facebook, and Vevo.[7] In other words, over 90 percent of the artists in their database would be considered undiscovered. Because of the small number of musicians who achieve the superstar dream or whatever their definition of success is, conventional wisdom says that your career-planning process should include both a Plan A – following your passion – as well as a Plan B – a fallback alternative, for example, obtaining a college degree – in case your Plan A fails. Chuck Harmony shared his perspective on Plan Bs when I asked him whether he considered music an avocation.

> *I don't have an outside job other than music. I've been that way since I was 17. I started as a musician at church and from that point on I've been feeding myself from music this whole time. I never really believed in Plan Bs. So as far as one-track mindedness can take you that's how I've been about music. It's just like this is it, win, lose, or draw, til death do us part; let's go this, this music.*

Taking a look at the trajectory of Chuck's career sheds additional light on his perspective. Chuck found tremendous success as a producer and is now a self-proclaimed Career Dualist who is spreading his creative wings as a producer-turned-artist plus music industry CEO. His passion has always been music, but it has not always been expressed the same. It has been multifaceted.

Can you pursue the creative path in a CD-like way? You can certainly choose to work another job in order to support yourself while pursuing your musical ambitions, as discussed in Chapter 2 and throughout this book. However, recall that doing so is not a CD choice; that is simply doing two things at once. Rather, if you choose the path of going for your creative career, that is a single-purpose road, while CD is not. A CD choice is one that pursues two careers simultaneously and is fully supportive of both. Whereas, the music industry creative path looks and feels like the opposite of a CD choice, as it will require the dedication of serving one and only one master – the musical dream.

This leads back to contemplating CD or duality. Having a Plan B is a kind of dual plan, but not the CD planning described in this book. Planning and goal setting are important to career strategizing. Depending on the type of artist career you want to have, there is a level of dedication, an investment of self that makes pursuing a *simultaneous* Plan B impractical, depending on your goals. You could pursue a college degree, but at the same time as the artist dream? You cannot serve two masters equally and simultaneously. If you want both the college degree and the music industry creative career, you can consider getting your degree first, then pursue the creative career without distraction after the degree is complete. If you do not achieve the level of success you self-define, you can identify your Plan B at that time with college degree in hand. Some parents will prefer the "college-first" path. Parents generally want what is best for you and usually have a wealth of wisdom and experience to share; therefore, talking with them about your ambitions is often a good idea (depending on your age). However, as an adult you will ultimately have to chart your own course, which is what this chapter is all about. The concepts offered in this book can help in determining where your authenticity lies. Making a choice to really go for the gusto on the creative side is a wonderful option that will be most authentic for some. Moreover, if this is your calling, you owe it to yourself to pursue it. For you, CD may wind up as a Plan B or future path. Others will choose the CD path. And others, moving from music industry logician to creative, or from music business creative to logician – one path at a time through career transitions – is the story some will choose to write.

Career Transitions

Solomon, believed by some to be the wisest king who ever lived, said "to everything there is a season and a time to every purpose under the heaven."[8] Some dualists will choose to pursue the full-time artist path for a season, then that season will give way to something different. When I was awarded tenure by my university, my sister congratulated me by sending me a beautiful plant basket with several different species. Historically, I have not considered myself to have much of a green thumb, sadly resulting in the demise of many plants over the years. But I was determined to keep this basket alive. Fast forward five years later, and it has been a rocky road, but it lives! Along the way, however, I have lost some species. After leaving the plants in their original basket for a couple of years, I finally decided to transplant them to a bigger pot. Not long after that I discovered a small, folded, green shoot emerging from the soil. It grew bigger and bigger and started to slowly unfurl until I could recognize that it was one of the "lost" species. You cannot imagine my excitement! That lone shoot is now a fully developed plant with many new leaves that I enjoy caring for. But more importantly, that little plant taught me something: Dormancy is a temporary state. The life is still there, and being revived may just be a matter of having the right soil, light, environment, food, and attention. The goal is not simply to make a CD choice, but to find the soil in which you will thrive. Transitions can be life-giving.

Career Transitionists

I had been noticing and even scouting newspaper articles about lawyer/musicians for a few years. Then one day in 2015 while reading the *Tennessee Bar Journal*, I saw a feature on an entertainment attorney who was a musician-turned-lawyer. Believing the lawyer's story would fit perfectly within the contours of this book, I clipped the article with the intention of meeting and interviewing her. That attorney was Meredith Collins. She was the first person I interviewed, yet her story appears nearly at the end of this book because her story of duality is different. Meredith is a career transitionist. The transitionist is not represented on the Duality Exploration Grid because the transitionist represents someone who focuses on one music industry career path at a time despite possessing A/A/D. Chuck Harmony and Claude Kelly were music industry creatives who transitioned to become Career Dualists. Meredith Collins was a music industry creative, then a Dualist Explorer, and now works outside the entertainment industry altogether.

Meredith Collins (Nashville, TN), Health Care and Corporate Transactional Attorney

I was really young when I was a full-time musician, my sophomore year in high school, which would have been 1998, I guess that's right. So I was 16 when I withdrew from my public school in Mississippi and pursued music full time. My mom was a teacher so she quit teaching, she taught fifth grade, she quit teaching and basically home schooled me for my last two years of high school while I traveled and pursued music. And that was sort of my journey, was very different in that it was very fast and opportunities, wonderful opportunities, were just handed to me. I was not the person who moved to Nashville and lived with six other people and slept on the floor and like stood on the street corner and played my guitar and really tried to make it. I just happened to know several people who were in the music industry and they were willing to give me opportunities and I simply accepted those opportunities. So everything was very fast and I was very green when I started the process. And you know, I was also very young. My mother, I remember her buying *Everything You Need to Know about the Music Business*, Volume 1,[9] you know, and just trying to read about it and learn about it and help me make smart decisions. All that to say what I knew about the music business was my experience, and nothing else. And so I had a record deal, I had a management agreement, I had a publishing deal right off the bat. And three years down the road when my option was up for renewal and my record deal, the label decided not to exercise my option. And in my mind at that time, especially if you're a country music singer and you don't have a record deal then how are you gonna do anything? And that was certainly before the age of like Napster and independent artists and I was just like how am I gonna do this if I don't have a record deal?… the timing of it worked out really well because I believe I lost my deal in May or June of 2001 or 2002, I guess it would have been 2002. And I would have otherwise been starting college the following August. So it just seemed to make sense for me to just apply to college and get an education. My parents were very adamant about that. They didn't care where I went, they just wanted me to go to college. So once I enrolled at Belmont I still sort of dabbled in the music industry and I was still performing and I still kept in touch with several people and I was still writing because I was still under my publishing agreement. But it just, I was in college and there was this whole other like life, and I felt like I had been burned by the music industry and it just wasn't appealing to me anymore. So I was 18 or 19 at the time and I said I'm going to do something else. And I've always been a pretty ambitious person in my mind. I was like I need to be successful and I'm obviously not successful at this music thing, so what else can I do to be successful?

Why did you decide to become a health-care and corporate transactional attorney?

When I was a summer associate at Bass, Berry, and Sims, which is where I practice now, the summer of 2008, so that was right before my 3L year at law school, the economy had not crashed yet at that point but I think things were starting to head south. And there are several different practice groups at our law firm… And I didn't want to do litigation so I was like what's going on in this corporate space. I knew Bass Berry had a health care group that was sort of imbedded in their corporate group. In my mind, as the economy was starting to sort of tank I thought well that seems like a stable area, health care law. There's always gonna be health care laws and regulations. People are always gonna need to understand those rules. That seems like something that could be very interesting and also stable. So I chose that practice group… Fortunately, they offered me a job and I considered myself to be very fortunate at that point, given the economy and the legal market. So that's how I initially got started. And it was purely because of my quest for a job, to have a job.

Would you ever switch entirely to music or entertainment?

No. Not at this point. Sometimes I think about what life would've been like had I just stuck with it. But I also believe that everything happens for a reason. And we certainly have free will and make choices but I think things were meant to happen the way that they happened. When I left Bass Berry in 2015 to try practicing entertainment law full time that was something that had always been in the back of my mind, given my background. Like "I wonder if I can actually do this," and it just sort of makes sense. Like I know music and I know music business. And so I had to try that and I did. I spent 22 months doing it and it became very clear to me that that was not where I was supposed to be either. But I had to do it. I mean I was very fortunate to be able to go back to my initial legal job. Yeah, I consider myself very fortunate.

If you had it to do all over again, which would be primary between music and law?

It's hard to say. I'm very fortunate, I'm very blessed currently. And so it's hard to say that I would do anything differently. I really like my job and I really like the people I work with. And as I have gotten older I have realized that for me that is a very, very important piece of the puzzle. Being in an environment, really 75 percent of your time, it is very important that I like the people that I'm around and enjoy the people that I'm around. And that's probably the primary reason that I like to do what I do right now, and then second being that I do like to practice. But the people and the environment is very important to me. I've always known that was important but it took me leaving Bass Berry to figure that out. 'Cause that's one of the reasons I did not enjoy practicing entertainment law. It's because it is very much it's a siloed profession, so much of it you can do on your own. I think many people are gifted at that and I could do it but I just didn't enjoy it.

Goals: I'm up for partner year after next. So I want to make partner... I don't necessarily care about the status or the money. It's just I want my colleagues to be able to rely on me and to respect me as somebody who can make those decisions, if that makes sense. So that's really at the forefront of my mind. Otherwise, I want to just be able to keep doing what I'm doing... and to be able to continue to help support my family.

Continuing to "keep doing what she is doing" is completely different from the life she once lived as a musician and no longer includes playing or performing music, even as a hobby. Now when she sings, it is for her young son.

Awards and honors: when I was younger I would win talent competitions all the time. I remember when I was singing, and you've probably had the same experience, but I was a member of the, whatever the association is that votes on the Grammys[10] and I remember seeing my name on the Grammy ballot and thinking that was the coolest thing. It's so odd, it was very unexpected, but I remember seeing it and thinking, wow, like I made it to appear on the ballot? And that was it, but it was still really cool. On the business side: I was just named one of *Nashville Lifestyle*'s rising stars in the legal industry for corporate and business law.

Career Decision Making and Making a Career Duality Choice

Saying yes or no to CD, or making a career transition – which way to go? These choices can actually be more complicated for dualists. Kathy J. Rysiew, Bruce M. Shore, and Rebecca T. Leeb took a comprehensive look at the research on multipotentiality (introduced in Chapter 2) and noted a common finding amongst researchers that career choice is particularly difficult for multipotentialed individuals because of their many interests and abilities.[11] Accordingly, they offered recommendations for helping multipotentialed persons, like dualists, navigate career choice. One of their recommendations is to lean into the multiplicity of interests through the use of concurrent career paths, i.e., pursuing more than one interest or ability at the same time, specifically through leisure activities or "job molding."[12] This suggestion is at the heart of CD, and is reminiscent of the job and leisure crafting suggested by Berg, Grant, and Johnson described in Chapter 6. Rysiew, Shore, and Leeb also recommended seeking career guidance (for example via a book like this one) that recognizes the complexity of decision making for the multipotentialed. Their third suggestion is that multipotentialed decision makers manage their career expectations. This recommendation is based on an analysis of literature that points to a perfectionistic outlook amongst multipotentialed persons, who are often looking for the "perfect" career.[13] It may sound obvious, but no career is perfect, including those in the music industry. So, it is unwise to tie vocation decisions to unrealistic career expectations. Instead, David Smith recommends remaining flexible.

Be open to the opportunities that come your way… Explore. Be interested. Be curious.

The simplicity of this perspective helps to cut through the complexity of multiple interests and perfectionistic tendencies. It is also a perspective that is working particularly well for David, who is living out his CD choices and for whom many opportunities have, indeed, come his way. After his interview for this book, this vice president of music entertainment at Pinnacle Bank was offered multiple publishing deals that would permit him to keep his job at the bank and write twice a week, which is precisely what he wanted. He signed a deal with Reviver Publishing in October 2018 and his Josh Gracin song "Good for You" was released on Spotify and Apple Music at the same time the deal was inked. He is writing his own tale, charting his authentic CD path.

Voices of Duality

All of the profiled dualists were asked about how they make career decisions. Specifically, I asked "What led you to pursue your primary vocation as primary?" I then gave them some responses to choose from, and asked them to rank the choices in terms of what most influenced the decision, to what was least influential. The response chosen by over half of the dualists was self-clarity, defined in the survey as "I know myself and my abilities." You may recall from Chapter 7 that self-knowledge is an aspect of authenticity. Therefore, these responses indicate that authenticity played an important role in their decisions.

I also asked, "On a scale of 1 to 5, how well does your primary vocation describe you?" This question assessed congruence, also described in Chapter 7 as a pillar of authenticity. The average score was 4, "It describes me pretty well." Another win for authenticity.

Their perspectives reflect the CD model introduced in Chapter 2, which ends with authenticity as the final tier. Each tier of the model builds on a prior one, offering a progressive way of thinking about CD and career decision making. CD/Di, the second tier of the model, is key in determining whether a CD choice offers a good fit for you. Of all the profiled dualists, those who fit within the CD quadrant are those who experience CD/Di, the decision-making quandary about A/A/D, most strongly. For example, Claude Kelly and Chuck Harmony felt the call to pursue their analytical propensity when they realized that the business of music was not working optimally to serve all their artistic or business needs. Nevertheless, they responded to that analytical call in order to advance their artistic drive, not to abandon it. When Kevin Bruener was a full-time artist, he was the band member who expressed analytical propensity in marketing the band and continues to express it as a marketing vice president for CDBaby. Yet he makes it clear that he can't ever let his artist dream die. Exercising a CD decision makes it possible for him to keep that dream alive and stave off CD/Di. David Smith knows CD/Di would be pronounced for him if he were not living out his A/A/D through CD. When these dualists employ CD it works for them, because they had unresolved CD/Di.

Therefore, if you have unresolved CD/Di, CD is intended to speak to you and to aid decision making. However, even if you are not currently experiencing CD/Di, if you have done the work of the preceding chapters to understand A/A/D, contemplate your calling, and identify your authentic values and beliefs, you have laid a solid foundation for charting an authentic career. When asked what advice the profiled dualists would give about duality and decision making, here is what they said:

Really believe in both things you're passionate about.

(Kim Lannear)

Don't let one [interest] kill the other… They can coexist. It's really hard, but they can coexist if you have a healthy respect for both.

(Chuck Harmony)

Making the decision to make one [interest] a priority is not a permanent choice not to do the other. Make sure you get the most out of whatever decision you make.

(Lana Detland)

If you have the interest, go for it… I think a lot of what drives the decision to have a blended career like this… is that you do have a strong interest in both. You definitely have to be ok with making changes… do personal evaluations about it. Where do you want that balance to be and where is your balance currently? Put yourself in a position where you're forcing yourself to do music or whatever that other interest is. I force myself to do something that I love.

(Jesse Bobick)

I would just say ask yourself why you're contemplating blending your career [being a dualist]. And if you have a good answer then there's no shame. And there's no shame in admitting that something didn't work or that… I hate to use the word "failure" but there's no shame in acknowledging failure… not making a career out of being a musician, not being able to make a living doing that, which to many that would not be failure at all.

(Meredith Collins)

Be authentic… You have to be you, no matter what. Be flexible and know that you may have a desire to be something you can't be in that moment.

(Gina Miller)

If it's natural for you [to be a dualist] to try to stop that is going to be stressful. Find a way to make it work. For folks for whom it's not really inherent, make some decisions.

(Joel Andrew)

I think it's a worthy pursuit. I think it helps you get a more well-rounded understanding of the business and I think a lot of the interesting business ventures that have happened in the last 10–20 years have been because of artists... people spanning both sides.

(Kevin Bruener)

Discussion Questions

1. Describe the two masters phenomenon.
2. What is the relationship between being a "Jack of all trades" and CD?
3. What does it mean to have an intrinsic challenge? What does it mean to have an extrinsic challenge?
4. What concepts do the challenges in (3) above relate to?

EXERCISE SET 8: CAREER DUALITY ASSESSMENT

The objective of this exercise is to ascertain whether to say "yes" or "no" to a CD choice, i.e., a dual call.

1 Review your responses to the exercises in Chapters 1 and 2.
   a. In Chapter 1, did you identify CD/Di? If not, this is a key indicator of whether a CD choice would be a good fit.
   b. From Chapter 2, reflect on your insights about your quadrant fit from the Duality Exploration Grid exercises.
2. Do you *want* to manage career activity in both worlds of analytical propensity and artistic drive?
3. Which call is strongest for you? Why?
4. What communities do you want to be a part of? This is different from asking yourself what communities you are currently part of.
5. Do you see analytical activities (e.g., working as an agent) as an intrusion on your artistic activities (e.g., playing your instrument)? Or do you see your arts activities as an intrusion on your analytical activity? A quick test: Do you sense internal *resentment* when you have to stop doing one set of activities to resume the other?
6. Create a plan for how you will implement your CD choice or other career decisions and insights identified through taking this journey.

Notes

1 Matthew 6:24. The New Testament in Modern English by J.B. Phillips copyright © 1960, 1972 J. B. Phillips. Administered by the Archbishops' Council of the Church of England.
2 "Bob Dylan Criticised as 'Impolite and Arrogant' by Nobel Academy Member," *Guardian*, October 21, 2016, www.theguardian.com/music/2016/oct/22/bob-dyla n-criticised-as-impolite-and-arrogant-by-nobel-academy-member.
3 "Bob Dylan Finally Accepts Nobel Prize in Literature at Private Ceremony in Stock-holm," *Guardian*, April 2, 2017, www.theguardian.com/music/2017/apr/02/bob-dyla n-finally-accepts-nobel-prize-in-literature-at-private-ceremony-in-stockholm.
4 https://feelinggood.com/.
5 A centering scripture from the Bible that has a CBT feel for me is Proverbs 23:7: "As a man (or person) thinks, so he is."
6 Alex M. Wood, P. Alex Linley, John Maltby, Michael Baliousis, and Stephen Joseph. "The Authentic Personality: A Theoretical and Empirical Conceptualization and the Development of the Authenticity Scale," *Journal of Counseling Psychology* 55, no. 3 (2008): 396.
7 www.nextbigsound.com/industry-report/2013.
8 Ecclesiastes 3:1, King James Bible.
9 I believe she is referring to the book *All You Need to Know about the Music Business* by Donald Passman, one of the first books to provide comprehensive information about the business of music in easy to understand language. Several revised editions have been published over the years.
10 National Academy of Recording Arts and Sciences.
11 Kathy J. Rysiew, Bruce M. Shore, and Rebecca T. Leeb, "Multipotentiality, Gifted-ness, and Career Choice: A Review," *Journal of Counseling and Development* 77 (Fall 1999): 423.
12 Rysiew et al., "Multipotentiality, Giftedness, and Career Choice," 427–8.
13 Rysiew et al., "Multipotentiality, Giftedness, and Career Choice," 425.

9

A COMMUNITY OF DUALISTS

com·mu·ni·ty | \kə-ˈmyü-nə-tē: a body of persons of common and especially professional interests scattered through a larger society.[1]

The music business is a subset of the broader entertainment industry, which is an amalgam of other industries to which Career Duality (CD) also applies. Filmmakers, actors, screenplay writers, novelists, playwrights, television and film producers, directors, entertainment company entrepreneurs, performing arts center executives, arts festival promoters, non-music entertainment technology entrepreneurs, visual artists, fashion designers, creatives and logicians in advertising, and other entertainment professionals all face the same question of how to most effectively engage their analytical propensity + artistic drive (A/A/D). Taken together, the entertainment industry is a community of dualists. Moreover, the dualist community is a global one. This chapter examines CD in the context of the broader entertainment industry, including its international reach, with a focus on film and live theatre.

The Wider Entertainment Industry

The sectors that collectively comprise the media and entertainment industry include books, newspapers, periodicals, motion pictures (with subsectors of cinema/theatrical releases plus home box office), television production, live music, recorded music, radio and television broadcasting, video games, and live theater, as in the production of Broadway-style musicals, dramas, and shows. Describing the details and complexities of each entertainment industry sector could constitute a series of books on its own. This chapter offers some general information about the wider entertainment industry to lay a foundation for how CD applies to it. Here are some comparative basics about the entertainment industry:

- All sectors require content, either original (created anew) or acquired (content purchased or otherwise obtained from a creative). In the world of music, the musical composition and the audio recording are both content. Whereas, in the world of film, movie content usually begins as a screenplay (sometimes made from a book) that leads to production of filmed images that constitute a motion picture. Television requires scripts and filmed content and requires enough to constitute a series, unless it will be a television movie. For live theater, the script is the content, as well as accompanying songs if the production is a musical. Video games are multimedia products comprised of images and sounds, often including recorded music.
- Television and film require locations for filming and legal access to the locations where filming will take place.
- All entertainment products require distribution systems to deliver the content to audiences. The internet and digital platforms, like mobile devices, are now most pervasive and disruptive to traditional delivery platforms. For example, prior to digital technology motion pictures were only available in movie theaters (and later via television), and musical recordings could only be purchased in stores or heard over the radio. Digital technology and the internet now make it possible to deliver content to any mobile device.
- Copyright law governs the definition, creation, and use of all entertainment products.
- Government regulation affects both the content and distribution of all products, with some industries having additional government oversight. For example, in the United States (U.S.) the Federal Communications Commission (FCC) regulates interstate and international communications by radio, television, wire, satellite, and cable. However, it does not currently regulate internet tv, e.g., Netflix or Hulu.[2]
- All sectors require personnel – whether production crews for movies and television, or studio musicians, or actors, etc. This is where career opportunities exist!
- Table 9.1 provides a comparative review of certain entertainment industry sectors. The chart does not include video games or literary publishing, though those are bigger slices of the industry pie than live theater.

The Global Entertainment Economy

In 2016, international entertainment revenues reached $1.9 trillion. In order of market size, the U.S. had the largest entertainment and media market, at $712 billion, followed by China at $190 billion. Japan was third, at $157 billion, then Germany, at $97 billion, slightly edging out the United Kingdom (U.K.) which earned $96 billion in revenues.[4] If your sense is that worldwide revenues from the media and entertainment industry – books, newspapers, periodicals, motion

TABLE 9.1 Entertainment industry sector comparisons

	Film	Television	Theatre	Music
(1) Access to business knowledge and skills required for logicians*	High degree of difficulty to acquire access to knowledge (funding movies, knowledge of the business and gatekeepers, etc.)	High degree of difficulty to acquire access	High degree of difficulty to acquire access	High to low degree of difficulty to acquire access
(2) Access to technical skills required for creatives	High degree of difficulty to acquire access to skills (screenplay writing, movie production, movie direction, camera operation)	High degree of difficulty to acquire access to skills (screenplay writing, production, movie direction, camera operation)	Moderate degree of difficulty to acquire access to skills (multiple skills required: dancing, singing, acting, script writing, theatrical production, lighting, sound)	Moderate to low level of difficulty to acquire access to skills (singing, playing instrument, songwriting, audio engineering)
(3) Level of risk to investors to fund creative products	Very high	High	Very high	High to moderate**
(4) Access to equipment required (expense, knowledge of what to obtain, and how to use it)	Very difficult to gain access	Very difficult to gain access	Difficult to moderately difficult to gain access	Easy to gain access
(5) Access to contacts, gatekeepers, and decision makers	Highly difficult to gain access	Highly difficult to gain access	Highly difficult to gain access	Highly difficult to gain access
(6) Level of funding required for creating a film/television show/theatrical show or production/ recording or live music event	Extremely high level of funding required	High level of funding required	High level of funding required	Moderate to low level of funding required, depending on scope of venture or event**

(Continued)

TABLE 9.1 (Cont).

	Film	Television	Theatre	Music
(7) Likelihood of success as an independent producer of the creative product (movie, theatrical production, television show, musical recording or live show)	Moderate to low	Low	Low	High to low

Note: *Although access to books about the entertainment business are ubiquitous and relatively easy to obtain, books are excluded from this table as a source of knowledge. They are a source of information, but knowledge is acquired in part through application of information, which leads to experience and practical expertise. The preface to the book *This Business of Television* points out "this book should not serve as a substitute for the expertise that can be provided only by an experienced specialist";[3] **when compared to the other industry sectors.

pictures, television production, recorded music, radio and television broadcasting, and video games – are big, you are correct. In fact, they are huge, which becomes even more apparent when you compare the U.S. revenues – the largest entertainment market – to those of other U.S. industries. For example, U.S. media and entertainment had higher exports (totaling $177 billion) than exports for aerospace products and parts ($136.4 billion) or pharmaceuticals ($58.3 billion).

In 2016–17, the top five export and licensing markets for the U.S. were: (1) the U.K. – its media and entertainment market was expected to increase by 3.4 percent to reach $99.8 billion between 2016 and 2017; (2) China's $209 billion market grew just under 10 percent from 2016 to 2017, a slight decline from 2015; (3) Canada was projected to reach $45.3 billion in 2017, an overall growth rate of 3.6 percent; (4) India grew 11.4 percent to reach $32.2 billion in 2017; and (5) Brazil grew 6.3 percent to reach $41.7 billion in 2017.[5]

Yet for all the money being made in the entertainment industries, these are uncertain times for market participants, i.e., those seeking to work in the industry. The uncertainty lies not in terms of whether revenue will be generated, for as these statistics show, revenues across all entertainment and media sectors are expected to increase around the world into 2019, for example, the U.S. media and entertainment market alone is anticipated to reach $771 billion by 2019. And according to the Motion Picture Association of America, the U.S. film industry (film alone, not including other entertainment sectors) accounts for $104 billion in wages, including $14.3 billion in exports.[6] However, uncertainty lies in being able to predict the primary sources of income, and in designing business models to maximize revenues and plan strategically for an ever changing business.

Like the music industry, the film industry is also shifting because of technology. Just as the music industry was once dominated by companies who could afford the best state-of-the-art recording equipment and controlled access to distribution, digital technology has been a leveler for the film industry, though not to the same extent as for the music industry. Movie cameras are prohibitively expensive and have historically limited those with compelling messages from making movies because they could not produce independent films easily or economically. Even when they did, the quality of the films was often reflected in the lens of lower quality cameras. But the advent of the smartphone and other digital cameras makes it possible for anyone to shoot a movie with more affordable equipment, including established filmmakers like Academy Award winner Stephen Soderbergh. Soderbergh's *Unsane*, released in March 2018, was shot entirely via an iPhone 7 plus. Malik Bendjelloul won an Oscar for *Searching for Sugar Man*, released in 2012, which was partially filmed using an iPhone. When Bendjelloul ran out of film for his 8mm camera, he shot the rest of the film on an iPhone using an iPhone app called 8mm Vintage Camera.[7] New technologies mean new possibilities, different career opportunities, and new economic realities.

An International Gig Economy and the Film Industry

A gig economy (discussed more extensively in Chapter 5) is the product of changes in the way organizations are making employment arrangements available, shifting from long-term, secure employment to short-term, contractual opportunities that require workers to find opportunities outside organizations. Individuals in highly skilled industries are also engaging in gig work on an international basis. For example, Expert 360 is an Australian-based company that offers to connect companies or anyone needing skilled work with consultants who can perform it. Figures taken from a 2016 report by McKinsey Global Institute estimate that 20 percent of the workforce in the U.S. and Europe were involved in independent work, using a broad definition of "independent."[8] And the number of independent workers is increasing, including in arts and entertainment.

The pervasiveness of the gig economy has increasingly become a focal point for discussions about careers. Like the music industry, the film industry has long operated on a short-term project – gig – basis. Candace Jones examined the film industry as a case study in boundaryless careers, a term that describes employment outside traditional organizational boundaries that operates within a gig economy.[9] Some interesting things she found: (a) 5–10 percent of students who graduate with film degrees gain employment in the film industry;[10] (b) you need a network of contacts to find projects; (c) the nature of the work is "complex and non-routine," so that acquiring the technical skills that are a precursor to finding gigs is challenging; (d) understanding industry culture is important since it governs values, rules, and relationships that allow professionals to understand how the industry operates;[11] (e) you must keep up with changes in film technology and be aware of shifting technical trends like lighting design and film composition;[12] (f) you must produce quality work and constantly challenge yourself in order to get more work — reputation is paramount; (g) more than one career strategy can provide entry to opportunities, e.g., working as a freelancer versus working with a team are two different approaches to market access.[13] Other researchers have also examined work arrangements in the film industry.

Helen Blair, Nigel Culkin, and Keith Randle conducted a comparative study of the U.K. and U.S. film industries. They found that although the U.S. film industry is better capitalized and more highly structured than the U.K. industry, both share these project-based and industry-specific commonalities.[14] Gaining access to film projects through film schools — as a way of developing a network of contacts — was more prevalent in Los Angeles than in London. Daniel Ashton examined the attitudes of students in the U.K. concerning having to climb the ladder in film and television, specifically by having to work as a show runner, an entry-level position that involves doing tasks like answering the phone and buying lunch for other team members but is considered a routine starting position from which to work. Some students in his study reported that they felt having a degree should exempt them from having to do the work of a runner, though they would do so if necessary.[15] Social contacts were critical to both U.S. and U.K. markets and are a key feature of working in the movie business.[16]

Though the gig economy has become a proxy for talking about boundaryless careers inside and outside the entertainment industry, research examining evolving ways to work in film is not new. Candace Jones and Robert J. DeFillippi were researching and writing about boundaryless careers in the film industry as early as 1996 as twenty-first-century concepts. They observed that the scope of boundaryless careers is expansive, reaching to industries they believe are similar to the film industry, which they identify as including "advertising, architectural design, biotechnology, computer software, consulting, fashion, law, medicine, public accounting and public relations."[17] According to Jones and DeFillippi, six competencies are required for survival in the project-based, boundaryless environment of the film industry: knowing what, why, where, whom, when, and how. Knowing what is encompassed in an understanding of the culture of the film industry as a project-based, network-driven environment. Of the other competencies, two have a direct connection to CD and related concepts of authenticity and calling: knowing how, and knowing why. Knowing why relates to calling, which is discussed in Chapters 4 through 6 as the directional axis of vocation. Know-how is important for every profession. The importance of acquiring technical skills is important for working as a creative in the film industry, particularly since a reputation for quality work can mean the difference between being offered a project or being unable to secure new opportunities. Additionally, the challenge of acquiring technical skills in film and television may account for the broader participation seen in music, rather than in film. How many aspiring to careers in movies have had access to learning about film production and writing screenplays, versus being able to download Garage Band and learning to play a musical instrument? How many have had access to the kind of camera equipment that has historically been used in making films? One industry is not better than the other, and the technical skills required for music are not "less" than those required for film. However, access to that technical knowledge is the issue as to barriers that must be overcome to manage a career in film.

These intricacies and challenges of penetrating the film industry require strategic perspectives and skills to navigate. Navigating an industry that is based on building networks while maintaining technical and creative skills invokes the application of A/A/D.

Career Duality across Industries

Within the film industry, use of A/A/D can mean channeling your creative juices as an actor, while being able to work on the business side of the industry as the head of a production company. Today, many actors – like Kerry Washington, Eva Longoria, and Drew Barrymore – own their own production companies. These are just three of 17 women featured in a 2018 issue of *Elle* magazine profiling women in film.[18] Some actors choose to both charter and star in their own films. *Biography.com* lists 57 actors who became noted directors, including Gene Kelly, Clint Eastwood, Sofia Coppola, Barbra Streisand, Ron Howard, Salma Hayek, and Robert Redford. Others not listed there include Jordan Peele, Spike Lee, and Oprah Winfrey. These transitions suggest that these actors are dualists, though in some cases they choose to focus on one skill set at a time, first expressing artistic drive as actors, then expressing duality through analytical propensity as directors or film company owners.

There is another career path in motion pictures that evidences a CD choice, namely, where one chooses the entrepreneurial route. Boundarylessness applies to entrepreneurship too. Charalampos Mainemelis, Sevasti-Melissa Nolas, and Stavroula Tsirogianni studied Oscar-nominated film directors for the period from 1967 to 2014. An objective of their study was to examine the way film directors cross boundaries.[19] When boundaries are crossed, e.g., from film to television and from director to producer to actor, duality is implicated. The auteur movement shifted the artistic expression of films to the director as the central artistic voice, but in today's industry directors are also expected to have business acumen and to also have some responsibility for the financial performance of a film. Mainemelis, Nolas, and Tsirogianni's study describes the business acumen of some highly successful directors. For example, Francis Ford Coppola, best known for directing *The Godfather* film franchise and *Apocalypse Now*, showed his regard for business matters outside of film in purchasing a vineyard some years ago with the express intention of having it finance his films.[20] Steven Spielberg described and thought of himself as a good businessman. Like the music industry, the nature of the film industry challenges A/A/D and can likewise facilitate the CD dilemma. Mainemelis, Nolas, and Tsirogianni found that directors seek creative renewal in any number of ways from producing video games and television animation series to touring with a jazz band, suggesting that A/A/D compels an outlet for expression, regardless of industry.[21]

Jordan Peele and Spike Lee chose expression of A/A/D by diving into directing as entrepreneurs while remaining actors, crossing professional role boundaries. For example, Spike Lee acted in his first ten films. Alternating between such boundaries is a CD choice. Both Peele's and Lee's films contain strong messaging about race relations in America, and being an entrepreneur-director gives you the artistic freedom to express a message that is consistent with your own vision, requiring no approvals except that of investors and the viewing public. This is a path of authenticity that is consistent with CD. Other entrepreneurial filmmakers have chosen the path of authenticity as well.

Authenticity in Film

Pedro Almodóvar is an internationally acclaimed Spanish filmmaker. In speaking of his work, he has said, "Experience has taught me that the more honest and personal my work is, the more successful I am."[22] Almodóvar's career reflects the fruit of that authenticity. He created the highest-grossing foreign film in North America in 1987 (*Women on the Verge of a Nervous Breakdown*). That year he also received the French Legion of Honor. He received the Gold Medal of Merit in the Fine Arts by the Spanish Ministry of Culture in 1999. He has won two Academy Awards, five British Academy Awards, six European Film Awards, two Golden Globe Awards, nine Goya Awards, and four prizes at the Cannes Film Festival. He was elected a Foreign Honorary Member of the American Academy of Arts and Sciences in 2001 and received an honorary doctoral degree in 2009 from Harvard University.[23] Overall, he is an immensely successful filmmaker, and the key to his success is rooted in authenticity.

Silviya Svejenova analyzed Almodóvar's career as a case study in how to develop an authentic artistic career. Specifically, he looked at a process by which "authenticity work" in the context of a creative career, specifically film, occurs. The process consists of four stages: (1) *exploration* – trying on different artistic and non-artistic roles and identities to ascertain what best expresses the creative individual's talent and aspirations; (2) *focus* – in this stage one adopts a particular role, e.g., film director in the context of film, or producer in the context of either film or music. This role is adopted as the identity by which one chooses to be known and build a reputation for having that experience, expertise, and interest; (3) *independence* – this stage sees the creative's quest for autonomy. This may be expressed as breaking from norms, expectations, or traditions in the art, or starting your own company. These are strategies for gaining control over both artistic expression and business aspects of career; and (4) *professionalism* – this phase represents mastery of the art form and signifies a level of maturity that is accompanied by success and recognition through awards or other acknowledgments of achievement. Because this phase focuses on career continuity, longevity, success, and notoriety, Svejenova suggests that this phase poses particular threats to authenticity.[24]

Although the path of authenticity reflected in Svejenova's four-stage model was created through his observations of the career of Almodóvar over time, the progression does not have to follow the order of the four stages set forth in the model. Instead, his model provides a process for how to shape a creative career and the sequence for the four stages depends on the individual and the context in which the individual works. Svejenova traced "the deliberate quest for authenticity of an actor who initially lacks power and credibility in the field." He found that "the actor's pursuit of authenticity paves the way to his recognition and legitimation."[25] It's a path to authenticity which is also a path to success; that is the beauty of authenticity. It's also kind of circular: authenticity yields authenticity. Nevertheless, channeling authenticity, discussed in Chapter 7, means that what constitutes success for Almodóvar may not constitute success for you or for another filmmaker. Authenticity, by its very nature, is uncopied and unique to you. It is a type of personal leadership that can be asserted in any sector of the entertainment industry that yields not only personal success, but can shape an industry. Every sector has exemplars of authenticity that have emblazoned bold, industry-altering trails.

Duality in the Theatre Business

Say the name Lin Manuel Miranda, or "*Hamilton*," and you have spoken volumes about trailblazing. This hip-hop musical has been a show-stopping gamechanger for the business of entertainment, leaving the industry some profound insights. First, hip-hop is a cultural phenomenon that crosses entertainment industries with astounding impact, both culturally and economically. Secondly, a Broadway production – and the live theater business in general – is capable of generating revenues that rival the revenues of the film and recorded music industries, with seemingly endless downstream revenue potential from future movies, touring productions, merchandise, etc. The third eye-opener is particularly relevant to a discussion of Career Duality, namely, a composer/actor/playwright/rapper/director/producer can revolutionize an industry. Manuel is a dualist, and it is his duality that makes him an entertainment industry revolutionary, much like the Hamilton personage he portrayed in the musical he created. Manuel fits the Artist Explorer category in the Duality Exploration Grid (see Chapter 2). He is primarily an artist, yet his analytical propensity is expressed in his vision of the musical as one that would have not only artistic significance, but social and cultural impact as well, for example, in his authorial intent to see diverse racial and ethnic casting for the musical. His roles exemplify how effectively A/A/D can be expressed to create authentic cultural and industry impact.

One of the profiled dualists I interviewed is a theater industry veteran who now works in theater on the business side as a logician, having transitioned from actor/dancer/singer to an executive. Living out duality in the theater business poses the same kinds of challenges as those within the music industry, as her story attests. Yet her duality has positioned her to be effective in her current role.

Lana Detland (not her real name), Executive Vice President of Programming and Sales, Arts Venue

The path that got me here was one that happened to me, not one that was chosen. When I decided to come off the road from performing and living out of a suitcase, [the venue] needed a ticketing manager, and I had already done ticketing off and on for years and had done settlements, was familiar with all those pieces of the puzzle. And went into that, and immediately became a manager, then became oversight of the entire venue's customer service program and training programs and left for a period of time and went to help organize a historic theater's patron service programs and their forward-facing programs. Ended up in marketing, ended up in board relations. Decided I needed to come back home because my parents were aging and not well and honestly just got stunningly lucky that my old job wanted to take me back because they were changing what they were doing and advancing the type of programming they were doing and needed somebody with my background, which was not a background in necessarily sales – other than what they had known me to do for 15 years for them previously – or programming, but it was the fact that I had been on the road, I had been a performer. I knew all those pieces of the puzzle. I was familiar with the scene, I knew all the players. So they figured between my know-how and experience with settlements and contracts and their ability to know the right places to be at the right time, then we could figure out how to do an ROI. So I landed in programming and the sales portion came later when our ___ department wasn't doing so well and they needed someone to turn the ROI around. So that has landed in my lap twice now. I've handed it back and got it back again.

I asked her why she decided not to be a full-time artist.

I was a full-time artist for six years. And like many good artists I had side gigs doing other things. [Name of city] was not as big of a city when I came back home. There was only one registered equity company here, now we have four or five. So when I decided not to live out of my suitcase anymore and I decided to come back home for a period of time, I still worked in theater quite a bit. Could have worked non-stop in it [in that city] and it really sort of came down to [name of city] wasn't there yet. If I had done it ten years later I probably would still be performing. But there just wasn't enough work. I will tell you that the other piece of it is after six years on the road and three years at home doing theater pretty much anytime I wanted to, to some extent it came down to ego. I was auditioning for the same directors and the same artistic directors over and over and over again who knew my repertoire very well, they knew what I could do, they knew where they were going to be comfortable placing me and yet I was still auditioning just like somebody who was new to town. And it was an uncomfortable situation with people I knew really, really well and decided it was best to get out while I wasn't bitter about it. So I made that break. I don't know that I intended it to be permanent, but it ended up that way.

I don't really get to express myself creatively anymore. Every once in a while I'll venture out, but it is a real commitment to say I'm gonna do a show. I mean that's rehearsals, that's a whole other cast of people relying on me to be available. The last time I did a show I can remember having to call them the day before rehearsal and saying I'm going to Washington, I just got a new show, I need you to change the rehearsal schedule. And they were willing to do it but that didn't make me very comfortable to put people in that position. Because putting a show together is really a team, and you need everybody involved.

Would you ever switch entirely to go back to acting, singing, dancing?

Yes... it's where my heart lies is in that piece of it. I often talk to our education programmer, I get a little jealous of her because she's right next to the art. She's programming and she's right next to it. I'm about four steps removed from it. So I know that I miss that creative environment. The practical piece of it is in a time where there were fewer theaters and fewer opportunities I was fortunate enough to work non-stop unless I just said I need a break for a minute. So I have to, on a practicality measure, say there had to be some talent there or that would not have happened. So it's obviously there. Am I supposed to be sharing that? Am I supposed to be doing something with that is sort of what always sits in the back of my head is: what am I supposed to be doing with that piece of it? And right now, I funnel it into looking at shows and being able to go "well, that was bad casting" or that was bad direction or that's just not a great piece, and I can take and see those pieces and that's how I apply the creative piece of it these days.

Though Lana did not use Kevin Bruener's words that "he can't let the artist dream die," the mutual sentiment is there. In fact, the desire to express A/A/D – particularly artistic drive – is a constant for all of the profiled dualists. And whether that expression takes place on location for a film or in a corporate office or in a recording studio, dualists seek authentic expression of their duality. It is just one of the commonalities we all share that makes us a community of dualists.

Community Impacting an Industry

You are in London. I am in Nashville. You work in television, or theater, or film. I work in the music industry. Yet we each experience the entertainment industry in ways that make us part of that body of persons of common and professional interests that defines a community. The entertainment industry is largely a community of dualists where the CD model applies across sectors to identify our commonalities, including: possessing A/A/D, experiencing CD/Di, having a desire to resolve CD/

Di and to actualize A/A/D, hearing calling within the entertainment industry, having the opportunity to live out authenticity through responding to calling, and possessing the opportunity to resolve CD/Di through CD. We don't all experience all of these components of the CD model in identical ways, but if we are dualists the CD model describes our common challenges and opportunities to resolve them.

If you are a dualist you are part of a collective who can identify with your experiences. We can support and empower each other and recognize the power in sharing our experiences and our collective wisdom, for example, in the ways Justin Longerbeam and Kevin Bruener are supporting a community of artists. Their artistic drive positions them to relate to the artistic challenges of working in the entertainment industry, while their analytical propensity positions them to contribute to another artist's success through their business acumen.

> *I've been making press releases for my friends because I've spent enough time in the back end of the industry to know what a press release needs to look like. So when my friend is confronted with a $3,000 price tag for a publicist for an album I might tell them to put that money to better use and give them my entire spreadsheet of all the media contacts that I have, and sort of sharing that information with the community without them investing massive amounts of money. [Do you charge them for that?] No. I think it's very hard to talk about your own work in a way that is translatable and I think there's been this interesting movement here where we're helping each other talk, we're being one another's champions and sharing resources so that the limited amount of funds that artists do have can go to things that create tangible product or put them on the road.*
>
> *(Justin Longerbeam)*

> *That podcast I did for CDBaby, that was the main reason I started it. I wanted to hear what other artists were doing… And tools they were using, and get them on the show and have them share with the whole audience… this community of people that are trying things and seeing what's working. So that's really driven me a lot, seeing this artist did this and it really worked with their fans, that's so easy, we can do that too. That's sort of on the community side, feeling closer to what's going on with artists and the reaction from their fans and how that's helping their career, and ideas they're trying.*
>
> *(Kevin Bruener)*

It takes boldness to live out your duality. Yet it is achievable, regardless of where you choose to plant your stake in the entertainment industry – whether in film, TV, music, theater, gaming, or elsewhere – and requires empowered decision making, as well as use of the kinds of strategies described in Chapter 8. It also requires connectivity, not just for landing the next opportunity but for mutuality of support, the connectivity of community. Just as importantly, the potential for impacting the entertainment industry through mutual support is powerful, as Kevin and Justin's efforts demonstrate. Each of them is incrementally changing the way the music industry works with respect to public relations, allocation of resources, and entertainment business models for communication. Like-minded others can even help you discover your own duality. Facilitating this kind of kinship dates back to bygone days of artistic performance: "The gleemen were bodies of minstrels, jugglers, and acrobats who combined together for mutual protection and support."[26] Perhaps it was their analytical propensity that led them to form a collective that would protect artistic drive. Let's encourage this community. These words about discovering duality in community are from the community of profiled dualists, from one dualist to another.

If you do both [express both sides of A/A/D], you need to have people doing what you do to talk to.

(Claude Kelly)

[It is] more important for you to know in your heart what feels right… Whatever that thing is, you've gotta do that. If it's two things that the world sees as opposite that doesn't mean that it's wrong, just means you've been given that. You'll find yourself gravitating toward people like that. I gravitate to people like me who are brilliant but also happen to be great musicians. If you're a dual person, you'll know.

(Loren Mulraine)

Discussion Questions

1.   Compare entertainment industry sectors. Where are the similarities? Where are the differences?
2.   How does your knowledge of industry sector distinctions affect your desire to work in the sector you have chosen for your career focus?
3.   How does the financial snapshot of the global entertainment industry affect your desire to work within it?

EXERCISE SET 9: ORIENTATION

The objective of this exercise is twofold: (a) for non-music industry dualists, to contemplate calling and authenticity outside the music industry context; (b) for all, to consider an action orientation to being part of a community of dualists.

1.   If you work outside the music industry in film, television, literary publishing, theater, video games, etc., the exercises in Chapter 8 apply throughout the entertainment industry, which means they apply to your career, so be sure to complete them if you have not done so. If you work outside the music industry and have been completing the chapter

> exercises, is there any additional strategy you need to make empowered career decisions?
> 2. If you are living empowered, what can you do to empower and support other dualists? How might that impact you, your calling, and your authenticity?

Notes

1 *Merriam-Webster's Collegiate Dictionary*, 10th edition (Springfield, MA: Merriam-Webster, 1993).
2 But see the article by Mary Trujillo, "FCC in Agreement: Agency Can't Regulate Netflix," *Hill*, March 3, 2016, http://thehill.com/policy/technology/274847-fcc-in-a greement-agency-cant-regulate-netflix.
3 Howard J. Blumenthal and Oliver R. Goodenough, *This Business of Television* (New York: Billboard Books, 1998).
4 U.S. Department of Commerce, International Trade Administration, "2017 Top Markets Report Media and Entertainment Sector Snapshot," June 2017 update, www.trade.gov/topmarkets/pdf/Top%20Markets%20Media%20and%20Entertinment%202017.pdf.
5 U.S. Department of Commerce, "2017 Top Markets Report Media and Entertainment Sector Snapshot."
6 U.S. Department of Commerce, International Trade Administration, "2016 International Trade Administration Media and Entertainment Top Markets Report," www.trade.gov/topmarkets/pdf/Media_and_Entertainment_Top_Markets_Report.pdf, 73.
7 Christy Carras, "12 Films That Were Shot on an iPhone," *Variety*, March 22, 2018, https://variety.com/2018/film/news/unsane-tangerine-films-iphones-1202730676/.
8 Chris F. Wright, Nick Wailes, Greg J. Bamber, and Russell D. Lansbury, "Beyond National Systems, towards a 'Gig Economy'? A Research Agenda for International and Comparative Employment Relations," *Employee Responsibilities and Rights Journal* 29, no. 4 (2017): 253.
9 See also Chapter 5 for a discussion of boundaryless and protean careers.
10 Candace Jones, "Careers in Project Networks: The Case of the Film Industry," in *The Boundaryless Career: A New Employment Principle for a New Organizational Era*, edited by Michael B. Arthur and Denise M. Rousseau (New York: Oxford University Press, 1996), 61.
11 Jones, "Careers in Project Networks," 63.
12 Jones, "Careers in Project Networks," 65.
13 Jones, "Careers in Project Networks," 69.
14 Helen Blair, Nigel Culkin, and Keith Randle, "From London to Los Angeles: A Comparison of Local Labour Market Processes in the US and UK Film Industries," *Journal of Human Resource Management* 14, no. 4 (June 2003): 622.
15 Daniel Ashton, "Making Media Workers: Contesting Film and Television Industry Career Pathways," *Television and New Media* 16, no. 3 (2015): 287.
16 Blair et al., "From London to Los Angeles," 631.
17 Candace Jones and Robert J. DeFillippi, "Back to the Future in Film: Combining Industry and Self-Knowledge to Meet the Career Challenges of the 21st Century," *Academy of Management Executive 10*, no. 4 (1996): 90.

18 Emily Zemler, "17 Actresses Who Started Their Own Production Companies," *Elle*, January 11, 2018, www.elle.com/culture/movies-tv/g14927338/17-actresses-with-p roduction-companies/
19 Charalampos Mainemelis, Sevasti-Melissa Nolas, and Stavroula Tsirogianni, "Surviving a Boundaryless Creative Career: The Case of Oscar-Nominated Film Directors, 1967–2014," *Journal of Management Inquiry 25*, no. 3 (2016): 264
20 Mainemelis et al., "Surviving a Boundaryless Creative Career," 276.
21 Mainemelis et al., "Surviving a Boundaryless Creative Career," 275.
22 Silviya Svejenova, "The Path with the Heart: Creating the Authentic Career," *Journal of Management Studies* 42, no. 5 (July 2005): 947.
23 Wikipedia, https://en.wikipedia.org/wiki/Pedro_Almod%C3%B3var.
24 Svejenova, "The Path with the Heart," 955–61.
25 Svejenova, "The Path with the Heart," 968.
26 "The Material of Music. IV (Continued)," *Musical Times and Singing Class Circular* 29, no. 542 (April 1, 1888): 204, doi:10.2307/3360806.

PART IV

Empowering Others and Living Empowered

10

TEACHING AND ADVISING FOR DUALITY

This chapter offers suggestions for teaching and advising for Career Duality (CD). It is directed to advisors, faculty, parents, mentors, and friends of dualists everywhere. Since this is a textbook for a college-level course, recommendations are framed with language that has college students in mind. However, as the Introduction points out, the goal of this book is to empower career exploration for dualists of every stripe regardless of age, country, or entertainment industry sector they aspire to work in. Consequently, feel free to replace the words "college student" with the name of whomever it is you seek to support and empower.

You Make a Difference

Make no mistake, you really do make a difference. During my high school years, I was thoroughly engaged around journalism, which I believed would be my chosen profession. I wrote for my high school yearbook and held a paying position as a reporter for a regional school newspaper called the *Region 5 Link* during my senior year. I was also a student reporter for *On Target*, a city-wide community paper that garnered an invitation for me to attend a city-wide journalism workshop. Students from schools across the city of Detroit who had been selected as reporters for the paper came together to meet and hear industry professionals speak on a range of topics that included feature writing, the role of women in journalism, and broadcast journalism. That spring we had the opportunity to meet local television anchors and print journalists. Speakers included Carmen Garcia, who worked for Channel 56 at the time, which was a UHF television station (if you are unfamiliar with VHF and UHF television channels, a quick internet search will solve that mystery and serve as a piercing insight into how much television has changed technologically in the past 40 years). Garcia went on to anchor the news on WDIV, an NBC-affiliated television station in Detroit. On the print journalism side, I was thrilled to meet and get an autograph (which I still have) from Fred Girard, a columnist for the *Detroit News*. The idea behind the *Link* newspaper was that students should have input in the educational process, and serving as a student reporter covering their schools and school districts was one way to facilitate achieving that goal while simultaneously providing journalistic opportunities and education. It was an immensely rewarding and very cool opportunity that made me feel like a professional. It also made me feel like I had a helm for my future, a sort of confirmation that journalism was the right path for me – even if it later proved not to be the path I chose.

Both these opportunities can be traced to two teachers: Jan Booth – my honors English teacher, and Valerie Bouler – the faculty advisor for the yearbook. Though I didn't always recognize it, I have always had support from people who believed in me. Ms. Booth and Ms. Bouler were two such teachers. Although neither of them was my designated advisor, their efforts to support me went beyond the classroom to direct me toward activities that had vocational, not just educational, value. As a result, I had unique, exclusive, edifying, and educational extra-curricular opportunities that would not have been afforded me without their interest in my long-term development. These teachers advised me to pursue these opportunities and made a difference that had a huge impact on me.

Teachers are not the sole source of career-building support. I possessed analytical propensity + artistic drive (A/A/D) in both high school and college but was not in touch with it at the time. This lack of self-knowledge is an example of the self-alienation that Alex Wood's research (introduced in Chapter 7) refers to. Though I knew I had singing ability and wanted to use it, my opportunities, open doors, and encouragement were directed at my analytical propensity rather than artistic drive, specifically within the context of writing and journalism. Why? No teachers – or many others – knew I could sing! Here, a side note is in order that serves as sage advice for us all. Are you familiar with the adage that God (or you) cannot steer a parked car? I rarely sang in front of others in those days, i.e., I was that proverbial parked car. I was afraid of what "driving" might mean. What if I believed I could sing but others didn't? When I tried out for the gospel team at my church during high school (described in Chapter 1), I did not make the team. Experienced vocalists, actors, musicians, and others who work in the arts know that not making an audition is just part of the journey. However, since I lacked confidence at the time (I was about 16), not making the team was a convenient reason to keep my voice to myself when it came to singing publicly, so I often did. Consequently, I never contemplated singing as a career back then. When I went to the University of Michigan I lived in Bursley Hall, located on North Campus very close to the School of Music. It was not until I walked to the School of Music from my dorm one day that I contemplated being a voice major, and even then it was no more than a passing thought. Yet there were these occasional glimpses of encouragement for singing, and this came only from those who knew of my artistic side, friends and peers.

The very first person who believed in me as a singer, who told me at age 15 that I could sing, was a friend of my older sister Yvonne. He was unequivocal and reassuring in his assessment; it was he that encouraged me to approach the church's minister of music to try out for the gospel team that he was already part of. First, there was a rapport that made me feel comfortable singing in his presence without a choir or others around me. Perhaps this is because he, with his gorgeous baritone voice so admired by me and others, sang with the shy, 15-year-old me when he visited our home. That rapport also meant that he heard me, really heard *me*. Some of your friends, children, and students simply need to be heard. Moreover, I knew that I could trust his input, for he very clearly let Yvonne know that singing was not *her* forte! This role that you can play – offering truthful, caring, attentive feedback – aids in the realization of A/A/D. Listening and encouragement may seem small, but for me it was the difference between beginning a life-long belief in myself versus wondering whether I had musical ability at all. Whether you are a parent, friend, advisor, or teacher you can make that difference for someone else.

Advising

For advisors and counsellors who work for an academic institution, whether secondary or at the college/university level, I recognize that the scope of responsibilities for advisors varies widely. As a college administrator, faculty pre-law advisor, and faculty member with academic advising responsibilities, I have advised hundreds of students over the years and understand many of the complexities of advising. Nevertheless, you have the best knowledge of the limitations of your resources as well as your scope of opportunities and should read these recommendations with those in mind, yet with an open mind to what may be possible.

Despite being selected for great extra-curricular opportunities, all was not roses and rainbows for me when it came to being advised during high school. Although I was enrolled in an honors college prep curriculum and a member of the National Honor Society throughout high school, I never took the Preliminary SAT (PSAT) or had any preparation for taking the ACT or SAT college admission tests. Much later I learned that the PSAT is co-administered by the National Merit Scholarship Corporation (NMSC) and that scholarship programs use the test to award college scholarships. Since I never took the PSAT I received no academic scholarship funds for college that might have been available through the NMSC. To this day, my mother believes this is because I was not properly advised. Perhaps. Maybe I was informed but did not understand the connection to scholarship eligibility. Fortunately, I had parental and other sources of funding for college. But for many students, being well advised can mean the difference between going to college or missing that opportunity as an avenue to pursue their dreams.

It can also mean the difference between experiencing that early spark of interest in a vocation that excites and motivates someone towards discipline and self-discovery, versus wondering where and whether they fit in the world. Vocational exploration is a journey that can take years to traverse. As a counselor or advisor, you are uniquely positioned to offer guidance, and students really need it. My PSAT experience is offered to suggest that if some advisors are not advising college-bound honor students about something like scholarships – seemingly a no-brainer – they, or you, may be missing opportunities to advise about career options and how to explore them, or helping students and others discover callings that may establish a guidepost for the future.

Seven Tips for Effective Career Duality Advising

NACADA, the Global Community for Academic Advising, proposes seven core values for academic advising: caring, commitment, empowerment, integrity, inclusivity, professionalism, and respect.[1] Although advising for CD is distinct in scope and purpose from academic advising, the NACADA values apply to lots of interactions, including CD discussions. In addition to those principles, here are some CD-specific recommendations:

Care

This is one of the NACADA values that bears repeating, as it is the basis for all other advising conduct. It lays a sound foundation for building rapport and for honest discussion about career exploration. Genuine caring fuels digging deep enough to see that an advisee may be experiencing the Career Duality dilemma (CD/Di).

Help Facilitate A/A/D Discovery

This book, particularly Chapters 1 and 2, includes exercises designed to facilitate exploration of A/A/D. Offer to act as an accountability partner for advisees to encourage their completion of the exercises. Check in with them about the exercises when they meet with you, to help them monitor their progress. The objective is not to chide or lay a guilt trip on an advisee who has not done their exercises. However, it is fine to challenge them to reflect on how they will constructively approach career decision making.

Do Not Tell Advisees What to Do

There may be circumstances in which giving advice approximates telling some-one what to do. As a lawyer, clients paid me to tell them how to solve or prevent a given legal problem. In the academic context academic advisors are often required to inform students what courses to take to finish their degree program.

However, even then students usually have a range of options from which to choose. Additionally, they must decide whether to accept or reject the advisor's recommendations. (If you serve as an academic advisor you know first hand just how frequently your advice is rejected!) Ultimately, each of us is responsible for making our own decisions and living out the consequences of our choices. This works no differently for college students. College is usually reached at the same time one is considered a legal adult. As such, it is more than an educational experience; it is a rite of passage, a marker for beginning to take responsibility for bigger, life-altering decisions. We undermine the chance to build this life skill when we opt to simply tell someone what to do. We also undermine critical thinking skills that educators work hard to instill. Additionally, there are practical reasons for not telling someone else what to do; If outcomes from following your advice go awry or differ from the advisee's expectations, you will be blamed. I am not referring so much to liability (though that is not a non-issue) as to the sense of regret the advisee may experience and attribute to you as the cause. I have had students seek advice from me on questions ranging from, "Should I take a break from college right now to pursue a stellar opportunity in the entertainment industry?" to "What do you think about me getting married before I go to law school?" Fortunately, no one has yet asked me whom to marry! Seriously, I am truly honored that students would entrust me with such important decisions, but these are not my decisions to make. Instead, I talk about my own experiences and what drove my decisions, and then let students know they are fully capable of deciding what is best for them. Our job as advisors, friends, teachers, and parents is to empower, not to control.

Likewise, in the context of duality, once a student is aware of their own A/A/D (if they possess it) they may ask you if they should switch majors to engage their analytical propensity instead of sticking with the major that engages their artistic drive, or vice versa. Instead of telling the advisee which major to pursue, ask questions about their preferences and interests. Help the advisee develop a robust sense of self-knowledge. As has been emphasized throughout this book it is self-knowledge that leads to authenticity and a sense of empowerment.

Be Informed

If you choose to recommend this book as a resource (and I hope you will), I strongly urge you to read it in its entirety yourself. In fact, I encourage you to complete the chapter exercises as well. The same holds true for other resources to which you choose to direct your advisees, in order to ascertain their helpfulness and to facilitate referencing them with conviction.

Listen and Ask Questions

Some years ago, I met with a student (Ruth, not her real name) who was from a family of lawyers and was taking one of my law courses. She came to my office to talk about careers and mentioned that she would probably become a lawyer too. When I asked why (or a similar question), the only answer she could give was related to being from a family of lawyers. Additionally, she did not seem too excited about the prospect. Sometime after that discussion she informed me that she had decided not to go to law school after all, and had identified another discipline that she was expressively enthusiastic about. Though I did not seek to influence her decision I believe it was appropriate to objectively ask questions to help her get in touch with her interests, not those of her family nor my interests for her. I believe our conversation was helpful in that regard. Ruth stands in contrast to another student I taught (Jack, not his real name) whose father was a lawyer, who also planned to attend law school. However, unlike Ruth, I detected in Jack a genuine interest in law that was not rooted in family tradition. Rather, he was clearly passionate about my class and about law school. He went on to attend law school. After he had begun his law school career he contacted me to share how things were going, and seemed totally enthralled with his studies. Ruth sought me out for general career counsel, perhaps because of her own misgivings about law school, whereas Jack also met with me about his future but focused the discussion more on the how of law school, rather than on whether to attend. For example, he asked me questions about the experience of taking the Law School Admission Test (LSAT), advice for success in law school, and wanted to hear about my experience as a lawyer. My discussions with Ruth and Jack were as different as their interests. What I learned and recommend is to listen for the heart, not just the head. An advisee may be telling you they think a business, science, or other degree is the most practical one. That may be the voice of a parent or someone else speaking through the student. Ask the advisee what *they* want. Then listen when they tell you, and ask more questions.

Wield Influence Truthfully, but Cautiously

This may sound like another version of "don't tell an advisee what to do," and maybe it is, but with a twist. What if you notice that a student has little artistic drive or ability, but is pursuing the path of a creative? Surely it is in the student's best interest for you to direct their A/A/D by pointing out to them they have no talent if they don't, right? Chapter 2 describes research associated with a concept known as "the talent account" and the detriments associated with giving advice based on an assessment of talent. Advisees should be free to chart their futures based on their own view of their potential, rather than yours. I once taught a voice major who was one of the best students in my law class, but who possessed very modest vocal talent, in my opinion. I never shared that opinion with the student, though it was tempting to do so. The student met with me on his own about attending law school and then decided to apply. He graduated as a voice major, went to law school, and contacted me later to let me know it was a good fit. He was able to figure it out on his own. Here is the twist: when he asked me about his potential for law school I was truthful. I pointed out his success in my class and encouraged him to pursue what interested him. However, I did not say "besides, you are not a very strong singer and would never make it in the music industry as a creative." My assessment would have been subjective and may not have been perceived by the student as particularly truthful because of its subjectivity. Our objective as advisors is to guide *the advisee*'s process of inquiry, ask insightful questions, help advisees get in touch with their interests, reach their own conclusions about their abilities, and empower them to make their own decisions. You *will* have your own opinions about what an advisee should do or be, and you may believe it is based on a "truth." I believe I have some innate ability to see what careers will be suitable for students, friends, just about anyone when I know some things about the person. However, I exercise a bit of self-restraint. Trust the advisee to find their own way when you share quantifiable truths, for example, how well the student has performed in various courses, or pointing out awards they have won as a creative. Redirecting the discussion to the concrete and verifiable helps avoid sharing perspectives that may be primarily subjective.

Share Your Own Experiences

Students are often appreciative of the insight they can glean from hearing about your own career journey. If you are a Career Dualist advisor (or an advisor who is a dualist) advising for duality may seem straightforward or even unnecessary to you because you have already made your own CD/duality career choices. As a result, you may actually be less sympathetic to a student's CD/Di. I hope not. It is especially important that you share your own tale of how you discovered your own A/A/D and why you have chosen your path. This kind of transparency also supports building a rapport with the advisee. Authenticity breeds authenticity.

The Prime Directive

If you are a fan of the Star Trek television series, the words "prime directive" mean something very specific to you. They may immediately evoke images of the crew of the starship *Enterprise* grappling with whether their interactions with another planet's inhabitants would violate that interplanetary treaty. The directive centers on the idea that exploring new worlds should not interfere with the natural course of events that would transpire on the planet but for that exploration. It is reminiscent of the wildlife films we watch wherein the filmmakers enter animal habitats for filming purposes, but do not intervene to rescue gazelles about to be eaten by lions. To do so would prevent filming nature as it really is. What does the prime directive (or a gazelle) have to do with advising for duality? It inspires me to address the importance of balancing an advisee's desire for input with a prime directive-like principle of providing advising interventions that are helpful yet minimally intrusive, that do not interfere with what is best for the one being advised. No list of tips for advising can cover every advisee, advisor, or scenario, and even if that were possible the list would still be imperfect since no one can prescribe these matters with complete accuracy or insight. There are grey judgments we must all make in advising, and sometimes the call may be difficult as to just what to say or do that will be most helpful. The research of Tamara Hagmaier and Andrea E. Abele is a simple but instructive place to start. In discussing the relationship between discovering one's calling and counseling they suggest: "To overcome the gap between knowing one's calling and realizing one's calling *an engagement orientation to happiness* might also be a key feature and starting point in counseling interventions."[2] Having the advisee's happiness as an end goal may not be a prime directive, but it is a sound guiding principle.

While he was a student of mine, Jesse Bobick, a profiled dualist, says that it was after he and I talked about A/A/D (though I didn't use that terminology at the time) that he decided to keep music close by to express artistic drive, even if working primarily as a music business logician.

> *The conversation that I had with you was extremely influential in that because I was really interested in the law side, and I was studying for the LSAT... [law] was something I was kind of heading towards. But putting it all in perspective... you're so much of a lawyer before you get to interact with the music side of business.*

Law schools may wish my discussion with Jesse had sent him their way, but I am gratified in the belief that he gained the kind of self-knowledge that will always be his. That's even better than a Juris Doctor. At least, for Jesse. Helping others to discover their A/A/D can be mutually rewarding.

Teaching

The following recommendations anticipate ways to use this book as a text for integrating CD concepts in existing courses and pedagogies. This book is suitable for use at the undergraduate college level within (a) a senior capstone course; (b) a course on careers; (c) a survey course on the music or entertainment industry; or (d) a course that explores biographical studies of music and entertainment industry professionals. If your program currently does not offer any of these courses, consider use of this book to begin a dialogue on the importance of providing a curriculum that provides career direction, like that discussed in this book, for students in music programs, business programs, entertainment/music business programs, arts administration programs, or other programs that offer instruction to students in the performing and fine arts, media studies, fashion industry, etc. The book is also appropriate for graduate study through use of the research and studies cited throughout the book. Moreover, the concepts in this book apply broadly outside the entertainment industry to career decision making and could be used for any careers or capstone course, with appropriate examples specific to that discipline.

The Senior Capstone Course

The capstone course is generally offered as a "culminating experience" class. What does that mean? It actually means different things for different disciplines. For example, if you teach in a motion pictures program the senior capstone course may consist primarily of a senior project that requires students to make a film or write a screenplay. Whereas, for an English major it might mean writing a directed paper. Whatever the discipline, the purpose of the course is to prepare students for departure from college and entry into the marketplace. In addition to skills-based, discipline-centered preparation, capstone courses offer students an opportunity to reflect on the past four years while looking intently into the future. Use this book in your capstone course to facilitate both the reflective and future planning components of the course.

Career Courses and Other Classes

To be the most forward-thinking and innovative entertainment business and arts program, offering a careers course is essential. As discussed in Chapter 5, an aspect of a changing technosphere that has disrupted the arts and entertainment industries is the shift in the way one works in the industry. Much of the work will be done either through entrepreneurship or through creative ways to supplement an arts-based income. Consequently, a course that has a career development title, is part of the regular curriculum, and is dedicated to exploration of these issues positions students for success. Such a course supplements, rather than works against, the school's career placement office, which serves a different purpose. When I was graduating from college all I knew was that I wanted to either work as a broadcast journalist or to work in public relations. I visited my university's career planning and placement office, as it was called at the time, for help. It was a place where I could find job postings and resources on interview and resumé development and I sorted through that information. Yet what I was really looking for was the kind of guidance one might find in a careers course (or other courses with a careers component), since I had no real roadmap. Consider pairing this book with a book on vocation, e.g., Parker Palmer's *Let Your Life Speak*.

Learning Objectives

In addition to content, the course outcomes you establish, i.e., the base of knowledge students should gain or skills they should possess as a result of taking the course, help to distinguish a capstone course from a careers course or a survey course from a biographical study class. The following are intended learning objectives (different from course outcomes) for each chapter, and apply to all course types. You may customize these learning objectives based on the course outcomes. After reading each chapter, students should be able to achieve the following objectives listed below.

- Introduction – (a) describe the book's scope and purpose; (b) explain how to get the most from the book.
- Part I
  - Chapter 1 – (a) describe the CD/Di; (b) relate the author's story to CD/Di.
  - Chapter 2 – (a) describe the CD model presented in the chapter and its purpose; (b) understand and describe the relationship between the components of the CD model; (c) understand the Duality Exploration Grid; (d) apply both constructs to the reader's own experience; (e) define and distinguish between music industry logician and music industry creative.
  - Chapter 3 – (a) describe ethnographic research; (b) identify the connection between the Duality Exploration Grid and the CD profiles presented in the chapter.
- Part II – give an exam or assignment that summarizes Part I concepts.
  - Chapter 4 – (a) define vocational calling; (b) describe research on vocational calling; (c) explain the relationship between calling and CD; (d) contemplate and identify a baseline calling.
  - Chapter 5 – (a) define context; (b) recognize and describe how calling applies to the music industry context; (b) identify the correlation between changes to industry context and calling.
  - Chapter 6 – (a) understand career decision-making research; (b) contemplate personal responses to calling.
- Part III – Give an exam or assignment that summarizes Part II concepts.
  - Chapter 7 – (a) explain the career authenticity research; (b) analyze the relationship between authenticity and CD and the significance of the correlation.
  - Chapter 8 – (a) identify strategies for managing CD challenges; (b) describe the research that examines intrinsic and extrinsic factors impacting career choice; (c) synthesize book principles and concepts; (d) apply chapter insights to contemplate an authentic career path.
  - Chapter 9 – (a) analyze the correlation between Chapters 5 and 9; (b) apply the book's concepts to the broader entertainment industry; (c) contemplate the reader's membership in a community of dualists.
- Part IV – Give an exam or assignment that summarizes Part III concepts and/or a final exam or assignment that summarizes and connects all book concepts; incorporate a particular focus on review of the Career Duality model and the Duality Exploration Grid.
- Chapter 10 – there are no learning outcomes for this chapter since it is intended for use by advisors and teachers.

For all parts and chapters – in addition to teaching Career Duality and the CD model, this text teaches about research and researchers within the fields of calling, authenticity, personality, multipotentiality, boundaryless careers, and other concepts. Accordingly, you may choose to increase the rigor of a course by digging deeper into the cited research and incorporating that as an additional learning objective for every chapter. This approach is also appropriate for a graduate-level course.

Assignment Ideas and Tips

Chapter exercises are found at the end of each chapter. These exercises are a fundamental aspect of the book's purpose and approach, and should therefore be utilized as essential, not optional, exercises. Each chapter also includes discussion questions suitable for stimulating class discussions, as a quiz, or as homework. Additionally, the following is a list of assignment ideas to supplement the chapter exercises and discussion questions. Customize as needed, and use as appropriate for your students, your pedagogy, and your course outcomes.

1. Students will need to keep a journal to complete the chapter exercises. This is an important aspect of the course.
2. Develop exams, quizzes, and journal assignments that facilitate achieving course and learning outcomes.
3. Assessment of A/A/D is important.
4. Use the Duality Exploration Grid to study the lives of dualists and the choices they have made. This can be a combination of celebrities or people students know, in the tradition of the profiles of Chapter 3.
5. Encourage critical thinking about the industry itself and how they can use A/A/D to bolster its innovation.
6. Challenge students to dig deeper. Use the Bibliography for further research of chapter concepts.
7. Encourage students to consider assessments (e.g., Myers Briggs Type Indicator, StrengthsFinder, etc.) offered by your career services office. These will not assess A/A/D, rather the goal is greater self-knowledge, which is an underlying theme of the book's message of empowerment.
8. Have students make a career plan that looks out one to three years, similar to a business plan.
9. Assign a two-part capstone (or other final if not a capstone course) project: one that engages their analytical propensity, and one that engages their artistic drive.
10. Assign a storytelling project about themselves and CD/Di or A/A/D.
11. Have students assess each other for A/A/D; give careful guidance from the principles in the book concerning which quadrant in the Duality Exploration Grid seems a fit.
12. Let students design their own project that engages the concepts of both calling and authenticity.

13. Provide a "virtual experience" – help place students in the environment where they can have a real look at their A/A/D, e.g., a job-shadowing experience, a live performance, etc.
14. Design an assignment that requires students to synthesize knowledge from other courses and apply it to insights from this course.
15. The "Why" map – ask students to review every required course taken for the major (or minor, whichever is most closely identified with this course) and identify why each assigned course was meaningful, then map that to an assessment of the student's A/A/D. In other words, how has each required course contributed to the development of either their analytical propensity, or artistic drive, or both?

A Few More Recommendations

- Not all of your students with be dualists, or some will be dualists without recognizing it. This is not an obstacle to achieving learning objectives. For example, if students say: "but I am not a dualist, so I do not see how this class or its assignments apply to me," these are tips for teaching the book to any student – teach students the value of self-knowledge, and the value of utilizing both analytical propensity and artistic drive by having students complete some analytical assignments as well as some creative ones.
- Most of the above tips concerning advising also apply to the classroom.
- Some of the end-of-chapter exercises (distinguished from the discussion questions) can be done during class, some can be done outside it as homework. Whenever exercises are to be done during class, create an environment for quiet reflection. Consider use of a class retreat.
- As the instructor, in addition to reading this book in its entirety, complete the exercises at the end of the chapters yourself. The exercises are an essential aspect of the book. Therefore, if you are going to teach or advise others using this book, experiencing what students will experience will make your teaching and advising more impactful. Take a journey of your own!

Notes

1 NACADA, "NACADA Core Values of Academic Advising," 2017, www.nacada.ksu.edu/ Resources/Pillars/CoreValues.aspx. See the webpage for a description of each core value.
2 Tamara Hagmaier and Andrea E. Abele, "When Reality Meets Ideal: Investigating the Relation between Calling and Life Satisfaction," *Journal of Career Assessment* 23, no. 3 (2015): 378.

EPILOGUE

Living Empowered

Living Called

Calling starts right where you are here and now. Sometimes we are inspired to act without fully understanding why. I may be inexplicably drawn to contact a friend, colleague, or relative with whom I have not spoken in a while. When I do, I learn they are experiencing a hardship, or simply needed to hear from me. Or you may be unexpectedly compelled to volunteer for a homeless shelter, or find a strong desire to give to a stranger whose need you sense. These short-term "calls" are not so different from the pull to apply for a position, or start a company, or be a creative. Calling is lived on a continuum, from small acts to bigger ones, from this moment to the next. Each time we respond to that voice, the more we understand how to respond to it and the clearer our callings become. Continuing, incremental revelations lead to larger flashes of insight.

Living Authentically

Jerry Maguire, one of my all-time favorite films, entertainingly illustrates what it means to live authentically. In the film a sports agent finds himself through an unorthodox philosophy of personal service to his clients. And through his newly adopted approach one of his clients, a football player who is small in stature, finds his authentic, most empowered self as a player and a deep bond between them is formed. But both men experience unfamiliar metamorphoses in the process, and the change is neither easy nor automatic. By experimenting with new aspects of themselves that are at first uncomfortable and unfamiliar, each discovers who he really is and genuinely desires to be. Strive for being true to self, recognizing that it is an evolving goal that can transform us to an even truer self. Give yourself permission to be the want-to, called you, even if it's not someone anyone else recognizes today. As the Career Duality model suggests, calling and authenticity are intertwined. The ought-to world represents inauthenticity, while responding to calling represents the expressed want-to of A/A/D that yields authenticity. Living called with authenticity supports living empowered.

Living Empowered

To law and pre-law students. The following words are intended to apply to all. However, because of my interactions with undergraduate and pre-law students and because I have made a number of my own career transitions in that field, this epilogue supplements the contents of this book with these words specifically directed to you: beware the subtle pull of escalation of commitment. In Chapter 1 I discussed that concept by sharing my story of the year I took off law school to contemplate pursuing a full-time singing career. I dismissed the idea of singing full time and chose instead to return to law school for many reasons, including the subtle pull of escalation of commitment. It is a pull, a draw, but its sway is different from calling because it is not driven by empowerment. Choosing law led to a worthwhile career destination for me, yet I have reflected on that decision many times over the years. Despite having had a meaningful legal career, there were times when I had a lingering sense of incompleteness about my choice. Was it because of the vocation I chose, or was it because it didn't feel like much of a decision at all? How a career decision is made is as important as the decision itself. If you embark on your journey from a place of authenticity and empowered decision making, as this book encourages, you are free to focus on your chosen work instead of preoccupation with the rightness or wrongness of the decision, which I now understand is what I experienced. Therefore, I encourage you to query (as legal minds do): are you following calling in an authentic way, or are you routinely doing "what's next" because of investments you have made in a particular direction, like time and money, or other "compelled" expectations? Or do you know just how empowered you really are?

To mid- to late careerists, retired and working lawyers, and to anyone else with a dream or who thinks you've missed your calling. Remember the story I shared in the book's Introduction about J.R., the retired lawyer I met when I first moved to Nashville? As you will recall from that chapter, I met a singer/songwriter/lawyer who had practiced law all his life and in his retirement (he was 65 when I met him) had moved to Nashville to pursue his songwriter dream, now that he could afford it and now that he had time to pursue it fully. Though I met him ten years ago I think of him often, and my thought is this: What a powerful decision! Far more powerful than regret or envy, and possibly the realization of a life-long calling. Living boldly, fully embracing the options you imagine, recognizing that self-imposed boundaries can be redrawn or dismantled entirely. That's what empowered decision making looks like.

It is not too late. It is not too late to make a Career Duality choice or any other career decision. Start today, right where you are, to plan and dream and live called, authentically, and empowered.

ABOUT THE AUTHOR

Cheryl Slay Carr, Associate Professor, Author, Attorney, and Vocalist, is Associate Dean of the Curb College of Entertainment and Music Business at Belmont University, Nashville, Tennessee.. She earned her Bachelor of Arts degree from the University of Michigan, received a Master of Public Administration from Clark-Atlanta University, and earned her Juris Doctor degree from the University of Maryland School of Law. Carr began her career with Belmont University in 2008. As a professor, she has taught and designed courses including Copyright Law, Music Industry Contract Law, Legal Issues in the Entertainment Industry, and Diversity in the Entertainment Industry: Understanding the Business of Jazz, as well as Diversity and the Film Industry. She is co-author of the book *Music Copyright Law*, and a contributing author to the book *Trademark Infringement Remedies*. She has published extensively on entertainment industry topics with a focus on business strategy, careers, and diversity in the entertainment industry, and recently received a grant to study women on music row. In 2016 she was appointed Associate Dean of the Curb College, where she supports the mission of the college through oversight of its operations and leads the college's diversity initiatives, strategic planning, curriculum development, and faculty development. Prior to joining Belmont, she worked as an intellectual property/entertainment law attorney, and has over 15 years of experience representing filmmakers, novelists, record companies, musicians, technology companies, and visual artists.

Professor Carr's entertainment industry experience is augmented by 17 years of experience in developing public policy through managing and advising public-sector programs. She commenced federal service through the Presidential Management Fellowship program at the Equal Employment Opportunity Commission under the chairmanship of Justice Clarence Thomas. During her years as a Fellow she also served at the National Aeronautics and Space Administration, and ultimately worked as Division Director for administrative appeals at the Centers for Medicare and

Medicaid Services. She currently serves on the board of directors for the Association of Popular Music Education and for Creative's Day, a non-profit organization formed in partnership with Nashville's Office of the Mayor. She has also served on the board of directors for Jazz Education Network, the Tennessee Jazz and Blues Society, and Maryland Lawyers for the Arts. She completed the Harvard Law School Program of Instruction for Lawyers in International and Comparative Intellectual Property, is a Maryland Bar Foundation Fellow, and is an alumna of the 2010 class of Leadership Music. Carr recently debuted Diversity and the Film Industry, a course focusing on issues that combine her public policy and entertainment backgrounds. She has been a performing artist for over 20 years, and released *Invocation*, an EP of jazz-inspired recordings, in 2015.

INDEX

Note: Page numbers in **bold** type refer to **tables**
Page numbers in *italic* type refer to *figures*
Page numbers followed by 'n' refer to notes

A/A/D 23–24
Abele, Andrea E., and Hagmaier, Tamara 81, 85, 131, 133, 134, 206
ability 21–2; calling 85–6; talent 24–9
actors 187
advising: be informed 203; caring 202; do not tell what to do 202–3; duality 199–210; facilitate discovery 202; listen and question 203–4; prime directive 205–6; seven tips for 202–6; share experiences 205; truth and caution 204–5
aesthetic legitimacy 150
agreeableness 30
alienation, self- 140, 200
Allport, Gordon 29
Almodóvar, Pedro 188–9
Alper, Neil, and Wassall, Gregory 35–6, 111
alter-egos 143
ambition 20
America, the Beautiful, descant 10, 14n4
American Idol 126
analytic self 13
analytical propensity 17–19, 38–40, 106–7, 123; mastery 157–61
analytical thinking 18
Andrew, Joel 62–4, 124, 165–6, 179
anxiety 167; managing 167

Apple iTunes 107
Armstrong, Louis 148
art, and commerce 149–50
art for art's sake 164
artistic ambition 20
artistic drive 19, 20–1, 40, 123, 142–3; mastery 158–60
Artistic Explorers 39, 46, 118, 157, 189
artistic propensity 19
artistic self 13
artists, jazz 147–8
Ashton, Daniel 186
assessments, tests 96
authentic career, charting 165–70
authenticity 165; calling 151, 211; cost of 149; cultural impact 145; defining and recognizing 140–4; definition 140; does it matter 144–7; film industry 188–9; hip-hop 147; living 151–3, 211; map *154*; mapping (exercise) 154; misinterpreting 143; personal impact 144–5; trap 151
Authenticity Scale 144–5
avocation 33–7
avocational approach 165

Baez, Joan 104
baseline calling 98

Behrend, Tara S., and Kaminsky, Samuel
E. 92, 98, 110
belief 127, 134
Bell Jones, Ashley, *et al.* 20
Bendjelloul, Malik, *Searching for Sugar Man* 185
Berg, Justin M., *et al.* 34, 131
Beyoncé, Sasha Fierce alter ego 143–4
Big Five Personality Factors 29, 30, 145
Blair, Helen, *et al.* 186
Bobick, Jesse 51–3, 178, 206
Booth, Jan 200
Bouler, Valerie 200
boundaryless career 108–9, 185, 186
Bourdieu, Pierre 149
brain: left/right 21–3, 42n7; and music 23
brain dominance theory 22–4
brain hemisphere 22–24
branding 152
Brookings Institution, The 18
Bruener, Kevin 37, 109, 113–14, 124–5,
169, 179, 192; career duality 65–7
Burns, David 167

calling 121; ability 85–6; additional 133;
alternatives 97–8; authenticity 151, 211;
baseline 98; belief, relevance, necessity
134; benefits 91–4; career control 93–4;
The Career Duality Model 81; career
management 93; challenges 88–91;
change context 109–10; components
102; confirmation 97; definitions 81–2;
difficult to discern 90–1; discernment 95;
divine 85; economic trade-offs 123–6;
feeling successful 94; hurdles, hitches and
hindrances 122–30; influences on 130–1;
inspiration 92; inspired career decision
making 92; living 211; measuring 133;
positive career expectations 92; positive
career experiences 93; preoccupation
with future or perfection 90; satisfaction
134; searching 84, 94–7; socially
beneficial 94; socio-economics 88;
sources 85–8; transcendent 85; tuning
into the presence 122; unanswered,
missed and unrealized 131–3; vulnerable
to shifting influences 90; *what if* versus
what is 133–4; work satisfaction 93
calling contemplation, exercise 99
calling guilt: obligatory work 89; social and
personal relevance 89
capital 149
capstone course 207
career, term use 83

Career Dualists 40, 65–76, 118, 157
Career Duality: across industries 187–91;
assessment exercise 41, 179; benefits
163–4; dilemma 2–3, 123, 156; extrinsic
challenges 162–3; framework 4; impact
on entertainment industry 4–5; intrinsic
challenges 158–62; life without 171–6;
saying no self-assessment 171; threshold
inquiries 3–4
Career Duality Model, The 17–21, *18*;
calling 81
Career Explorers 39, 46–8, 118, 157
Career exploration 37, 98
career theory (Holland) 23
careerists, mid- to late 212
Carr, Cheryl Slay: administration training
11; biography 213–14; CD dilemma
12–13; early musical experiences 9–10;
entertainment law 12–13; escalation of
commitment 11–12; *Invocation* 214;
journalism 16; law practice 12; law
school 11–12; poetry 17
Carter, Shawn *see* Jay-Z
CDBaby 60–7, 113–14
CEO career path 129
challenges 166
Chance the Rapper 106
Chandler, Dawn E., and Hall, Douglas T.
94, 109, 110, 121, 125–6
choice 33
cognitive behavioral therapy (CBT) 167
Collins, Meredith 173–6, 178
community 181; affiliation 161; impacting
industry 191–3
competition 126–7
competitive industries 129–30
concert, holographic 106
concurrent career paths 34
confirmation 97
conscientiousness 30
consumer demand, music industry 107–8
contacts 185, 186
content creation 182
control, career 93
convergent thinking 18–19, 31–32
Copland, Aaron, *What to Listen for in Music* 148
Coppola, Francis Ford 187
copyright law 150, 182
courses, career 207
crafting: career 108; job 132, 134, 165;
leisure 132, 165
creative economy 5
creative personality, measuring 20

Creative Personality Profile 20
creativity 18, 19–20; Big Five 30; paradoxical 21; scheduling 169
credibility, street 146
critical processes 18
Critical Thinking Test 18, 42n4
Cropley, Arthur 18, 20–1, 31, 32
cultural capital 149
cultural impact, authenticity 145
customizing context, exercise 118

decision making: career 2, 92, 176–9; influences 139–40
decisional quandary 21
Decoded (Jay-Z) 148
DeFillippi, Robert J., and Jones, Candace 186
delegation 169
Detland, Lana 178, 190–1
Dik, Brian J., and Steger, Michael, F. 122
directional axis of vocation 98, 186
directives 139–40
directors 187
discernment 95, 121; fuel for 97
distribution systems 182
divergent thinking 19
divine calling 85
Dobrow Riza, Shoshana: and Heller, Daniel 86, 88–9, 102, 110, 123, 127–8, 130; and Tosti-Kharas, Jennifer 81, 86, 110
Drake 104
drive, artistic 19, 20–1, 158–9
Dualist Explorers 39, 48–64, 118, 157
dualist, general 5, 16–17, 33, 37, 77
dualists, profiling process and protocol 44–5
duality 16; color 37–40; soul of 40–1; theater business 189–91; voices of 177–9
Duality Exploration Grid, The 37–40, *38*, 45, 46, 122, 157; amplifying 77; flexibility 170
Duffy, Ryan D., and Sedlacek, William E. 92, 122
duty 140
Dweck, Carol, *Mindset: The New Psychology of Success* 27
Dylan, Bob 104, 159–60, 180nn2&3

economic capital 149
economic trade-offs, calling 123–6
econosphere, music industry 107–8
employment, self- 112
empowerment: living 211–12; overpowered 161–2
engagement orientation to happiness 206

entertainment economy, global 182–7
entertainment industry: community of dualists 181–2; revenues 182, 184; sector comparisons 182, **183**
Entertainment One-Nashville 53–6
entrepreneurship 115–18, 187
esteem, self- 167
Expect to Win (Harris) 25
expectations 25, 166, 176; managing external 163
experiences, career 93
exploration 188
Explorer grid label 38–9, *38*
exports, US 184
external input, self-perception 28
extroversion 30

Feist, Gregory 30
Feldman, D., and Katzir, Tamar 25
Fierce, Sasha (Beyoncé) 143–4
film industry 184; authenticity 188–9; gig economy 185–7; technology 185; US and UK 186; women 187; working arrangements 185–6
financial problems 123
Five Factor Model 29, 30, 145
Fixed Mindset 27
flexibility: The Duality Exploration Grid 170; Smith on 176–7
flow theory 26
focus 188
Forbes 150
Fortune 500 companies 129
Foundation for Critical Thinking 18
freelance options 128
freelancing 111
funding 201–2

Gabor, Elena 28
Gazipura, Aziz, *Not Nice: Stop People Pleasing* 170
genius 26
German Association of Nurses, study 133–4
Gibson, Michael 146, 147, 150
gifts, natural 28
gig economy 110–12, 115; international 185–7
glee club 9, 14n2
goal setting 164
God 130–1
Godfather, The (1972) 29
Google Glass 107
Gorelick, Kenneth 147–8

Graduate Management Admissions Test (GMAT) 11, 19
Grisham, John, *A Time to Kill* 10
Growth Mindset 27
guilt 89

Hagmaier, Tamara, and Abele, Andrea E. 81, 85, 131, 133, 134, 206
Hall, Douglas T. 95; and Chandler, Dawn E. 94, 109, 110, 121, 125–6
Hamilton (Miranda) 189
happiness, engagement orientation to 206
Harmony, Chuck 71–3, 86–7, 94, 125, 127, 178; Plan B 172
Harris, Carla, *Expect to Win* 25
Heller, Daniel, and Dobrow Riza, Shoshana 86, 88–9, 102, 110, 123, 127–8, 130
hip-hop 146; authenticity 147
hobbyists 36
Holland, John: career theory 23; vocational fit 31
Holland Self-Directed Search (SDS) 23, 24
Hollister, Virginia, and Throsby, David 28, 35–6, 123
holographic concert 106
Hoque, Faisal, *Ten Paradoxical Traits of Creative People* 31
Howe, Michael, *et al.* 24, 26
Hubbird, Ben 59–61, 87, 149–50
Hughes, Everett 125
Human Information Processing Survey (HIPS) 23

Ibarra, Herminia 142
identity 141
Impressionism 145–6
incomes, second 35
independence 188; music industry 115
independent workers 185
Infinite Companion 59
innovation 115–18
inspiration, calling 92
intrinsic challenges, managing 166
Invocation (Carr) 214

Jack of all trades 158, 166
Jay-Z 106; *Decoded* 148; fortunes 150
jazz artists 147–8
Jeffries, Herb 58
Jerry Maguire (1996) 211
Jesus, *Sermon on the Mount* 156–7

jobs: crafting 132, 134, 165; creative economy 5; moulding 176
Jones, Candace 185; and DeFillippi, Robert J. 186
Jordan, Michael 25
Juilliard, student work outcomes 127
Jung, Carl 29

Kaminsky, Samuel E., and Behrend, Tara S. 92, 98, 110
Katzir, Tamar, and Feldman, D. 25
Kelly, Claude 71, 73–6, 81, 109–10, 114, 116–17, 193
Kenny G 147–8
knowledge *see* self-knowledge
Kunda, Ziva, and Markus, Hazel 141

Labor Statistics (US Dept. of Labor Bureau), American's work hours 91
Lannear, Kimberly 46–8, 124, 178
late careerists 212
law profession 1, 12
Law School Admission Test (LSAT) 11, 19, 204
leadership 115–18
Lee, Spike 188
left brain/right brain 21–3, 42n7
Leider, Richard J., and Shapiro, David A. 151
leisure crafting 132, 165
Let Your Life Speak (Palmer) 84, 207
living empowered 211–12
logical reasoning 19
Longerbeam, Justin 48–51, 83–4, 95, 115, 124, 164, 192

McKenna, Robert, *et al.* 85, 130
management: career 93; self- 168; time 162–3, 167–70
Markus, Hazel, and Kunda, Ziva 141
Martinsen, Oyvind 20–1, 30
Masekela, Hugh 104
masters *see* two masters
mastery 158–9; analytical propensity 159; artistic drive 158–9; duality 166
mathematical ability 23
measuring creative personality 20
mid-careerists 212
Miller, Gina 53–6, 82–3, 178
Mindset: The New Psychology of Success (Dweck) 27
Miranda, Lin-Manuel, *Hamilton* 189
money 95, 123–6, 150; art for art's sake 164

moonlighting 35–6
Morrissey, Monique 112
Motion Picture Association of America 184
Mowday, Richard T., and Sutton, Robert
    I. 102
Mozart, Wolfgang A. 27, 32
Mulraine, Loren 56–9, 96, 169, 193
multipotentiality 22, 176; career satisfaction
    34; gift 165
music, and brain 23
music business: benefits of understanding
    115; logicians 18, 107; creatives
music industry: being who an industry
    needs 112–14; changing context 103–8;
    consumer demand 107–8; distribution
    105; econosphere 107–8; independence
    115; listening 105; live experience
    105–6; protection 114; recording 105;
    satisfaction 114; sociopolitical changes
    103–4; technological changes 104–7
Myers-Briggs Type Indicator 29

Napster 107–8
National Merit Scholarship Corporation
    (NMSC) 201
natural gifts 28
Naxos Records 51–3
necessity, calling 134
neuroticism 30
Next Big Sound 171
Not Nice: Stop People Pleasing (Gazipura) 170

obligatory work 89
openness 30
optimism 167
orientation, exercise 194
ought-to-world 139–40

page 9, 16, 44, 81, 121
Palmer, Parker 145; *Let Your Life Speak*
    84, 207
part-time options 128
passion 83–4; source or calling 86–8
Pavlov, Ivan 22
Peele, Jordan 188
perception, self- 28
perfection 176
personality 21–2, 29–32; creative 20;
    predicament and paradox 30–2; trait
    theory 29, 30, 145; types 23
perspective 125
piracy 107
pivotal moments, exercise 13

Plan B 172
Plato 103–4
prayer 96
problem solving 18
procrastination 167
production companies 187
professionalism 33–7, 188
profit 95
protean career theory 109
protection, music business 114
purpose, finding 82–3

racism 129
rap 146
reasoning 18; logical 19
regret, staving off 163–4
rejection 10
relevance, calling 134
response to calling, exercise 135
retirement savings 112
Rettig, Hillary, *The Seven Secrets of the
    Prolific: Guide to Overcoming
    Procrastination, Perfectionism and Writer's
    Block* 168
revenue, creative economy 5, 182, 184
RIASEC types 23, 31
Roach, Max 104
Rysiew, Kathy J., *et al.* 22, 176

safe career 10
satisfaction: calling 134; multipotentiality
    34; music business 114
savings, retirement 112
scheduling creativity 169
scholarships 201–2
Scripturally Sound 47–8
searching, calling 84, 94
Searching for Sugar Man (Bendjelloul) 185
second incomes 35
Sedlacek, William E. 89; and Duffy, Ryan
    D. 92, 122
self 13; artistic 13; malleability 141;
    true 141–4
self-alienation 140, 200
self-concept 141
self-congruence 133
self-employment 112
self-esteem 167
self-knowledge 22, 25, 29, 86, 96, 122,
    161, 200
self-management 168
self-perception, external input 28
selling out 147–50

semi-professionalism 33–7
Sermon on the Mount (Jesus) 156–7
Seven Secrets of the Prolific: Guide to Overcoming Procrastination, Perfectionism and Writer's Block, The (Rettig) 168
sexism 129
Shapiro, David A., and Leider, Richard J. 151
Shoals, Drew 63–4, 78n
Silent Night, descant 10
Smith, David 67–71, 87, 125, 153, 169; on flexibility 176–7
Smith, Ron 32
socio-economics, calling 88
Socrates 22
Soderbergh, Stephen, *Unsane* 185
Sperry, Roger 22
Spielberg, Steven 187
Spotify 114
Springsteen, Bruce 104
stage presence 143
Steger, Michael, F., and Dik, Brian J. 122
Story, Joseph 1
strategies: career 172; charting an authentic career 165–70
streaming 107
street credibility 146
studying 32
success 94, 153
Sutton, Robert I., and Mowday, Richard T. 102
Svejenova, Silviya 188–9
Swift, Taylor 129
Szirony, Gary, *et al.* 22–4, 28

talent 24–9
talent account 24
teaching career duality 199–210; assignment ideas and tips 209–10; learning objectives 207–9; recommendations 210
technology, film industry 185
telling your own tale, exercise 77
Ten Paradoxical Traits of Creative People (Hoque) 31
tests 96
theater business, duality 189–91
thinking 18, 19

Throsby, David: and Hollister, Virginia 28, 35–6, 123; and Zednik, Anita 38
time: constraints 123; management 162–3, 167–70
Time to Kill, A (Grisham) 10
Tosti-Kharas, Jennifer, and Dobrow Riza, Shoshana 81, 86
transcendent calling 85
transitionists 173–6
transitions 173
true self 141–4
two masters 156–8; feeling 160–1; phenomenon 158–60

Uber 111–12
United Kingdom (UK), film industry 186
United States of America (USA): entertainment revenue 182; exports 184; film industry 186; work hours (Labor Statistics) 91
Unsane (Soderbergh) 185

Van Gogh, Vincent 32
Vanilla Ice 146
Varga, George 148
vocation 83; book 207; directional axis of 98, 186; primary 95
vocational authenticity 145
vocational fit (Holland) 31
Voice, The 126

Wakin, Daniel J. 127
Wassall, Gregory, and Alper, Neil 35–6, 111
Weirdo Workshop 71–6
well-being 144
What to Listen for in Music (Copland) 148
women, in film 187
Wood, Alex M., *et al.* 140, 144–5, 200
work: American hours of 91; drivers 95; obligatory 89; satisfaction 93; volition 89
workers, independent 185
Wrzesniewski, Amy: and Dutton, Jane 132; *et al.* 81, 85, 93, 95

X Factor 126

Zednik, Anita, and Throsby, David 38